Revolt in the Provinces

Revolt in the Provinces

The People of England and the Tragedies of War
1630–1648

SECOND EDITION

JOHN MORRILL

Longman
London and New York

Addison Wesley Longman Limited
Edinburgh Gate,
Harlow, Essex CM20 2JE,
United Kingdom
and Associated Companies throughout the world

*Published in the United States of America
by Addison Wesley Longman Inc., New York*

First published 1976 by George Allen & Unwin in the *Historical Problems* series
as *The Revolt of the Provinces: Conservatives and
Radicals in the English Civil War 1630–1650*
First published by Longman Group 1980
This Second Edition published 1999 by Addison Wesley Longman

ISBN 0 582 254884

Visit Addison Wesley Longman on the world wide web at
hhtp://www.awl-he.com

British Library Cataloguing in Publication Data

A catalogue record for this book is available from the British Library

Library of Congress Cataloging-in-Publication Data

A catalogue record for this book is available from the Library of Congress

Set by 35 in 10/12pt Baskerville
Printed in Malaysia, LSP

Contents

Acknowledgements (1976)

This book is one of the products of my three years as a Research Fellow at Trinity College, Oxford. I should like to express my appreciation to the President and Fellows for their goodness in electing me to a post which afforded so much time for leisured thought, and for providing so stimulating and friendly an environment in which to work. I dedicate this book to them, in gratitude.

Many individuals and bodies helped me to find and allowed me to use material in their care. I am thinking particularly of the staffs of the Public Record Office, British Library, Bodleian Library, John Rylands Library and several local record offices. In addition, I am happy to thank several local history societies for allowing me to cite, in the documents section of this book, extracts from material in their copyright. These are Norfolk Record Society, Somerset Record Society, Wiltshire Record Society, Worcestershire Historical Society and Pembrokeshire Record Society (also Mr B.E. Howells, the editor of 'Pembrokeshire Life 1572–1843', Dyfed County Council, owners of the relevant document, and Pembrokeshire Record Office, where it is deposited).

I am grateful to Robert Ashton, Hassell Smith, Mike Mahony and David Underdown for help on specific points, and to Ian Gentles, Mark Kishlansky and Christopher Thompson for allowing me to read and use unpublished material. John Cooper, Derek Hirst, Donald Pennington and Blair Worden all read the synopsis or drafts of the first two chapters. They have saved me from grievous failings of fact and presentation. I should also like to thank Geoffrey Elton for performing his duties as editor so sympathetically and generously. Above all, I wish to record my indebtedness to John Cooper for his encouragement, stimulation and friendship over many years.

My wife's tireless enthusiasm in typing several 'final versions' of each chapter is but the most visible of the willing sacrifices she made to get this book written. Most wives would have mutinied long ago.

In the course of writing this book, I have consulted the following theses with great profit.

B.G. Blackwood, 'The Lancashire Gentry, 1625–1660', University of Oxford D.Phil. thesis (1973)

J.B. Crummett, 'The Lay Peers in Parliament, 1640–1644', University of Manchester Ph.D. thesis (1970)

G.A. Harrison, 'Royalist Organisation in Wiltshire, 1642–1646', University of London Ph.D. thesis (1963)

P.G. Holiday, 'Royalist Composition Fines and Land Sales in Yorkshire', University of Leeds Ph.D. thesis (1966)

C. Holmes, 'The Eastern Association, 1642–1646', University of Cambridge Ph.D. thesis (1969)

A.M. Johnson, 'Buckinghamshire, 1640–1660', University of Wales MA thesis (1963)

A.M. Johnson, 'Some Aspects of the Political, Constitutional, Social and Economic History of the City of Chester', University of Oxford D.Phil. thesis (1971)

M.V. Jones, 'The Political History of the Parliamentary Boroughs of Kent, 1640–1662', University of London Ph.D. thesis (1967)

G.J. Lynch, 'The Risings of the Clubmen in the English Civil War', University of Manchester MA thesis (1973)

M.P. Mahony, 'The Presbyterian Party in the House of Commons, 2 July 1644 to 3 June 1647', University of Oxford D.Phil. thesis (1973)

B.S. Manning, 'Neutrals and Neutralism in the English Civil War', University of Oxford D.Phil. thesis (1957)

A.M. Morton-Thorpe, 'The Gentry of Derbyshire, 1640–1660', University of Leicester MA thesis (1971)

J.T. Pickles, 'Studies in Royalism in the English Civil War', University of Manchester MA thesis (1968)

B.W. Quintrell, 'The Divisional Committee of Southern Essex During the Civil Wars', University of Manchester MA thesis (1962)

B.W. Quintrell, 'The Government of the County of Essex, 1603–1642', University of London Ph.D. thesis (1965)

I. Roy, 'The Royalist Army in the First Civil War', University of Oxford D.Phil. thesis (1963)

C.M. Thomas, 'The First Civil War in Glamorganshire', University of Wales MA thesis (1963)

G.R. Thomas, 'Sir Thomas Myddleton, 1588–1666', University of Wales MA thesis (1967)

R. Yarlott, 'The Long Parliament and Fear of Popular Pressure, 1640–1646', University of Leeds MA thesis (1963)

Acknowledgements (1998)

It gives me great pleasure to acknowledge the advice and encouragement of friends and colleagues in the preparation of this remade book. The following read the first draft of 'The Intellectual Origins of *The Revolt of the Provinces*' and all advised me substantially to revise and reshape it: Glenn Burgess, Christine Carpenter, Colin Davis, Rosamond McKitterick, Jonathan Scott, David Smith, and Jonathan Steinberg. Three are former graduate students and now close colleagues and friends, one an especially close and honest and straight-speaking colleague in the field, and the other three are non-specialists in the early modern period but friends with whom I have regular 'brown-bag lunches' during which we explore our mutual passion for the discipline of History and our dismay at the external pressures on the academic community of the 1990s. The encouragement of all these friends on the enterprise and their counsel on how *not* to go about it is more deeply appreciated than any of them will ever know. Yet there is a debt deeper yet. Since 1976 I have had the privilege of supervising large groups of graduate students – sixty-seven by 1 January 1998 – most of whom now hold the Ph.D. degree. My growth and development as a scholar owes far more to them collectively and individually than to anyone or anything else – whether or not they completed their theses and whether or not they sought and secured positions which allowed them to continue the pursuit of historical truth. It has been the great privilege of my academic life to accompany them on their intellectual journeys, even if there has been heartache too at careers denied to some of them and miscarriages of justice along the way. I dedicate this book to all of them, with gratitude for their friendship and admiration of their achievement in compelling the past to yield up its secrets.

JOHN MORRILL
Feast of the Annunciation 1998

List of Maps

Introduction: The Intellectual Origins of The Revolt of the Provinces

Preface

This is a new edition of a book more than twenty years old. It is not simply a reprint and yet it tries not to change the argument of the original. It has a new name and a new structure and it contains two new essays: this introductory essay which seeks to explain why it was written as it was written; and a concluding essay which offers an author's comments on which parts of the argument survive late 1990s scrutiny and which do not. But at its heart is an unrepentantly unchanged argument. It is a curious and possibly risky hybrid produced at the suggestion of forthright friends and colleagues and with the encouragement of my publisher. It is reappearing in new livery because I am persuaded that although quite a lot of what was very new in 1976 (such as the discussions of neutralism, provincialism and localism in 1642 and of the Clubmen movements of 1645–46) has been absorbed into the general literature, other parts that seem to me just as important have not had the impact that I had hoped, and this edition is intended to make them more accessible.

The Revisionist Moment

The Revolt of the Provinces was written in 1973 and 1974 and published early in 1976. It immediately established itself as one of the canonical works of the 'revisionist' school of historical writings. When, at the close of the 1980s, Glenn Burgess looked back at the phenomenon of revisionism[1] in early Stuart historiography, he noted that it appeared

1. I will make use of the term as representing a body of writing that offered a new and initially coherent response to the prevailing dominant historiography: others

1

to have sprung fully-armed from the womb between the years 1976
and 1979 and from a disparate group of scholars. Especially influential was the article by Conrad Russell – 'Parliamentary History in
Perspective, 1604–1629';[2] the collection edited by Kevin Sharpe –
Faction and Parliament;[3] the work of Mark Kishlansky[4] – both his work
on *The Rise of the New Model Army* and his articles on 'the rise of
adversary politics'; Robert Ashton's *The English Civil War 1603–49*;
a special edition of the *Journal of Modern History* in 1978; and *The
Revolt of the Provinces*. The appearance of Conrad Russell's *Parliaments and English Politics 1621–1629* (1979) seemed to crown the
triumph of the new approach. Burgess has defined revisionism as
the construction of

> a new and non-anachronistic social history of politics [that] should
> (a) be appropriate to a stable, aristocratic *ancien régime* society;[5] and
> (b) recognize that politics has its own structures and patterns that
> are *irreducible* to other things. In other words, its major targets have
> been anachronism[6] and reductionism (perhaps also holism).[7]

The genre of writing to which *The Revolt of the Provinces* was quickly
assimilated certainly began as a rebellion against the attempt to
graft onto an anachronistically-conceived political history some sort
of social dimension. It was quickly seen as a genre of writing, yet
one of the striking things about this revisionist reflex of the mid-
1970s was that the protagonists hardly knew one another. Sharpe
and I overlapped in Oxford – he began his D.Phil. while I was a
Research Fellow – but we were not then close friends. I had met

deny the value of the term – see, for example, G. Burgess, 'On Revisionism: An Analysis of Early Stuart Revisionism in the 1970s and 1980s', *Historical Journal 33/3* (1990),
pp. 609–28 at 616–17 and the works there referred to.

2. C. Russell, 'Parliamentary History in Perspective 1604–1629', *History* 61 (1976),
pp. 1–27.

3. K.M. Sharpe, *Faction and Parliament: Essays in Early Stuart History* (Oxford, 1978).

4. M.A. Kishlansky, 'The Case of the Army Truly Stated: The Creation of the New
Model Army', *Past and Present* 81 (1978); *idem*, 'The Army and the Levellers: The
Road to Putney', *HJ* 22 (1979); *idem, The Rise of the New Model Army* (Cambridge, 1979).

5. Here, in a discursive footnote, Burgess singles out the work of Paul Christianson
(especially his 'The Causes of the English Revolution: A Reappraisal', *Journal of
British Studies* 15 (1976), pp. 40–75).

6. Perhaps the most important contribution of Burgess's article is his discussion
of 'whig history' and the fact that it is *not* its addiction to teleology so much as its
willingness 'to use present-day standards and concepts to organize our study of the
past which is the essence of whig history and of the 1970s revolt against it' (Burgess,
'On Revisionism', pp. 614–15 and especially nn. 23 and 24).

7. Ibid., p. 612. At the end of the passage cited, Burgess draws attention to the
remarks of Mark Kishlansky in 'Ideology and Politics in the Parliamentary Armies,
1645–9', in J. Morrill (ed.), *Reactions to the English Civil War 1642–9* (London, 1982),
p. 164.

Kishlansky through David Underdown, but our discussions had centred on the nuts and bolts of using the Commonwealth Exchequer Papers, and we had met perhaps three times before 1978. By the time that *The Revolt of the Provinces* was published, I had only met Robert Ashton twice, Anthony Fletcher once – when he interviewed me for a job in Sheffield – and Conrad Russell not at all. Revisionism was not a collective response to a historiographical impasse. Revisionism in the 1970s – like Ranterism in the 1650s – was a mood and not a movement.

In the first draft of his article,[8] Burgess looked for an *Ur-text* from which the revisionists took their inspiration. He was puzzled by this coincidence of inspiration and the only book he could think of as a possible source of *positive* inspiration was Peter Laslett's *The World We Have Lost*, a book which challenged so many of the assumptions underlying the social interpretation of the Civil Wars that it seemed a likely candidate for having inspired others to draw political consequences from it. This is retrospectively plausible but not how I remember it. I browsed *The World We Have Lost* in 1973 and remember being at once puzzled and appalled by it. I retained only a hazy notion of it until early in 1975 (*after* I had completed *The Revolt of the Provinces*), when I constructed a reading list for a course on early modern society in Britain and France for a third-year option at the University of Stirling. I then added it rather as an afterthought, and it was only in teaching that course that its overstated brilliance was borne in upon me.

Glenn Burgess's draft essay on revisionism set me thinking, however. What had triggered my own discontent with the existing frameworks of interpretation? If it was not Laslett, could it have been Geoffrey Elton? His essay on the *Apology* of 1604, 'A High Road to Civil War?', first published in 1965,[9] certainly challenged the whole tradition of a progressive breakdown of Crown–Parliament relations in the early seventeenth century and I *now* realize that his judgement on Gerald Aylmer's *The Struggle for the Constitution*, which first appeared (very obscurely) in 1964[10] and more influentially in his collected essays in 1974,[11] was a veritable prospectus for revisionism:

8. Partly at my insistence, that section was dropped from the published version of the article.

9. It first appeared in C.H. Carter (ed.), *From the Renaissance to the Counter-Reformation: Essays in Honor of Garrett Mattingley* (New York, 1965), pp. 325–47 and was reprinted in G.R. Elton, *Essays in Tudor and Stuart Politics and Government* (4 vols, 1974–93), Vol. 2 (1974), pp. 164–82.

10. *Annali della Fondazione italiana per la storia amministrativa*, 2 (1965), pp. 759–65.

11. Elton, *Essays*, Vol. 2, pp. 155–63.

Thus the prehistory of the civil war should certainly be read as the breakdown of a system of government. But it did not break down because it had been unworkable from the first. It had depended for its working on the recognition that political conflict – disagreement over interests and issues – is a natural state of affairs, requiring detailed, day-by-day management from those charged with the conduct of affairs, that is the Crown and its ministers, as well as some mutual accommodation to other people's views and desires. It broke down because the early Stuart governments could not manage or persuade, because they were incompetent, sometimes corrupt and frequently just ignorant of what was going on or needed doing. This is not to deny the existence of difficult and critical problems (every age has those) nor the often factious and bigoted and ill-conceived opposition which those governments encountered. Certainly they had quite a job on their hands, but that is what they claimed to be there for. What matters is their repeated inability, for reasons also often factious, bigoted and ill-conceived, to find a way through their problems.[12]

But Elton had no seventeenth-century students in Cambridge[13] and was utterly distrusted by the Oxford establishment, many of whom saw him as an intellectual bully and a crude myth-maker.[14] His work had no effect on the development of my thinking about the seventeenth century that I am conscious of. I have checked this at various times with other 'revisionists' and they concur. Conrad Russell, for example, later told me that the crucial influence on his thinking was not Elton, but Joel Hurstfield, whose *The Queen's Wards* (1958) he found 'said it all'. It was, he implied – and I think I agree with him – the way properly-researched administrative (in the best sense) studies subverted the work of the high-road-to-civil war conventions that mattered. And thinking of the way I was puzzled, disturbed, made uneasy by books like Tony Upton's study of Sir Arthur Ingram confirms this.[15] Thus, while engaging in and with the genre of local studies was clearly important in shaping my views, it was not the essence of what caused me to write *The Revolt of the Provinces* as I did.

It is also too easy to put the emphasis on the localist perspective – there had been studies previously (and by good and thoughtful *historians* rather than by local antiquaries-historians such as Mary

12. Ibid., p. 161.
13. The outstanding seventeenth-century scholars of my generation in Cambridge all worked with (Sir) John Plumb (Clive Holmes, Derek Hirst, John Miller) or with the Cambridge Population Group (e.g. Keith Wrightson).
14. It was an enduring source of grievance to Elton and of shame to Oxford that Elton was not – until the eve of retirement – asked to examine a D.Phil.
15. A.F. Upton, *Sir Arthur Ingram* (Oxford, 1961).

Coate[16]) which had operated within a 'whig' framework. Of course it mattered that the great issues of principle dominating the accounts of 'national' politics looked very different once diffracted through particular regional experiences. Of course the kind of work I had already done on civil-war Cheshire had undermined my faith in the kind of aggregative analysis underlying the prevailing social interpretation of the period. But more important, I suspect, in triggering my own rethinking of the paradigms of interpretation was dissatisfaction with the triumphalism of certain writings that took the preoccupations of the 1960s – social determinism, the righteousness of the radical cause, the progressive nature of parliamentarianism – too far. It was not the embracing of the ideas of any particular historian – Laslett or anyone else – that triggered revisionism: it was a reaction against the writings of Christopher Hill and Lawrence Stone.

In the early 1970s the dominant figure in civil-war historiography was Christopher Hill. He was a colossus for the seventeenth century in much the same way that Geoffrey Elton was a colossus for the sixteenth century. Almost every year he produced another book and almost every year he gave one of the prestigious named lectures in History in universities around the English-speaking world. His radio lectures on *The Intellectual Origins of the English Revolution* had inspired me as a sixth-former; his *Society and Puritanism in Pre-Revolutionary England* had been the single most exciting book I had read as an undergraduate. But by about 1973 the bubble was bursting. I felt increasingly dissatisfied with the narrow evidential base for his socio-political account of the Revolution. I was increasingly impatient with his exclusive reliance on printed sources, and with his skewing of the history in favour of the marginalised and the marginal.[17] I was very influenced by the powerful review by John Kenyon of *The World Turned Upside Down*. Kenyon wrote of Hill's sectarian heroes:

16. M. Coate, *Cornwall in the Great Civil War and Interregnum* (Oxford, 1940). Also A.C. Wood (previously the historian of the Levant Company), *Nottinghamshire in the Civil Wars* (1934). In 1973 David Underdown had published *Somerset in the Civil Wars and Interregnum* (Exeter, 1973). A deep immersion in provincialism has never made David Underdown a revisionist.

17. When I encountered the Clubmen and felt their rage and desperation I remember being really angry with Hill, very judgemental about his disregard for the victims of the war and glorification of the mad and the marginal. I do not admire or commend those feelings, but they helped me to decide to write this book. By the late 1980s I was capable of a more just and reasonable judgement on his work from this period: see 'Christopher Hill's Revolution', in John Morrill, *The Nature of the English Revolution* (1993), pp. 273–84.

that some of them were mad we have always impatiently known but Dr Hill positively glories in it. What is not in serious dispute, though the mention of it occasions understandable asperity in the practitioners of this particular sub-genre of history, is that the ideas of and efforts of these left-wing radicals had no discernible effect on the subsequent course of English development except that it perhaps made the ruling classes and the established church a mite more reactionary than they might otherwise have been . . .

He concluded that:

this was not really a proletarian movement at all. It was an unexpected opportunity for failed shopkeepers, lazy artisans and eccentric academics to find their voice.

And he went on to call for Hill to devote his energies to an equally skilful reconstruction of the royalist mind.[18] That review had a wonderfully liberating effect on my mind. I can remember thinking that it was not only – not particularly – the royalists whose mental world needing re-creating; it was the mental world of those who sought to avoid taking sides, who were pushed around by events. It was that review which set me thinking about the Clubmen and which encouraged me to agree to give a paper to an undergraduate history society in Cambridge on the Clubmen.[19] Others too must have had a moment of recognition that those groups who had come to dominate the historiography of the 1960s were the epiphenomena of the Revolution and that there were much larger groups whose actions determined its course and consequences much more fundamentally.

Just four weeks after Kenyon's courageous challenge to the Hill thesis, there was an even more eye-opening review, that in *The New Statesman*, by Blair Worden, of Lawrence Stone's *The Causes of the English Revolution 1529–1642*. That book had made me viscerally angry and frustrated, with its easy assumptions, elisions and leaps of reason. There was something triumphalist and hollow about it. Blair Worden's review appeared under the title 'In a White Coat'[20] and I

18. John Kenyon, 'Christopher Hill's Radical Left', *The Spectator* (8 July 1972), pp. 54–5.

19. I spoke at the invitation of Blair Worden to the Selwyn College History Society in November 1973, an event that was crucial to the offer of a Fellowship there the following year when Worden left to return to Oxford.

20. *The New Statesman* (4 Aug. 1972), pp. 167–8. Another early revisionist, Paul Christianson, also rose to the challenge represented by Stone's book and wrote a 12,000-word review essay that seemed a bit wacky when it appeared but subsequently proved to have diagnosed most of its frailties: 'The Causes of the English Revolution: A Reappraisal', *JBS* 15 (1976). In a sense that review was the harbinger of revisionism.

remember feeling liberated by Worden's mockery of it and of Stone's sociologese. *The Causes of the English Revolution* was a collection of three essays, but it was the third, which looked at the long-term causes, at the 'precipitants' and triggers, that generated the reaction. It read like a distillation of then-current thinking, a stock reduced by a fierce boiling on top of a stove. The work of at least some of the other 'revisionists' in the later 1970s had as a starting point a rejection of the model proposed by Stone in that work.

Perhaps most important was what came to seem the utter falsity of what Stone himself called the 'basic presuppositions' of the book:

> the first and most fundamental is that there is profound truth in James Harrington's assertion that 'the dissolution of this Government caused the War, not the War the dissolution of the government . . . The second is that this is more than a rebellion against a particular king . . .'[21]

While disclaiming (thirdly) that this was a class war in the Marxist sense,[22] Stone went on to pass a social determinist judgement on its origins:

> new social forces were emerging, new political relationships were forming and new intellectual currents were flowing, but neither the secular government nor the Church was demonstrating an ability to adapt to new circumstances.[23]

Does this not represent very precisely the targets which drew the revisionist fire most consistently for a decade after the book's appearance?[24]

Another negatively important aspect of the argument of *The Causes of the English Revolution* is its attempt to incorporate the notion of a growing split between 'Court and Country'. This is how Stone explained it:

---

21. Stone, *Cause*, p. 48.   22. Ibid., p. 54.   23. Ibid., p. 114.
24. In commenting on a draft of this introduction, Glenn Burgess wrote: 'how much have we lost in the reaction to Hill and Stone? For all of their many faults, both integrated into one picture economic, social, political, religious and intellectual history. Who does that any more?' He is, of course right. 'Revisionism' challenged the political and intellectual (legal, constitutional, religious) assumptions of the 'whig' historians, and sought to replace it, but having destroyed the taxonomic base and the empirical superstructure of their social determinism, it effectively ignored the social *context* of the English Revolution. Meanwhile, the magnificent reconstruction of the social realities of early modern England by historians headed by Keith Wrightson has tended to be written as though there was no major political cataclysm at the heart of the seventeenth century. Here, if anywhere, is an opportunity for and an obligation of academic ecumenism.

The country . . . defined itself most clearly as the negative of this
negative reference group[25] [= the Court] . . . It was a vision of moral
superiority over the Court; the country was virtuous, the court wicked;
the Country was thrifty, the Court was extravagant; the Country was
honest, the Court corrupt; the Country was chaste and heterosexual,
the Court was promiscuous and homosexual; the Country was sober,
the Court was drunken; the Country was nationalist, the Court
xenophile . . .

And so on.[26] Just to make the most obvious of the many objections:
if this has any truth as a comment on 'country' perceptions, it is a
truth about the reign of James I and emphatically not about the
reign of Charles I. Yet Stone portrays this as a key element in the
'mentality of *the opposition* [*sic*]'. Rejecting that term – '*the* opposition' – was also absolutely central to the revisionist revolt and actually
it is quite hard to find others beside Stone using it in the 1960s.

Namierite historians had made Court/Country divides an axis of
eighteenth-century political history, and the pre-history of the term
had been explored by others, especially in their contributions to
the debate on the nature of the General Crisis of the Seventeenth
Century. In 1969, Perez Zagorin had published a book on the reign
of Charles I to 1642 entitled *The Court and the Country*. Completed
almost a decade earlier and fiddled around with for too long, it was
a well-researched and elegantly-thought-through book which had
missed its moment. But it gave Stone another idea to exaggerate.

In preparing this introduction, I have been going through my
own imperfect archive, including the first draft of *The Revolt of the
Provinces*. The very opening of the first draft began:

> The gentry controversy is dead and buried and has been given a
> decent funeral. However, historians walking back from the funeral
> have climbed aboard a new band-waggon playing a tune called 'Court
> and Country' and not for the first time they have become so dis-
> tracted that they have not yet realized that they are heading in the
> wrong direction.

This conceit did not survive its very first scrutiny – by Blair Worden
– although the surviving version, after the revised introduction,
does go straight into the limitations of 'court and country'; and a

25. An excellent example of the kind of ugly term which was mercilessly flogged
by Blair Worden in his review: 'historians will have to be retrained. They will need to
master a new and exacting vocabulary, consisting of terms like *dysfunction, J-curve*,
and *decremental deprivation*. They will need to discover the point at which multiple
dysfunction becomes incurable' (*New Statesman* (4 Aug. 1972), p. 167).
26. Stone, *Causes*, p. 105.

rejection of this model was the starting point for most of the essays in Kevin Sharpe's *Faction and Parliament* and also for much of Russell's work in the 1970s.

The lineaments of revisionism lay, then, in a fairly self-conscious rejection of the model so boldly summarised in *The Causes of the English Revolution*. I have just chosen that word 'lineaments' with care. It did not 'cause' revisionism, but *shaped* it. It is a revisionist ploy to look for the contingent, after all. Revisionism of a recognisably comparable kind can be found in almost every branch of history. But early Stuart (and more generally early modern) revisionism was quicker from the blocks, more systematic and more contentious than most kinds of revisionism. As far as early modern revisionism is concerned, most of its early champions were UK-based and most of its early critics – Rabb, Hexter, Zaller, Hirst[27] – were US-based.[28] That may say something about the political culture of 1970s Britain and America, of course; or it may say something about availability of the sources. The political, constitutional and religious history of the period – and to a lesser extent the social history of the period – was written either exclusively from printed sources or from 'official' government sources. There was a strict hierarchy of sources (and I was taught to respect it): first in importance were papers in the Public Record Office, then papers (best if in the British Library or the Bodleian) which were the papers kept by ministers which ought to have been (had, in a sense, escaped from) the Public Record Office. And then there were the rest. With the exception of Stone, few of the major figures in the previous generation had ever entered a local Records or Archives Office – certainly not Hill, Trevor-Roper, Elton or the authors of any of the standard

27. T.K. Rabb, 'Revisionism Revised: The Role of the Commons', *P. and P.* 92 (1981), pp. 55–78; D. Hirst, 'Revisionism Revised: The Place of Principle', *P. and P.* 92 (1981), pp. 79–99; J.H. Hexter, 'The Early Stuarts and Parliament: Old Hat and the *Nouvelle Vague*', *Parliamentary History* 1 (1981), pp. 181–216. The most interesting of these biographically is Derek Hirst, who wrote a distinctly 'revisionist' essay in K. Sharpe (ed.), *Faction and Parliament* shortly before leaving Cambridge, England for St Louis, Missouri and thereafter became one of the most effective and telling of the anti-'revisionists'.

28. Furthermore, at the heart of the revisionist revolt against 'whig' and positivist historiography were a group of Oxford-trained émigrés (Russell, Fletcher, Sharpe and myself, most prominently, I suppose), which may be related to the fact that so much of the history that we were attacking was Oxford-generated (the work of Christopher Hill and Lawrence Stone in particular). As I pointed out earlier, the puzzling figure here is Hugh Trevor-Roper, at least as implicated in many of the errors of method and presuppositions exposed by the 'revisionists' as Hill and Stone. He was the one insider to Oxford whose work might have come under fire, but criticism in the later 1970s and early 1980s was in fact very muted.

textbooks – and local archives were seen as the preserve not of real historians but of local antiquaries. The work of Everitt was challenging that view, but *The Revolt of the Provinces* was the first book to address central problems in the early modern period by a broad sweep around the country that *privileged* local records, put them on a par with 'national' archives. It is this, I suspect, which gives the book much of the freshness and vividness on which so many reviewers commented. This restructuring of the importance of types of evidence can be seen in the work of Fletcher, Sharpe and contributors to his *Faction and Parliament*, and it allowed Russell – not himself a pioneer in regional record offices – to build his profoundly influential *Parliaments and English Politics 1621–1629* (1979) around the proposition that 'the difficulties of the early Stuarts were not difficulties with their Parliaments; they had difficulties which were reflected in their Parliaments'.[29]

The Genesis of The Revolt of the Provinces

This then was the historiographical *climate* of the mid-1970s. It helps to explain the sort of approach to the period that drove me. But it does not explain why I wrote on the precise subject of this book. That had to do with my own training and intellectual formation.

I was brought to seventeenth-century history by two brilliant teachers: Norman Dore, who taught me for four years at Altrincham Grammar School (1959–63) and who introduced me to the Civil Wars and trekked me and my fellow sixth-formers across civil-war sites in Cheshire; and John Cooper, who both inspired me and awed me[30] as an undergraduate (1964–67) at Trinity College, Oxford.[31] My special passion was nurtured, however, by the opportunity the former gave me to assist him – in the mine-month interval in 1964 between my election to a scholarship at Oxford and my taking it up – in researching his book *The Civil Wars in Cheshire* (Chester, 1966). I sat day after day in the local history section of

29. C. Russell, *Parliaments and English Politics 1621–1629* (Oxford, 1979), p. 417.
30. He taught me Europe and a Wider World 1415–1640 for the Preliminary Examination; for British History 1603–1832, General History 1648–1715 in my second year, and English Constitutional History 1559–1783 and Commonwealth and Protectorate 1647–58 in my final year, more than half of all my tutorials.
31. I have written a memoir of Norman Dore in the *Transactions of the Historic Society of Lancashire and Cheshire*, Vol. 11 (1996), pp. 1–12; and of John Cooper in J.S. Morrill and G.E. Aylmer (eds), *Land Men and Beliefs: Studies in Early Modern History* (1985), pp. 11–20.

Altrincham Public Library and in the Central Reference Library in Manchester trying to plot the allegiance of the Cheshire gentry and to look for patterns that would explain their behaviour. There I made the first significant discovery of my career: that allegiance was far more fluid than existing models – those generated by the protagonists and antagonists of 'the gentry controversy' – would allow. Many gentry whose behaviour appeared to be best described as 'a desire to avoid becoming involved' were treated by one side or the other as obstructive and therefore as on the other side. I also discovered John Bretland of Thorncliffe, an attorney and estate manager who got caught up in the crossfire within the parliamentarian party and was sequestered as a delinquent by the friends of Sir William Brereton for his attempts to broker, from within the parliamentarian camp, a ceasefire with the local royalists.[32]

I had continued to work on the allegiance of the Cheshire gentry fitfully in the vacations from Oxford during my undergraduate years, and the resultant 12,000-word essay was submitted as an optional extra element in the Honours School in 1967.[33] It was inevitable that when I went back to Oxford to study for the D.Phil. I should decide to develop that work. Initially, Sir John Habakkuk was designated as my supervisor and it was fortunate in one sense that he withdrew from graduate supervision upon his election as Principal of Jesus College and that Donald Pennington was appointed in his stead. If I had worked with Habakkuk I would have been confirmed in an ill-advised plan to enter into economic history and into problems of land-ownership and land transfer. I do not think it would have been my scene.

I had attended Donald Pennington's shrewd and sardonic lectures in my second year as an undergraduate. He had the great ability to get inside institutions, to see how the constraints of situation affected men's behaviour. His course of lectures had been on the Long Parliament and on its committee structure, and this – together with his book on the workings of the county committee of Staffordshire during the civil wars[34] – was more influential in the way my doctoral work developed than I realised at the time. The approach fitted well with my earlier work on the complexities of allegiance, and his

32. Most fully discussed in J.S. Morrill, *Cheshire 1630–1660: County Government and Society during the 'English Revolution'* (Oxford, 1974), pp. 216–22.

33. A version of this, drafted by me and developed by Norman Dore, appeared as 'The Allegiance of the Cheshire Gentry in the Great Civil War' in the *Transactions of the Lancashire and Cheshire Antiquarian Society*, Vol. 77 (1967), pp. 47–76.

34. D.H. Pennington and I. Roots, *The Committee at Stafford 1643–1645* (Manchester, 1965).

work emphasised the significance of happenstance in determining how men – and it was just men – coped with the reality of civil war in their local communities. His supervision was not pro-active (that is not a euphemism for inactive – he always listened, responded, supported) but it was far more influential in shaping the ideas in the thesis – 'The Government of Cheshire during the English Civil Wars and Interregnum' – than was the work of Alan Everitt, often seen as the inspirer of the 'county community' school of civil-war history. Indeed, by the time I submitted my thesis I was convinced that its *target*, its negative reference point, was Everitt's *The Community of Kent and the Great Rebellion* (Leicester, 1966). Everitt, indeed, was the one man I feared having as an examiner. That was because I believed that I had shown that under the pressure of war, the gentry community fragmented and new men with new ideas, who were less county-minded, more bureaucratic and less pragmatic, seized power. Why I thought Everitt would dislike this, I have no idea. Graduate students are inclined to become touchy about those working close to their territory, and more often than not there is a dash of paranoia too. I suppose that I was no exception. I was suffering from a form of myopia, failing to recognise how much I was working within the paradigms created by Everitt; but the fact remains that a character-istic saying of mine at the time – that the gentry were not ignorant of or indifferent to national issues, but that local power structures caused national issues to be *diffracted* into unique local patterns – owed much more to Donald Pennington than to Alan Everitt.[35]

And so my thesis was finished in just three years, with many cut corners and much clumsy writing. But it somehow caught the mood of the moment. My examiners were generous in their comments and the book was recommended to the Oxford Historical Mono-graphs series.[36] It took me 18 months to tidy it up and get it ready for press. It was published in 1974.

Meanwhile I had become a Junior Research Fellow in Oxford and had been looking for a new subject. I decided to work on a book provisionally entitled 'The Royalists in Defeat', which would have been a study of the way they were treated – that is, a study of the machinery of sequestration and composition – and through that a study of just how diffuse and unsatisfactory was the catch-all

35. Everitt probably had more influence on me through his short study of *Change in the Provinces 1600–1660* (Leicester, 1968), which I hailed as an 'indispensable work' a few years later (J.S. Morrill, *Critical Bibliographies in Modern History: Seventeenth-Century Britain* (1980), no. 650).

36. J.S. Morrill, *Cheshire 1630–1660: County Government and Society during the 'English Revolution'* (Oxford, 1974).

category 'royalist'. It would have looked at regional patterns, at how men who had been non-aligned, or passively behind a dominant parliamentarian movement in their own area, or even active royalists only briefly, or perhaps parliamentarian rather more often than they had been royalist, all finished up being sequestered as delinquents. I spent a great deal of time in the Bodleian Library, in the Public Records Office, and in the Additional Manuscripts in the British Library laying the foundations of this study, and then, quite suddenly, I went off it. It seemed a sledgehammer to crack a nut.

I cannot remember quite what made me think about the Allen & Unwin series 'Historical Problems: Studies and Documents' as a vehicle for the book shaping up in my head. I suppose I was attracted by the idea of the documentary appendix as a pedagogic device, and I may also have wanted to write a book that would be read first and foremost by students, while being research-rooted. The prospectus I wrote certainly seemed a way of getting at that central nagging question which had been with me since 1963 or so, the need for a conceptual framework within which to analyse civil-war allegiance, a framework that was far more complex, supple and *real* than the prevailing one. I therefore wrote a book plan in 1972, sent it to Geoffrey Elton, drank his whisky in the austere eyrie he had on the fifth floor of the then brand-new History Faculty Building in Cambridge and signed up to write a book in 70,000 words – one third of them in a documentary appendix. It was to be called, I think, *Allegiance in the English Civil War*.

By then I was myself tutoring for 6–8 hours a week, although, given the strength of Tudor/Stuart history scholarship in Oxford, I was mainly teaching European history (the papers spanning 1559– 1648 and 1648–1715) and that was making me think through my views on the nature of the early modern state. A key question in the historiography at the time was the so-called 'General Crisis of the Seventeenth century', based on Hobsbawm's Marxian model and Trevor-Roper's Marxian-Doppelgänger model,[37] and the subject of an extended and lively debate in the pages of *Past and Present*.[38] The

37. Trevor-Roper is a figure whose importance is exceptionally difficult to pin down. In essence a Tory Whig rather than a Whig Whig, he enjoyed subverting the work of those he disapproved of by adopting their methodology and turning their own arguments on their heads. He is one of the few figures at the centre of the Gentry controversy, the General Crisis furore and the Court-and-Country debates. An intellectual historian of rare distinction, he was capable in his contributions to the above debates of the crudest forms of positivism. His influence may have been influentially negative.

38. The principal essays were brought together in T. Aston (ed.), *Crisis in Europe 1560–1660* (Cambridge, 1965).

more I taught that topic the more aware I became of English excep-
tionalism. None of the things that linked the crises of the continental
monarchies – above all the overreach of monarchs seeking to finance an unprecedented scale of warfare – affected England. And
the ideological differences within the English political nation seemed
insufficient to generate the greatest of all the constitutional, institutional and politico-religious revolutions of the period. In notes I
made in late 1972 I started using the term 'the functional radicalism of the civil wars themselves', and I began to explore the way the
revolution of 1649 was the product of the events of the 1640s, and
not the culmination of processes at work long before 1640.[39] I gave
a paper on this theme of the functional radicalism of war to the
Oxford branch of the Historical Association in late 1972, and,
emboldened by this exercise, offered a series of lectures to the
History Faculty in the winter of 1973–74 under the title 'Some
Unfashionable Thoughts on Seventeenth-Century English History'.
Thus did revisionism arrive in Oxford. And out of those lectures
came *The Revolt of the Provinces*.

I wrote most of the book in the period from January to August
1974, in my final year in Oxford before I left for a teaching post at
the University of Stirling. I had by then a draft of all four chapters
of the book now entitled *Conservatism and Revolution in England,
1625–49* – the four chapters being versions of the three reprinted
below and a fourth specifically concerned with the second civil war
of 1648 and with the chapter title 'The Revolt of the Provinces,
1647–49'. The text was 75,000 words and the documentary appendix another 25,000 words. Chapter 2 was the problem, a shapeless
30,000 words, but it was, as I believed, the kernel of the book. I
spent several months in Stirling cutting and trimming chapter 2
down to 15,000 words and the whole manuscript to 55,000 + 25,000
words, and I posted it to Geoffrey Elton in January 1975.

Within days I got a very enthusiastic letter back from Elton, full
of kind words about the way I had developed the argument, and
approving of the stances I had taken, but saying that it had to be
shoe-horned into the contracted 70,000 words. I sat down in some
despair and then decided – and I cannot now remember why, but

39. These ideas were first worked out in a paper to Keith Thomas's graduate
seminar in (I think) 1970 or 1971. I took a short section of my thesis on army
mutinies in Cheshire in 1647 in which there was no apparent Leveller involvement
and put them into a national context as a part of a study of how the Army was
radicalised more by happenstance than by the Levellers. The resultant paper was
published first in *P. and P.* 56 (1972) and then as ch. 17 of Morrill, *Nature of the
English Revolution*.

'the quick and easy solution' might be why – that I would remove chapter 4, and summarise it as a codicil to chapter 3. I also trimmed the documents and the whole thing went back quickly to Elton. He had also objected to the title and I came up with an alternative which I cannot now recall – something like *Royalists, Parliamentarians and Neutrals in the English Civil War.* Within 48 hours Elton phoned, accepting the revised typescript and rejecting the new title. We discussed it briefly and I can clearly remember saying to him that we could call it *Revolt in the Provinces 1630–1650*, and him saying he could live with that title.[40] It is a source of abiding mystery to me how that got changed in the copy-edited text to *The Revolt of the Provinces* and how it was that it was never spotted by me. Thus the title dreamt up on the phone got transposed into the original title of the suppressed fourth chapter and the book – to its commercial benefit and intellectual confusion – known as *The Revolt of the Provinces.* That title drew attention to the tension between centre and localities, and appeared to be a new overarching term describing the essence of the 1640s. It will be recalled that I had originally thought of the term as descriptive of the events of 1648, when defeated royalists and disgruntled parliamentarians in many regions – exhausted by high taxation, marauding troops, grasping committees answerable only to the centre – rose up against the refusal of the Long Parliament to make a settlement with the king. Since the argument of the book was that 'provincialism' in the years 1640–49 bred neutralism and a desire to *limit* the effects of the fighting, it was a misleading title, whereas the tamer *Revolt in the Provinces* lacked explanatory force and authority but had the benefit of describing what the book was about.

The Revolt of the Provinces: Conservatives and Radicals in the English Civil War 1630–50[41] was published in 1976 and quickly sold out in both hardback and paperback. Because Allen & Unwin had decided to close down the series, they refused to reprint it and Andrew MacLennan of Longman, with whom I was discussing other projects, quickly offered to take it over. It appeared in Longman livery in 1980 and stayed in print with them for more than a decade. For that edition, a very revisionist preface was added. I was to live to rue

40. Indeed that is the title scribbled on the top copy of the typescript in my possession.
41. The dates may also be worth dwelling on. They were deliberately chosen to avoid implying even cover of a recognised period. The original dates were 1629–49, but those dates arouse an expectation that the book would concern itself with (a) the character of the Personal Rule and (b) the Regicide, neither of which would in fact be central to the story I wanted to tell.

some of the more immoderate statements in that preface, especially repeating the joke of Norman Dore that I appeared to have established why the civil war did not happen.[42]

In a sense my mistake was to draw attention to the debate on the pre-war sections of the book, and that was to compound the problems created for the book by its appropriation to a revisionist canon. *The Revolt of the Provinces* had grown out of research into the papers of the parliamentary committees of sequestrations, compositions and accounts – in effect papers from the years 1643–54. The whole centre of gravity of the book lay in the 1640s and on the radicalising effects of living through so costly a war. The first chapter was an impressionistic, under-researched base upon which to rest the argument of the book. In the event, the book came to be seen as a text in the debate on the origins of the civil war. It has been most praised and most criticised for its speculative introduction and not for its well-researched essays on the 1640s. I myself believe that chapter 2 of the book – 'The progress of war' – is the best thing I have ever written.[43] It is a discussion of the 'functional radicalism' of the war, the first systematic attempt to look at *how* Parliament fought the war – how it raised its troops, paid, supplied, fed them; at how national plans were mediated down to a local level; and at how this effected the lives and well-being of local communities. Particular local studies provided much of the evidence, but not the concepts. Above all, I remain committed to the contrast between a royalist administration that sought after a modified constitutionalism that degenerated into chaos and a parliamentarianism that was rooted in a controlled reliance upon *droit administratif* that split the movement but won the war. It is the chapter many skip through, but I believe that its importance remains to be tested. It is my hope that this revised edition will rectify that neglect.

The Revolt of the Provinces *and Revisionism*

What then are the links between my own development and the revisionist moment that explain the success of *The Revolt of the Provinces?*

42. *Revolt of the Provinces* (1980 edn), p. x (the 1980 preface is not included in this edition).

43. I base this on the volume of citation and discussion of the book in other scholars' work and on a quick glance at scored and annotated library copies I have encountered. I would estimate that half of all references are to ch. 1, and almost all the other half to the 'Clubmen' sections of ch. 3. In my view the proportions ought to be 10% of citations to ch. 1, 50%+ to ch. 2 and 40%– to ch. 3!

First and foremost it was written to be a logical extension of my first book – a demonstration at a national level of the case I had argued in *Cheshire 1630–1660*:

> In Cheshire, as elsewhere, local tensions and local preoccupations proved more important than national issues or abstruse constitutional principles [in determining patterns of allegiance]. The overriding political unit was the county community, and the particular situation in Cheshire diffracted the conflicts between King and Parliament into an individual and specific pattern. As a result, all rigid, generalized, explanations, particularly of the socio-economic kind, are unhelpful if not downright misleading.[44]

I now recognise the inadequacy of each sentence in the foregoing. Above all I now recognise that when I set out to make sense of the dynamics of political choice across England, the Cheshire model remained too strongly with me.[45]

Secondly, *The Revolt of the Provinces* was a revolt against social determinism and against *The Causes of the English Revolution*. It is true that the sterile debate known as the 'gentry controversy' was imploding by the early 1960s, but that sense that there was a necessary link between social change, intellectual fervour and *necessary* political revolution linked the 'pre-revisionist' work not only of those historians on the libertarian left influenced by – drawn to – the student revolution of the later 1960s[46] but also those who were on the libertarian right – Trevor-Roper and Hexter, for example. They squabbled with one another, but within a framework which simply did not provide categories helpful to those of us undertaking serious empirical research rather than engaged in smash and grab raids on the archives.

Thirdly, its distinctiveness from other examples of early revisionism in its subversion of existing accounts lies in its concentration on the 1640s. The biggest battlegrounds in the years after 1976 lay with the study of the parliaments of 1603–29 and with the *discontinuity* between the reign of James I (or at any rate the reigns of James and Buckingham) and the reign of Charles I. *The Revolt of the Provinces* was conscripted into those debates, but it was ill-equipped

44. Morrill, *Cheshire*, p. 330.
45. See below, pp. 194–7, especially for the way in which the writings of Ann Hughes have acted as a corrective to the exaggerations of this account.
46. I have a clear memory of Christopher Hill and Lawrence Stone enthusiastically debating on Radio 3 in (I think) 1969 the fact that student radicals in Princeton wore the same green blazes as the Levellers as a suggestive link between two 'with-it' movements.

to be a major participant. Rather it took seriously the oddly neglected decade of the 1640s. Stone called his book *The Causes of the
English Revolution* but he too was really explaining the isolation of
Charles in 1640. Stone, and more surprisingly Hill – whose work
covered either the period up to and including the 1630s or the
period from the end of the civil wars to the Restoration and beyond
but who never worked systematically on the 1640s or wrote about
the Regicide and Revolution of 1649 as against the stillborn sectarian alternatives – never really addressed the *nature* of the Revolution, and certainly no one had seriously attempted to trace the link
between the revolt of 1642 and its *denouement* in 1649. By far the
most important book in that regard for me was David Underdown's
Pride's Purge published in 1971. His was an unparalleled account of
the *hows* of the later 1640s and it was richly suggestive of the *whys*
without providing any sustained explanation.

The radical issue my work raised – rather obliquely perhaps in
The Revolt, but more and more directly in the years that followed –
is whether the English had – in any sense – a 'Great Revolution'
comparable with the French, Russian, Chinese (etc.) Revolutions. It
was an unargued assumption in the work of Hill and Stone and
many others that the abstract social sciences offered semantic tools
for linking events widely spread across space and time. The revisionist challenge to that assumption had to be a prolonged one,
because it meant taking on a methodology as well as a questionable
assumption. With History under siege as a discipline, the repudiation of modish allies was risky. But behind that unargued secondary
assumption in the work of Stone was that even more entrenched
one – that there was an English Revolution comparable with more
recent 'Revolutions'.

A mark of how unsatisfactory that was can be found when we ask
not the *how* or the *why* but the *when* question. When was this revolution supposed to have occurred – 1640–42, 1642–49, 1648–49,
1649–60 etc.? *The Revolt of the Provinces* distinguishes sharply between what made people act as they did to create the political crisis
of 1640, the resort to arms in 1642 and the 'revolution of 1649'.
And the consequence of this was that I abandoned the use of the
word 'Revolution' as being a term too loaded with anticipation, too
weighed down by anachronistic resonances, helpfully to describe
the political, religious, intellectual maelstrom of the 1640s. I never
doubted the fundamental significance of the period as a hinge – if
not quite a fulcrum – in English (for which twenty years on I would
say British and Irish) history. To deny that England had a Revolution

in 1649 was not and is not to deny that it had a transforming moment. There was an earthquake in Britain in 1649. But it may not be helpful to call that earthquake a revolution. The point is that both terms are metaphors and that my book rejected the second without quite coining the first.

From the beginning, I was uncomfortable with the term 'revolt of (=in) the provinces' as a conceptual substitute for 'The English (or Puritan) Revolution'. But the search for such a term was a concern that dominated the next major phase of my intellectual development and produced some influential but very contentious articles in the early 1980s. As a peroration to one of them, I had written:

> Have we been so confused in seeking parallels between the British Crisis of the 1640s and the wave of rebellions on the Continent (brought on by war and the centralising imperatives of war), or between the English Revolution and the events of 1789 and 1917, that we have missed an obvious point? The English civil war was not the first European revolution: it was the last of the Wars of Religion.

I wish I had written 'not so much the first . . . as the last . . .'. That would fulfil the rhetorical expectation of the penultimate sentence and would represent my views more exactly. The desire to end in a flourish landed me in a controversy based on an insupportable overstatement acceptable in context but misleading out of context.[47]

Fourthly, then, *The Revolt of the Provinces* sought to explain how a rebellion against the misgovernment of Charles turned into something much more potent. It explored what I called the 'functional radicalism' of the war years. This is why chapter 2 was and is so important – why that chapter begins with Lord Wharton's assertion that 'they were not tied to a law for these were times of necessity and imminent danger' and ends with the claim that the experience of war and the burdens of war were 'either to incline men to cling more closely than ever to known structures, known ways, or it could cut them loose, freeing them to seek a happier future through new political eschatologies. In the event, the radical conservatism of the Clubmen was to be more characteristic of the later 1640s than the iconoclasm of the Levellers.'[48]

Finally, this is essentially a book that seeks to explain complexity of belief. It is a book that set out to establish a new and positive

---

47. The essay – 'The Religious Context of the English Civil War' – is most accessible in Morrill, *Nature of the English Revolution*. The quotation is from p. 68. For some recent comments on the controversy this passage stirred up, see ibid., pp. 33–44.
48. Below, p. 122.

account of the dynamics of men caught up in the maelstrom of war. It showed that the civil war was more than a conflict that divided royalist gentry from parliamentarian parvenus and middling sorts, or which was a struggle within a nation or just within an élite divided between a radical south and east and a conservative north and west. And it asked whether, if the war was not generated by revolutionary impulse, the war itself might have generated revolutionary potential. Furthermore it did all this while stressing that there was a provincial as well as a centrist dimension to the process. To have been a 'revolution' there would have had to have been a transforming of provincial consciousness as well as those of the Army and of aspiring revolutionary courtiers. I found no evidence of such transformations and indeed found middling sorts of rural England already to have the mental antibodies to prevent an epidemic of Levelling and sectarian ideas, except in the laboratory conditions present in the Army and London.

The Revolt did not deal with all groups equally. It assumed that some parts of the story had been well enough told. Thus, there seemed to be more than enough books that explored the nature of 'puritanism' and the contribution of puritan dynamism to the outcome of the civil war. This was a book which looked at those who became involved in the war – as victims, as reluctant participants, as active proponents of peace and of local settlement – who could not tidily be stuffed into one of two catch-all boxes marked 'royalist' and 'parliamentarian'. Later I was to turn my attention to a closer scrutiny of the 'activists' but I was already perfectly explicit about who they were: 'what emerges quite clearly from a study of the activists in the summer of 1642 . . . is that for them, religion was the crucial issue.'[49] It is simply not true that 'revisionists' fell back on religion when they could find no other reason for explaining why there was the civil war that they had argued was not inevitable, predictable or necessary.[50] This is a book which aimed to say, 'not everyone was as clear, committed or militant as the current writing presumes. Let us look at what those who were more hesitant, uncertain and above all convinced there were remedies for England's ills short of a civil war did about it, and let us see what the consequences of their actions were.' I hope there is still meat on the

    49. Below, p. 68.
    50. G. Eley and W. Hunt (eds), *Reviving the English Revolution* (1988), p. 9 (of the 1980s writings of myself and Blair Worden: 'it comes as something of a surprise to find two of the most inveterate revisionists . . . rediscovering the centrality of religion . . . the irony is worth savouring').

bone of that argument in this book and that it might still benefit a new generation approaching it with their own questions demanding their own answers.

Preparing this Edition

This book was the product of a historiographical moment and of a particular stage in my own intellectual development. For that reason, I do not believe it can be 'brought up to date'. Normally the wheat and the chaff of any well-established book are sorted out by reviewers and readers, and the worthwhile material incorporated into the textbook literature and into the contexts of other monographs. But sometimes a book retains a centrality because it is on a core topic and addresses a set of questions that retain interest in a way that other and subsequent works do not do. I have been persuaded that this is the case with *The Revolt of the Provinces*. I have therefore decided to produce a new edition. But – as I said earlier – this is not *that* straightforward. I had intended to republish the original text supported by a new introduction. That quickly gave way to the idea of a contextualising introduction and a reviewing conclusion.

I had one other major decision to make: whether or not to restore the abandoned fourth chapter on the events of 1648.[51] It had only been dropped because of the requirement that the book stay within the 70,000 word limit. Being an admirer of Anton Bruckner's symphonies, and aware of the benefits gained by the modern reconstruction of the 'original versions' which restore the music he was persuaded by foolish friends to cut out so as to shorten his works, I was drawn to the idea. But I have not been able to bring myself to do it. I still have the text of that chapter; but I am no Bruckner and I cannot find the original ending of chapter 3 removed when the 1648 material was condensed down to form section IX of chapter 3. And more importantly I feel that it was the least impressive part of the whole draft, the most determinedly and least convincingly 'provincialist' of all the parts of the book, and that it would not have achieved anything which the existing shortened version does not achieve.

The new introduction and conclusion add some 20,000 words to the original text. Going through that text to update the footnotes

51. See above, pp. 14–15.

(e.g. by replacing references to unpublished theses by references to subsequently published books-of-theses) I realised that there were a number of factual errors I needed to correct.[52] This already represented some form of violation of the integrity of the text, and yet it seemed entirely sensible and necessary. What then about the status of the documentary appendix? It was clear to me from the reviews, from the comments of friends and from using this book in teaching situations, that the documentary appendices had not had the pedagogic effect I had hoped for, that they were little read and were not seen as an integral part of the book.[53] Yet the book was designed so that the matter in the appendices was an essential part not only of the *argument* but of the attempt of the book to re-create the mental worlds and real choices of actors at the time of the civil war. My own sense is that one of the most powerful and effective things the book does is to locate decisions that determined people's actions and reactions in real situations. These were not men and women making armchair choices on the basis of prayer and a reading of the diurnals and the pamphlets of Henry Parker or John Bramhall. They were constrained but real choices. It needed the rhetorical force of their own words in explaining what those choices were and how they were made to get this part of the book right. And there it was buried away in thumbed but unread appendices. After due thought and experimentation, I decided not to change anything in the structure of the *argument* but frequently to insert in direct quotation or paraphrase extracts from the appendix previously simply referred to by cross-reference from the end-notes. The result has been to stay faithful to the intention of the 1976/80 version without developing or altering the argument by a jot or a tittle.

Very late on I made one more change. I have always been puzzled by the relative lack of interest in the central chapter – 'The progress of war'. Reading it again after many years I realised how dense it was and hard to follow, at least in comparison with the surrounding chapters. It had been severely pruned to fit into the space the original publishers would allow me. In the hope that clearer signposting and guidance would make it more readable and effective, I have changed the subsection numbers into subtitles, written new linking passages at three points and replaced a particularly constricted passage on the nature of parliamentarian finance

52. For example, see p. 55 or p. 90.
53. A point most forthrightly made to me by Keith Thomas when I met him in St Giles (Oxford) not long after the book first came out and which has remained with me ever since.

with two paragraphs based on original material I had suppressed in 1975 (the passage in question is that represented by the paragraph(s) containing notes 14–16 in both versions). The aim once more was to increase clarity without changing the argument.

This is then at once an old and a new book. At its heart is a text which tells us much about the historical climate of the 1970s as well as something of the history of the 1640s. It is sufficiently developed and reshaped to be allowed a different title, the one it was supposed to have had from the beginning. I can only hope that it proves able to meet the historical needs of the year 2000.

CHAPTER ONE

The Coming of War

Introduction

There could be no civil war before 1642 because there was no royalist party. The origins of the English civil war are really concerned less with the rise of opposition than with the resurgence of loyalism; loyalty to a King who appeared to have disregarded the rights of his subjects, and support for a Church which had combined the persecution of an old nonconformity (puritanism) with the championship of another (Arminianism).

Most historians have in effect concerned themselves with the crisis of 1640; with the isolation of Charles I from the great majority of his people. The events of 1640–42 are treated as of secondary importance, the falling away of the faint-hearted as the crisis worked itself out. The royalists are portrayed, even by those without ideological axes to grind, as men lacking both vision and the stomach for a fight – men unable to overcome an inbred respect for authority and the hierarchy of values expressed in the Great Chain of Being.

Furthermore, the events of 1640–42 are still interpreted almost entirely in terms of a succession of crises at Whitehall and Westminster, as though the political convulsions there were neatly counterpointed by parallel crises in provincial communities. It will be the primary task of this section to examine what was happening in the partially autonomous shires and boroughs of England and Wales before and during the years 1640–42. It will also attempt to show that while men – above all those prominent gentry families who ran local government – shared many assumptions about the nature of the crisis, their response was largely conditioned by local events and

24

local power structures. It will be about the interaction of national and local politics.

Alan Everitt is the leading exponent of the concept of 'provincialism' and its significance for an understanding of early modern England. In several persuasive works he has argued that 'most towns and counties were more interested in living a life of their own, in which politics played merely an intermittent part . . .'.[1] His theme has been taken up and developed by other historians and incorporated into their more general treatment of the period. Thus Lawrence Stone has written:

> when an Englishman in the early seventeenth century said 'my country', he meant 'my county'. What we see in the half century before the civil war is the growth of an emotional sense of loyalty to the local community, and also of institutional arrangements to give that sentiment force. The county evolved as a coherent political and social community, with reference to – and potentially in rivalry with – both other counties and the central executive and its local agents.[2]

I am not, of course, going to argue that this provincialism excluded concern for general or national political and constitutional issues, but rather that such issues took on local colours and were articulated within local contexts. The gentry did not consider dispassionately such problems as those arising from the Book of Orders, ship money or the Nineteen Propositions. They did not attempt to weigh their legality or necessity in the light of abstruse general constitutional principles. Rather, they evaluated the effect such measures would have on the peace and security of their local communities. Only occasionally did county factions adopt positions in relation to national issues based on local opportunism rather than on conviction. However, they did often reshape the points involved and invested them with a more local significance. It is in this light that I accept Alan Everitt's assertion that 'though the sense of national identity had been increasing since the early Tudors, so too had the sense of county identity, and the latter was normally the more powerful sentiment in 1640–60'.[3]

1. A.M. Everitt, 'The County Community' in E.W. Ives (ed.), *The English Revolution, 1600–1660* (1968), p. 49; see also by him, *Change in the Provinces: The Seventeenth Century* (1969): 'The Local Community and the English Civil War', in *Historical Association Pamphlet*, G. 70 (1969). He has also written a brilliant case study, *The Community of Kent and the Great Rebellion* (1966).

2. L. Stone, *The Causes of the English Revolution* (1972), p. 106.

3. Everitt, 'The Local Community', p. 5.

Court and Country

One dominant theme of work in the 1970s on the origins of the
English civil war was the attempt to tie in the sentiment of provincialism with the notion of twin polarities in English politics in the
period 1621–42, the polarities of Court and Country.

Modern use of the terms derives first from the writings of Hugh
Trevor-Roper, who has employed them to illustrate a basic flaw in
the structure of the states of early modern Europe, including England. He sees the concept of Court and Country as representing
'the tug of opposite interests' within the ruling orders, between the
'Renaissance state', that 'ever-expanding bureaucracy which, though
at first a working bureaucracy, had by the end of the sixteenth
century become a parasitic bureaucracy', and the Country, 'that
undeterminate, unpolitical, but highly sensitive miscellany of men
who mutinied not against the monarchy . . . nor against economic
archaism, but against the vast, oppressive ever-extending apparatus
of parasitic bureaucracy which had grown up around the throne
and above the economy'.[4] The attractiveness of the idea for historians of England was greatly enhanced by Perez Zagorin's demonstration that the terms had been widely used at the time to describe
the polarisation of the political world, particularly in the 1620s.
Zagorin argues that the terms represent the essential conflicts of
political interest in pre-revolutionary England. He described the
polarities as 'diffuse, yet real, not fictitious collectivities [between
which] . . . only hostility could prevail'.[5] A further important dimension has recently been added by Peter Thomas, who sees the two
terms as reflecting the disintegration of the cultural latitudinarian-
ism of the Elizabethan Court and the emergence of an élitist court
aesthetic in the reign of Charles I.[6] Court and Country represented
the distinction between the adherents of the new and the old cultural tastes and forms.

All these writers, and others who have taken to employing the
terms, have been more interested in the Country than in the Court;
the concept of the Court has never been fully worked out. In general, historians have been content to take the opposition's view of

4. H.R. Trevor-Roper, 'The General Crisis of the Seventeenth Century' in T. Aston
(ed.), *Crisis in Europe, 1560–1660* (1965), pp. 114, 78, 94.
5. P. Zagorin, 'The Court and the Country: A Note on Political Terminology in
the Seventeenth Century', *EHR*, Vol. 77 (1962); *The Court and the Country* (1969),
p. 32.
6. P.W. Thomas, 'Court and Country' in C. Russell (ed.), *The Origins of the English
Civil War* (1973).

the Court at face value. In reality, however, the Court was pursuing a coherent, if irresponsible, programme of economic, political and ecclesiastical reform throughout the 1630s. The programme proved to be beyond its administrative resources, but it was neither ineffectual nor hand-to-mouth (at least not until 1638 or 1639).[7]

Furthermore, with the exception of Hugh Trevor-Roper, historians have tended to assume that Court and Country were synonymous with the 'ins' and the 'outs', between whom rugged barriers were fixed. Thus, for Perez Zagorin the Court 'was the traditional collective designation of the monarch, his residence, council, officials and courtiers. But coupled as a term with the Country, it meant [they] . . . had become recognised partisans in a political struggle.'[8] There has been a tendency to overlook the ease with which men who had been leaders of the Country opposition in Parliament moved into office, and also to ignore the number of men within the bureacracy who shared the views (or even enjoyed the patronage) of the leading Country lords. Sir Thomas Wentworth was a leading 'Country' politician in the 1620s and an architect of 'Thorough' in the 1630s, and William Noy, who designed the ship money writs, had earlier acted as a legal and constitutional adviser to the Country party in Parliament. Some of those (like Sir Benjamin Rudyerd or Sir Henry Vane) who spoke out most forcefully about the policies and practices of the Court in the parliaments of 1640, had remained office-holders within the Court throughout the earlier period.

One of the reasons why political life in the 1620s and 1630s was more deeply troubled than hitherto was that Charles I, unlike his predecessors, excluded from office representatives of some of the main currents of political and religious opinion. One of Elizabeth's greatest achievements, surely, had been to contain within her Court and administration representatives of every significant current of thought. Through her careful handling of patronage, she had prevented (until 1601) any group from feeling isolated and left out. Conservatives and radicals in Parliament all felt that they had allies at Court, and the result was that struggles there mirrored those at Court and were one element in an institutionalised contest in which each group sought to win the Queen over to its views. Opposition was 'earthed' to Court faction. It was directed not *against* the Court,

7. The chapters by Hawkins and Tyacke, and to some extent Hill and Corfield, in Russell (ed.), *Origins*, largely remedy this. But we still await a more up-to-date account of Court faction and policy-making in the 1630s the match that written nearly fifty years ago by H.R. Trevor-Roper, *Archbishop Laud* (1940).

8. Zagorin, 'The Court and the Country', p. 310.

but at promoting particular policies and groups already represented
within it. It is not the case that political conflicts in the 1620s were
more dangerous than those which divided Leicester and Walsingham
from Cecil in the 1570s and 1580s. By the reign of Charles I, however, groups were forming around prominent Lords who were
excluded from the Council and from positions of influence. The
leaders of these groups held deeply felt political viewpoints not
represented by any of the cliques in power. Yet despite a growing
divergence over constitutional questions, the key to the 1620s lies
in the belief of the opposition groups that the solution to misgovernment lay not in constitutional change but in their own attainment of office. Unlike Elizabethan factions, they could only make
themselves heard by adopting a strategy of confrontation. The extent to which the parliamentary politics of the period revolve around
the tactical use of parliamentary power has recently been elucid-
ated by Mr Thompson. He has argued that at least one opposition
group used its strength in the Commons as a platform from which
to negotiate its way to office, and he has shown that it nearly succeeded. Much the same group, which included men like the Earl of
Warwick, the Earl of Bedford and John Pym, made another bid for
power in 1640–41. It is not surprising that such men, excluded
from office for so long, should add a hard constitutional edge to
their political beliefs.[9] It is about such groups as this that Zagorin
is thinking when he writes: 'the Country was the first opposition
movement in English history whose character transcended that of a
feudal following or a faction. . . . If faction and party be considered
as alternative types of political structure then the Country approx-
imated more nearly to party.'[10] The papers of the Earl of Bedford
are full of schemes for fiscal, economic, social and political reform.
What he represents is an alternative Court, a shadow cabinet; he represents the articulate minority whose interests were power and the
just exercise of power. I shall call such men the 'official' Country.[11]

But those historians who have used the concept of Court and
Country want it to mean more than this small number of frustrated
courtiers. They want it to mean a broad coalition of interests within
the ruling class. Alongside the 'official' Country was to stand a 'pure'

9. For the 1620s, see C. Thompson, 'The Origins of the Politics of the Parliamentary Middle Group', *TRHS*, 5th ser., Vol. 22 (1972); for the same group's pursuit of
office in 1640–41, see Russell (ed.), *Origins*, pp. 110–16 and *passim*; and 'The Aris-
tocracy and the Downfall of Charles I' in B.S. Manning (ed.), *Politics, Religion and the
English Civil War* (1973).
10. Zagorin, 'The Court and the Country', pp. 74–5.
11. For Bedford's schemes, see Russell (ed.), *Origins*, pp. 112–15.

Country, an alliance of provincial squires fed up with misgovernment and with the corruption and expense of the Court. The concept of a 'Country alliance' has been most clearly laid out by Lawrence Stone. He sees the Country as a yearning for a rustic arcadia, a vision of the moral superiority of the simple country life over the diseased, venal, degenerate Court; it was loyalty to and affection for 'particularist local interests and institutions'. This mentality was combined with 'an increased sense of national identity and an increased respect for its head, the Tudor monarchy, and for its most representative institution, Parliament'. From here, however, Stone makes a great leap to the claim that this 'pure' Country mentality found expression in 'a national programme' put forward by articulate and politically sophisticated spokesmen.[12]

I object to this final leap. I shall argue that if the term 'Country' is useful at all it can be applied only with the proviso that it comprehended two distinct things: a mentality shared by a large number of gentlemen and others (a majority of the political nation by 1640), and a political designation for those groups prepared to use Parliament as a path to office. The former involved an aversion to all politicians. Had Bedford become Lord Treasurer, this great Country party leader would have implemented policies which would have incurred the wrath of the pure Country as surely as had the policies of that other great former Country politician, Strafford. Indeed, one of Bedford's main projected reforms was the introduction of a new parliamentary tax to replace the subsidy. The machinery of Assessment and the very nature of this tax closely resembled that of ship money, the most hated of all the expedients of the personal rule. When we come to consider the nature of the opposition to ship money, we shall see how the 'pure' Country would have reacted to Bedford's scheme.

The great benefit of the concept of the Country is that it helps to explain the political crisis of 1640. For a brief period after Charles's invasion of Scotland the two 'Countries' did make common cause against an isolated and impotent administration, so isolated that it had no existence outside Whitehall (and not much of one within a deeply divided government and household). The gentry and freeholders returned to the parliaments of 1640 those who told them they knew how to put an end to misgovernment. But once the means to be employed became apparent, the alliance broke down. In the summer of 1641 the Country split, and it was out of the split

12. Stone, *Causes*, pp. 98–117.

that the parties of the civil war emerged. At that juncture the terms Court and Country became a liability, and I believe that at this point both Lawrence Stone and Perez Zagorin become misleading. Stone tells us that the existence of the Country is a precondition of the revolution; Zagorin that 'in the strife of the Court and the Country the English revolution had its origins'.[13] Such statements are dangerously inexact. The term is helpful in explaining the crisis of 1640, but not that of 1642.

Two simple illustrations may clarify this point. John Crummett has drawn up lists of those peers who can be considered Courtiers in 1640 (those who identified themselves with the policies of the government during the personal rule, and who held high political or household office) and Country peers (those who disassociated themselves from the politics and life-style of the Court). Of the twenty-eight lay peers closely associated with the Court, fifteen subsequently fought with the King, seven against him; of the thirty-one Country peers, eleven were subsequently royalist, sixteen parliamentarian.

It might be assumed that electors in the two-member constituencies would return men of similar political views, particularly in a year during which national issues were at the forefront of most election campaigns. Indeed, in most constituencies candidates stood as pairs. The county seats in particular could be expected to return men for the Country interest. Yet in half the shires, one member in 1642 joined the King, while the other remained at Westminster. Men like John Fettiplace and Henry Marten, members for Berkshire, or Arthur Capel and William Lytton, members for Hertfordshire, or Peter Venables and Sir William Brereton, members for Cheshire, had all been outspoken critics of royal policies in the 1630s. Yet, in each case, the former became a royalist, the latter a parliamentarian in the years after 1642. No English county except Middlesex returned men to Parliament for its shire and borough seats in 1640 who spoke with one voice in 1642 or later.[14]

Nevertheless, the 1640 elections wherever there was a large or open electorate do show a united front by the electors against the Court interest. There was common agreement about what was wrong, yet even within the 'official' Country leadership there were critical

13. Ibid.; Zagorin, 'The Court and the Country', p. 32.
14. The figures for the Lords are taken from appendices in J.B. Crummett, 'The Lay Peers in Parliament, 1640–1644', University of Manchester Ph.D. thesis (1970); for the Commons, from evidence contained in M.F. Keeler, *The Long Parliament, 1640–1641* (1954), *passim.*

differences of opinion and emphasis. Such colonial ventures as the Providence Island scheme and the Saybrooke Adventurers have often been interpreted as interlocking enterprises, an outpouring of puritan nationalism into the New World, the creation of refuges for the victims of persecution and as blueprints for a reformed English society and institutions. Recent research, however, suggests that there were considerable differences between the aspirations of the leaders of the two schemes. The Saybrooke settlers did indeed pursue a policy of rigid puritanism and political experimentation, reproducing a Zion in America which would later be held forth as a model for England (with regular parliaments of fixed duration, a negative voice in each House, and officers answerable to the legislature). The Providence Island scheme, meanwhile, initiated by the old parliamentary middle group of the 1620s, was pursuing a policy of compromise, resisting attempts to undermine the rites of the Church of England, and only resuming militant privateering schemes against the Spaniards after the failure of the attempt at a peaceful settler economy.[15] Although the leaders of these two groups made common cause against royal misrule in 1640, they represent different visions of the future, as indeed does a third group within the 'Country alliance', that led by the Great Tew Circle, men like Lord Falkland, Sir Edward Hyde and Sir John Colepepper, whose austere concern for constitutional propriety and religious moderation were to make them resolute opponents of the Crown in 1640 and increasingly determined royalists after 1642.

Some men defy a simple Court and Country label. Sir Benjamin Rudyerd was a long-time client of the Earl of Pembroke, both when he was in and out of office, yet he had retained a position as surveyor of the Court of Wards continuously since 1618. In 1640 he adopted a hard-line Country position in politics and religion, and he defiantly christened himself a puritan:

> We well know what disturbance hath been wrought upon the Church for vain, petty trifles. How the whole Church, the whole kingdom, hath been troubled, where to place a metaphor – an altar . . . These inventions are but sieves made on purpose to winnow the best men, and that's the devil's occupation. They have a mind to worry preaching; for I never heard of any but diligent preachers that were vexed with these and like devices. They despise prophecy . . . They would evaporate and dispirit the power and vigour of religion, by drawing it

15. The above is largely based on a paper delivered to Keith Thomas's graduate seminar at Oxford in January 1974 by Mr Christopher Thompson, by whose kind permission I am able to use it here.

into some solemn, specious ceremonies, new furbish'd up . . . They
have so brought it to pass that, under the name of Puritan, all our
religion is branded, and under a few hard words against Jesuits, all
popery is countenanced. Whoever squares his actions by any rule,
either divine or human, he is a puritan. Whoever would be governed
by the King's laws, he is a puritan . . .[16]

Yet within twelve months he had become an opponent of root and
branch reform of cathedrals and cathedral chapters:

Although cathedral churches are now, for the most part, but recept-
acles for drones and non-residents, yet some good men may be found,
or placed there to be assessors with the bishops . . . Burning and
shining lights do well deserve to be set in good candlesticks . . . I am
as much for reformation, for paying and maintaining religion as any
man whatsoever: but I profess, I am not for innovation, demolition
nor abolition.[17]

Rudyerd's rhetoric, like that of Sir Edward Dering and Sir Edward
Hyde, shifted as the social dangers of the root and branch movement
became apparent. The essence of his message was for a magnanimous Parliament to ease the King's burdens, earn his gratitude, make
him see the benefits of working with them and not against them:

A king, Mr Speaker, doth not subsist, untill Hee bee able to lyve
splendidly, magnificently, At Home. Untill Hee be able powerfully
and proportionably To bear up with his neighbours, other princes
Abroad . . . It wilbe our Honor, Mr Speaker, To sett up the king, as
an emulous, envious Pattern to all the Princes of Christendom,
in such a way as Hee shall never want Love nor Money, a playne,
English homespun way, without foraine, highstrained sublimated
inventions.[18]

By the summer of 1642, he was wringing his hands and watching
the movements of his patron. He stayed on in Parliament, one of
the chorus of voices in the wilderness calling for peace and accommodation in the years of war.[19]

Rudyerd understood something of the dynamics of politics. He
had little in common with men like William Davenport of Bramall
Hall, Cheshire, who stands as a paradigm of the pure country squire;

16. BL Tanner MS 65 fos 178–9. See J.S. Morrill, *The Revolt of the Provinces*, previous editions 1976, 1980 (henceforth *RP*), doc. 6a.

17. BL Tanner MS 65 fo. 184. See also *RP* doc. 6c.

18. BL Tanner MS 65, fo. 46.

19. For example W.M. Lamont, 'The Squire Who Changed Sides', *History Today*
(May 1966); D. Hirst, 'The Defection of Sir Edward Dering', *HJ*, Vol. 15 (1972);
B.H.G. Wormald, *Clarendon* (1951), pp. 1–157.

of the mere Country, perhaps. He was the son of a Cheshire squire who sat as a JP, served as sheriff, and built on to his manor house in north-east Cheshire in a style just going out of fashion; the representative of a cadet line of a Domesday family; a squire with one manor and other scattered lands worth £400 per annum, just about in the top fifty of the Cheshire gentry. But he was also a man who kept a commonplace book in which he recorded all the news from London which interested him. The material varied enormously in quality, authenticity and length, but it does reveal the nature of his political interests. With the exception of some scurrilous and obscene verses – usually aimed at royal favourites like the Earl of Somerset and the Duke of Buckingham – most of the material adopted a high moral tone, and was (until 1641) consistently anti-government and specifically anti-Court. For example, a large section dealt with the squalid divorce of the Earl and Countess of Essex and the 'murder' of Sir Thomas Overbury. Much of the material was used to imply criticism of the Court as a whole. It was but part of Davenport's wider interest in Court scandal (much later he recorded details of Lord Castlehaven's trial for sodomy).

Throughout the 1620s, Davenport recorded speeches made in Parliament. But his choice is revealing: he made no reference to the most significant constitutional clashes of the decade (over the Protestations of 1621 and 1629 or the Petition of Right), and concentrated on those issues which concerned personalities, such as the Spanish marriage project and the impeachment of Buckingham (of less constitutional importance than the earlier parliamentary trials of the monopolists and Bacon, 1621, or Cranfield, 1624, in which the Commons had revived its judicial powers).

Most of the remaining material reflects a conventional protestant nationalism. Davenport included sections on the state of the navy in 1624, on the condition of Mansfeld's army in 1625 (at that time acting unsuccessfully on James's behalf), on the disastrous Ile de Ré expedition of 1627, and (in contrast to these feeble efforts by the Stuarts to further the Protestant cause) accounts of the campaigns in Germany of Gustavus Adolphus, King of Sweden and Protestant hero.

The transcripts all reflect a profound disenchantment with the Court, its policies and practices. They also reflect an anti-Court mentality rather than a pro-opposition one. There is not a single reference to any of the activities sponsored by the leading opponents of the Crown, and there is little concern with the very real constitutional issues raised by the crises of 1621 and 1626–29.

By 1640, Davenport was disillusioned with the Crown and its policies, but his antipathy was undiscriminating and superficial. There is no evidence that he was connected to any organised faction, interest or party. Indeed in 1641–42 he was to campaign for a purely local group which consciously disassociated itself from both Crown and parliamentary policies and which ultimately tried to keep Cheshire out of the war as a neutral enclave. When war came, he was strictly passive. Furthermore, on the few occasions on which he revealed anything of his own views, it is clear that his reading had not led him to adopt the language of the 'official' Country. He simply described the Ile de Ré expedition, for example, as 'the most unfortunate journey'. Much clearer was his comment on the distraint of knighthood proceedings. This was one of the many devices by which Charles I strained his traditional rights in the quest for a balanced budget during his personal rule. In 1631, the King appointed commissioners in every county to discover and collect fines from all those gentlemen who had failed to sue for knighthoods at his accession. It was the revival of a half-forgotten royal right. Davenport's general comment was that he was recording 'the strange commission that came down into Cheshire'. To Davenport it was 'strange': a novel unwonted exercise of the Royal prerogative; to the 'official' Country, as portrayed by Zagorin and Stone, it was anything but strange. They could and did see it as part of a consistent programme of illegal and arbitrary action by a government bent on destroying the traditional constitution. Davenport resented royal policies but he did not articulate this resentment within a radical framework of reference, or fit it into a general intellectual mould. It is a crucial distinction which separates him and a majority of the provincial squires from men like Pym and Hampden, who claimed to understand royal policies and who sought to promote their own coherent philosophy of law and government.[20]

We are thus presented with a paradox. By the 1630s there were more sources of information than ever before available to the gentry, who were also far better educated than any previous generation. But it is far from clear that this permitted them to understand the crisis which confronted them in 1640. What made the provincial gentry so formidable and united them in their opposition to the

20. Davenport's commonplace book is in Chester City Record Office, CR/63/2/ 19. For a much fuller account of the man and his career, see J.S. Morrill, 'William Davenport and the "Silent Majority" of Early Stuart England', *Jnl. of the Chester Arch. Soc.* (1974), and for an account of the local environment in which he moved, see J.S. Morrill, *Cheshire, 1630–1660* (1974), chs 1 and 2.

Crown in 1640 was their *lack* of understanding of royal policies. What Charles's ministers were doing was innovative, eroded local traditions and conventions, and produced many social tensions. It deeply troubled the provincial communities and they reacted by using their power to paralyse local government. When Parliament did meet, they sent to Westminster members of the 'official' Country, men who appeared to know how to stop the dangerous and incomprehensible policies, the justification for which was so unclear. Their attitude has been admirably summarised by Ivan Roots: the provincial governors, the justices and the gentry, saw in Strafford and Laud 'dangerous advocates of national unity through uniformity, men quite unfit for the state of England as they knew it and liked it'.[21]

In this respect, their response to the Book of Orders of 1630–31 by which the Privy Council sought to regulate minutely the enforcement of social legislation in every county (particularly the poor laws) is instructive. It was resented less because it imposed intolerable administrative burdens than because it required local justices to carry out the provisions of statute to the letter. It is clear that, particularly in the northern and western shires, local benches had established conventions and customs to meet local needs, many of which ignored or went against the provisions of statute. Thus in Cheshire bridge repairs were undertaken by methods at variance with those prescribed by law, while many counties developed their own methods of ensuring parental care for illegitimate children. Similarly, what enraged county opinion about the monopoly of Sir Giles Mompesson for which he was impeached in 1621 was that it gave him power to license alehouses, a power which bypassed the justices at quarter sessions. One assize grand jury spoke of 'the great inconveniences attending it, both in the execution thereof and in the ymployment of men ill acquainted with the precedents of this county'. Resistance to the Book of Orders thus can largely be explained in terms of Charles's semi-conscious assault on local autonomy and his insistence on obedience to the letter of the statute law.[22]

21. In Ives (ed.), *English Revolution*, p. 42.
22. See the chapter by G.C.F. Foster in A.G.R. Smith (ed.), *The Reign of James VI and I* (1973); by L.M. Hill in Russell (ed.), *Origins*; and by I. Roots and A.M. Everitt in Ives (ed.), *English Revolution*. For a case study see T.G. Barnes, *Somerset, 1625–1640* (1961), ch. 7. See also F. Bamford (ed.), *A Royalist's Notebook* (1936), for example p. 12. Dr Hassell Smith has persuaded me that this pattern is truer of the north and west than of the south and east, and has argued that this was because the practices of these latter regions were more faithfully reflected in the legislation.

The gentry responded to the *effects* of royal policies rather than to their origins or purpose, which remained concealed. On wider political issues, too, they remained surprisingly ill-informed. Although there were no newspapers dealing with English affairs until 1641, an increasing number of illicit broadsheets and pamphlets reporting scandals at Court, speeches by the parliamentary opposition, and other inflammatory material did circulate round the provinces in the 1620s and the 1630s. The fact that Davenport copied out all the papers that interested him might suggest that he was one of a reading circle who received the latest piece of news and then passed it on. Certainly members of a local community seem frequently to have collected copies of recent pamphlets and despatched them home whenever they were in London.[23]

Yet the letters sent home to friends and relations treated great affairs of state in a surprisingly trivial manner. Sir Thomas Knyvett, the cultured Norfolk squire who was frequently in London on legal business, affords a good example. Many of his letters contain news about events in London, but all are purely anecdotal. Thus on 8 June 1629 he wrote to describe the extreme heat and dust of his journey, to give an account of the health of his mother-in-law, and then he comments on the Queen ('the Queene is abroade againe & lookes they say better than she did by farre, so she dazells all men's eyes that looke on her') and on the continued imprisonment of the MPs arrested for their part in holding down the Speaker and seeking to prevent the dissolution of the third Parliament ('The Parlament men are yet in prison & lyklye to lye there still. Saturday next is appointed to heer councel on both sides, but it is thought thay wilbe delayed. You make me merrye with the discourses of that shee Divell . . .'). And on 11 November 1637 he wrote to say that 'the busines nowe talkt on in towne is all about the Question of the shipp money'. But apart from telling his wife that 'Mr St John hath allready spoken for the subject very bould and bravely', he dwells on his failure to attend the day's hearing (despite being 'up by peepe of day') because the crowds ahead of him were so vast. He then discusses the fact that the most fashionable place to dine is with the Moroccan ambassador, and he closes with the latest news about the building of "a new maskqing house" within the Palace of Whitehall'.[24]

23. See for example J. Frank, *The Beginnings of the English Newspaper, 1620–1660* (1961), *passim*, and Zagorin, 'The Court and the Country', pp. 106 ff. For some examples, see B. Howells (ed.), *A Calendar of Letters Relating to North Wales* (1967), pp. 47–9.
24. B. Schofield (ed.), *The Knyvett Letters* (1949), for example, pp. 75–6, 91; *RP* docs 1a, 1b.

Philip Moreton, son of a minor northern gentleman, on the make on the fringes of the Court, sent home a succession of letters in which the affairs of Ireland and the continent were incongruously mixed up with speculations about promotions within Charles I's Household, the success and failure of courtiers in their gambling enterprises, and the state of the London marriage market. The reporting of the news from London and Whitehall throughout the 1620s and 1630s is almost invariably at this level.[25]

The evidence in general suggests that Davenport was typical of the upper gentry in knowing a good deal that was distasteful and unpleasant about the Court, but knowing and understanding less about the real constitutional issues, leaving that to the experts. Here I think it is important not to over-emphasise the educational sophistication of the country gentlemen. It is true, of course, that there had been a remarkable expansion in the number of gentlemen who had attended university or the Inns of Court – over 85 per cent of the justices of the peace by the 1630s, for example. But it should be remembered that the majority went there not to obtain a degree, but a veneer of polite learning. Wilf Prest has added the following caveats against the trend of other recent writers:

> In many respects law then occupied much the same place in the popular mind as economics has enjoyed during the present century. Yet we would not necessarily expect our contemporaries who freely used terms drawn from the language of economics to have had any formal acquaintance with the subject; no more should we regard the litigious Jacobean who speaks portentously of actions, entails and fines as peculiarly gifted with an understanding of the technicalities of the common law.... The instruction provided [by the Inns of Court] concentrated on the minutiae of real property law rather than the broad issues of constitutional jurisprudence . . .[26]

The cultural revolution involved in this expansion of educational facilities and methods is important, but it must not be overrated. It is true that puritan influences were never eradicated from the universities. But neither were the forces of conservatism. The puritanism even of Cambridge in the early seventeenth century was narrower in its emphasis and far less radical than that of the 1570s or 1580s. The point is that a minority took the opportunity to explore political, social and religious ideas, but the majority were probably not affected. Such formal instruction as they underwent would have emphasised obedience to authority and the habit of reading. And

25. BL Add. MS 33936–7, *passim*.
26. W. Prest, *The Inns of Court, 1590–1640* (1972), pp. 152–3.

the sort of reading thereafter pursued by most of them was mani-
festly non-controversial; astronomy, geography, topography, history,
all these had a psychological effect in building up the gentleman's
critical faculties and powers of thought, but hardly afforded a direct knowledge of the constitution and the workings of the government.[27] Antiquarianism had its uses, as in the parliaments of the
1620s where both sides inaptly produced precedents to bolster their
arguments, but most squires were less interested in antiquarianism
as such than in genealogy. This led to some trenchant attacks on
Stuart innovations – above all on the baronetcy;[28] but it seems rarely
to have led to speculation about constitutional issues, except amongst
the 'official' Country intellectuals.

To test these ideas, let us examine provincial reaction to one of
the most controversial of all the government's expedients in the
1630s, ship money. Based on precedents as recent as 1594 and
1626, this was not a tax but a rate levied by the King, by virtue of his
emergency powers, to safeguard the narrow seas. Opposition to it
mounted, but only when it became apparent that the rate was to
become an annual one, and the King's discretionary power to proclaim a permanent state of emergency was questioned in the courts
by John Hampden. But it was not until the summer of 1639 that
opposition became effective. Between 1634 and the autumn of 1638,
90 per cent of the assessments were paid, an extraordinary achievement by seventeenth-century standards, and a far higher percentage than was later achieved by the parliamentary subsidies and poll
tax of 1640–41.[29]

Provincial opposition mounted from 1636 onwards. Yet the crisis
seems to have come not when the judgement in Hampden's case
became known, but when the King compounded his folly by demanding coat and conduct money for the army he intended to use
against Scotland. Professor Barnes believes that the judgements of
the two judges who found for Hampden on constitutional grounds
were widely circulated,[30] but their views seem to have made less

27. For example M. Curtis, *Oxford and Cambridge in Transition, 1558–1642* (1959);
H. Kearney, *Scholars and Gentlemen* (1970); Prest, *Inns of Court*, compare H.A. Lloyd,
The Gentry of South-West Wales, 1540–1640 (1968), pp. 111, 120.

28. Bamford (ed.), *A Royalist's Notebook*.

29. For the Hampden case, see C. Russell, 'The Ship Money Judgements of
Bramston and Davenport', *EHR*, Vol. 77 (1962); W.J. Jones, *Politics and the Bench*
(1971), pp. 126 ff; J.S. Cockburn, *A History of English Assizes, 1558–1714* (1972),
pp. 214–17; for the amount collected annually in each county, see M.D. Gordon,
'The Collection of Ship Money in the Reign of Charles I', *TRHS*, 3rd ser., Vol. 4
(1910), pp. 156–62.

30. Barnes, *Somerset*, pp. 225–8.

impact than we might have expected. The case aroused intense interest, and the court was packed to hear the cut and thrust of legal argument.[31] Yet the King's right to levy the rate was rarely questioned in the provinces. Ship money was hated for its costliness and its disruptive effects on the social and political calm of the communities, but remarkably few references to Hampden's case can be found in the records. Many, reasonably enough, delayed making payment in the hope of a favourable opinion for Hampden which would absolve them from paying. Yet once the King had won, the great majority did pay. The efficiency of the tax in the year of the Hampden case (October 1637–September 1638) was still over 90 per cent. Thus in Yorkshire, where a sheriff had earlier reported that the Hampden case 'did much retard the service in respect of the greate expectation men had thereof', almost eleven of the twelve thousand pounds assessed were eventually collected.[32] Sir Francis Thornagh, Sheriff of Nottinghamshire, was the only one to report that the outcome had actually stiffened resistance.[33]

One reason for the fiscal success of ship money in the early years was the studiedly moderate policy adopted by a government which, for once, was determined not to create martyrs. Refusal to pay led to the unpleasantness of distraint, but not to arrests or imprisonment. Lord Say and Sele, who made a great fuss about refusing to pay, was left to bluster, while payment was exacted by distraining and selling his cows on an outlying farm.[34] As the sheriff of Merioneth reported, 'I believe it is his Majesty's pleasure that his subjects shall be mildly dealt with, which makes me presume to levy the mize [assessments] more leisurely of the poorer sort, but I shall have the money to pay in such time as shall be acceptable'.[35] Even Hampden was left undisturbed after his counsel had charged the King with constitutional impropriety. The King could afford to be magnanimous; he was winning.

The pattern of opposition is curious; many of the men who were later to become prominent in the opposition within the Long Parliament were diligent ship money sheriffs (these included Sir Simonds d'Ewes in Suffolk and Sir John Gell in Derbyshire),[36] while

31. For example Schofield (ed.), *Knyvett*, p. 91; *RP* doc. 1c.
32. See for example J. Cliffe, *The Yorkshire Gentry from the Reformation to the Eve of the Civil War* (1969), p. 309; Russell (ed.), *Origins*, p. 87; *CSPD, 1637–1638*, p. 327.
33. Ibid., p. 443.
34. C.V. Wedgwood, *The King's Peace, 1637–1641* (1955), pp. 156–8.
35. *CSPD, 1637–1638*, p. 328.
36. According to Mary Keeler, *Long Parliament*, p. 14, forty-six members of the Long Parliament had served as ship money sheriffs, yet only fourteen were reprimanded

many future royalists appear amongst its most trenchant opponents (these included Sir Marmaduke Langdale in Yorkshire, Sir Thomas Aston in Cheshire, and Sir Francis Seymour in Wiltshire). There is a further point: in many places such opposition as existed in 1634–38 came not from the county leadership but from the yeomanry and tenant farmers. In Lancashire, only three gentlemen can be found who were actively opposed to ship money, and popular resistance was confined to the backward and largely recusant Lonsdale and Amounderness hundreds. The heavily puritan area around Manchester paid up apparently without trouble.[37] Only one Yorkshire gentleman appeared in opposition before 1638, a recusant who claimed he was being made to pay twice.[38] Sir Francis Astley, Sheriff of Norfolk, listing defaulters in May 1638, could name no one more prominent than four head constables, two attorneys and a clergyman. In 1636, a report from Dorset claimed that 'the greatest part of the arrears falls among the poorer sort'; East Anglia generally paid above the national average until the end of 1638; and as late as 1640, the escheator of Worcester wrote that the gentry were not to blame for the remissness of the county.[39]

Some reports do mention gentry leadership, but they were a minority until 1639. Hampden, then, represented the articulate, official opposition position, but it is not clear that the provinces as a whole were behind them on the issue. A great county leader like Warwick could instigate a tax strike as early as 1636, but he backed down when the King threatened to break his local power by dismissing his nominees from local posts, and the county paid up throughout 1637–38.[40] What produced the collapse of co-operation in 1639–40 was not a growing awareness of the great constitutional issues raised by Hampden's lawyers, but a growing fear of the

---

for dilatoriness and none for actually opposing the service. Significantly, no action was instigated by the parliament into the activities of even the most zealous sheriffs. For d'Ewes, see *RP* doc. 4e.

37. *CSPD, 1640*, p. 229; G.H. Tupling, 'The Causes of the Civil War in Lancashire', *Trans. of the Lancs. and Cheshire Antiq. Soc.*, Vol. 65 (1955), pp. 23–9; B.G. Blackwood, 'The Lancashire Gentry, 1625–1660', University of Oxford D.Phil. thesis (1973), p. 179.

38. Cliffe, *Yorkshire Gentry*, p. 313.

39. *CSPD, 1637–1638*, p. 395; *CSPD, 1636–1637*, p. 151; *CSPD, 1640–1641*, p. 61. It is, of course, arguable that local officials deliberately set out to protect their friends and neighbours by concealing gentry leadership, but I am not convinced by this view.

40. C. Holmes, *The Eastern Association and the English Civil War* (1974), pp. 20–1. This book appeared after the completion of this introduction. I had, however, earlier read Holmes's thesis (University of Cambridge Ph.D. thesis (1968)). Wherever possible, I have amended footnotes, but have been unable to take account of the new evidence and emphases contained in the book.

consequences of ship money for the economic and social stability of each county community.

As Tom Barnes has pointed out, the earliest complaints about ship money were made not on constitutional but on administrative grounds;[41] the instructions of the Privy Council were contradictory and confusing. Sheriffs were instructed to proceed on the basis that ship money should be assessed like any other county rate (such as those for poor relief or for the repair of highways and bridges). But because of the scale of the ship money rate (equivalent to more than two parliamentary subsidies) and because it was recognised that many local rating lists were out of date, sheriffs were given discretionary powers to make adjustments. This allowed endless disputes to develop within each county with the possibility of an appeal over the sheriff's head to the Privy Council. Delays, disputes and violence were the natural outcome and almost all the opposition in the years 1635–38 can be said to have arisen from this confusion. One prevalent source of dispute was the distribution between boroughs and county; another was that between different hundreds.[42] The system required the sheriff to divide the total for his shire between the hundreds and then, assisted by the head constables, to subdivide these sums amongst the parishes and townships. He was then required to assess individuals within each village by calling on the help of 'the most substantial' inhabitants, and he would frequently find himself being offered contradictory advice by different groups within a village.[43] Indeed it is surprising that the consequent administrative chaos did not lead to even greater trouble. Many of the problems were intractable. A sheriff of Lincolnshire inquired whether newly drained fens were to be assessed according to traditional rates or new ones;[44] the assessments in Huntingdonshire in 1637 were delayed by disputes about which local rates were to be employed (some townships paid their tithes and ecclesiastical rates, including poor rates, to one parish, other 'leys' to another). The sheriff defended his delay, pointing out that he had 'to take special care lest he should break their ancient customs, which would much disturb the business'.[45]

41. Barnes, *Somerset*, p. 209 ff; Gordon, 'Collection of Ship Money', pp. 145–8; *CSPD, 1635–1640, passim.*

42. Good examples include *CSPD, 1636–1637*, p. 445; *CSPD, 1639–1640*, p. 345; Barnes, *Somerset*, pp. 209–15; J.R. Philipps, *The Civil War in Wales and the Marches* (2 vols, 1874), Vol. 1, pp. 71–4. See also *RP* doc. 4c.

43. For example *CSPD, 1636–1637*, p. 408 (petition of the inhabitants of Brigstock, Northamptonshire).

44. *CSPD, 1637*, p. 56.   45. *CSPD, 1636–1637*, p. 440.

Many of these disputes reawakened dormant but profound jurisdictional conflicts. The city of Chester, for example, had long wanted
to destroy the independence of the enclave of Gloverstone which
lay within its walls but which was excluded from the jurisdiction of
the corporation by a clause in the city's charter. The enclave was a
haven for unlicensed, unincorporated tradesmen and retailers. The
city used the ship money writs as an excuse to reopen the whole
question. Similarly, the city sought to treat all dean and chapter
revenues as liable to assessment towards the city's rate, and also to
assess the county gentry on their business interests within the city.
The Privy Council, by deciding against the city on the first two
counts and against the county on the third, succeeded in alienating
everybody.[46]

Many prominent opponents of the Crown were only concerned
with such issues. Robert Phelipps, a leading member of the parliamentary opposition in the 1620s,[47] and William Strode[48] were only
interested in protecting their own hundreds from over-assessment,
and Phelipps's son expressed an open willingness to pay so long as
customary procedures were followed.[49] Sheriffs had a vested interest
in exaggerating rather than minimising the extent of opposition,
yet they all agreed that rating disputes were the real, not just the
feigned, ground of opposition. The sheriff of Shropshire in 1637
wrote that only 'the inequality of assessments has caused delay'.[50] A
sheriff of Somerset expected no opposition once he had completed
his adjustment of the assessments,[51] and others concurred.[52]

Ship money opposition was first evident amongst the middling
sort because this was the first heavy burden paid by them to the central government for decades. Except for the now defunct fifteenths
and tenths, the burdens of taxation had come increasingly to fall
on a smaller percentage of the freeholders. The subsidy rolls now
included about 10 per cent of all householders, far fewer than those
assessed for local rates, such as those for the poor or for bridge
repairs. It may be true that the burden of the subsidies fell heaviest
on the poorer of those included, but a majority of freeholders
escaped altogether. Ship money was the first rate or tax ever paid

46. See A.M. Johnson, 'Some Aspects of the Political, Constitutional, Social and
Economic History of the City of Chester, 1550–1662', University of Oxford D.Phil.
thesis (1971), ch. 3; BM Harl. MS 2093 fos 90–173; BL Harl. MS 2173 fos 19–40. For
a rating dispute at Hereford, see *RP* doc. 4a.
47. *CSPD, 1635*, pp. 409, 495, 502, 575; *CSPD, 1636–1637*, pp. 15, 31, etc.; Barnes,
Somerset, pp. 216–19.
48. *CSPD, 1636–1637*, pp. 400–1, 522.   49. *CSPD, 1637*, pp. 18–19.
50. *CSPD, 1637*, p. 378.   51. *CSPD, 1636–1637*, p. 428.
52. *CSPD, 1636–1637*, p. 3. See *RP* docs 4a, 4d.

by a majority of freeholders for a use outside the shire. In Essex, for example, where only 3,200 names occur in the 1640 subsidy roll, 14,500 families were assessed for ship money.[53] Elsewhere the rating books for the poor, for landscot or other local rates unquestionably brought thousands of families into a national rating system for the first time.[54]

Such opposition as was dignified by legal arguments was concerned more with questioning the sheriffs' powers and authority to enforce payment than with the legality of the rate itself. The Privy Council had characteristically decided to issue ship money writs to the sheriffs rather than to the justices in the hope that a single man would be more easily browbeaten than a bench. But the sheriffs' powers to modify rates and to sell distrained goods were far from clear, and there was a growing feeling that the Council's instructions required sheriffs to exceed their legal powers. In 1640 for example, Sheriff Warcopp of Oxfordshire reported that 'no constable will assist distraint, as they will be sued by those claiming the sheriffs' warrant not sufficient to bear them out'.[55] Pleas by the sheriffs to the justices for help were rebuffed with the claim that they had no power to intervene.[56] The much-harassed sheriff of Lincolnshire for 1640 – John Brownlow – reported that not only was he thwarted by the non-compliance of corporate boroughs, in which 'I have noe power to levye', but by the obstruction of those employed to assess and collect the rate in the county itself:

> the officers usually imployed to distreyne doe most of them pretend a feare that they should thereby make themselves lyable to actions and suits, and therefore refuse the service unlesse they maye be secured and divers of them certifie me that offering to distreyne they have been threatened and had violence offered them and that havinge distreyned they can find none that will buy distresses . . .[57]

The position of sheriffs once they had left office was particularly difficult.[58] Wherever magistrates can be found intervening, their

53. PRO, SP 16, Vol. 357; see B.W. Quintrell, 'The Government of the County of Essex, 1603–1642', University of London Ph.D. thesis (1965), ch. 9.

54. *CSPD, 1636–1637*, pp. 3, 211. For a discussion of the different bases used in different counties, see Cliffe, *Yorkshire Gentry*, pp. 141–2.

55. *CSPD, 1635*, p. 505; *CSPD, 1640–1641*, p. 70. See also *CSPD, 1636–1637*, p. 291 (Derbyshire); *CSPD, 1639–1640*, pp. 105–6 (Devon); F. Jessup, *Sir Roger Twysden* (1965), p. 36.

56. J. Hurstfield, *Freedom, Corruption and Government in Elizabethan England* (1973), p. 278.

57. PRO, SP 16, Vol. 457/92. See also *CSPD, 1635–1636*, p. 221 (Merioneth).

58. *CSPD, 1639*, p. 413.

actions appear to reflect a sincere desire to uphold custom and law and order. There is little evidence that they were concerned to use ship money as a cover for deeper political designs. There is also a great difference between this concern with local traditions and local stability, and the preoccupation with fundamental laws and with the belief that ship money constituted an instrument of absolutism which some historians have discerned in their actions. Ship money created feuds between town and country, hundred and hundred, village and village; it angered and embittered the poorer members of the community; it required the sheriffs to strain their powers; above all it exemplified the government's insensitivity towards localist sentiment and belief. No wonder that by 1639–40 the gentry were united in their determination to halt the progress of a regime bent on novel, socially disruptive policies. The constitutional propriety of ship money was not the main reason for the opposition to it. What had changed between 1634 and 1639 was not the gentry's opinion of Charles's constitutional arguments but the breakdown of peace, quiet and order in the local communities. The gentry were less concerned with the theoretical implications of Charles's use of his prerogative than with the unacceptable consequences of his actions. Even if Charles's *constitutional* position had been impeccably orthodox and uncontroversial, he would still have been faced by a tax strike in 1640.

The growing unrest finally found expression in outbreaks of popular violence and in the non-cooperation of county governors during the summer of 1639. The turning-point came not with the judgement in Hampden's case but with Charles's fresh demands for men and money for his war to enforce obedience and the new Prayer Book on the Scots. Sheriffs, now faced with the responsibility of helping to raise and equip (by coat and conduct money) men for the war, could no longer put pressure on their subordinates to gather ship money. 'I could not possibly effect it now, having been employed . . . in impressing soldiers out of the trained bands for his Majesty's service in the Northern parts,' wrote the sheriff of North-amptonshire.[59] The sheriff of Worcester even released constables whom he had imprisoned for opposing him over ship money: 'in respect of this great service concerning the soldiers I thought fit to set them at liberty, that there might be no neglect in the execution of that service.'[60] The mayor and sheriffs of Bristol sought to 'ex-cuse their neglect in omitting to give an account of the ship money

59. Ibid., p. 21.   60. *CSPD, 1640*, p. 300.

by the time spent in collecting the late coat and conduct money and exercising the soldiers'.[61] In Denbighshire the sheriff was powerless to prevent the constables using the money they had collected as ship money to cover coat and conduct money assessments.[62] The Bishops' Wars brought fresh local grievances: the use of the carefully stored arms of the county militia, and of the militia itself, was resented not only because of the drain on resources, but because the gentry (already anxious about rumours of invasions from Ireland or the Continent) found the prospect of being left without local defence intolerable.[63] Many regiments raised for the campaign mutinied, and riots by troops were reported from over twenty counties, the soldiers destroying altar rails and stained glass windows in the churches, symbols of the new Laudian idolatry, or joining the enclosure rioters to pull down hedges.[64] The winter of 1639–40 was a bleak time as local government ground to a halt and the economic depression, particularly in the clothing areas, led to a fresh wave of rioting. Yet throughout 1640 Charles intensified the crisis; a new writ for ship money, the largest yet (after a lowering of his demands in 1639); fresh levies for a second war against the Scots; fresh initiatives from the King and his clerical advisers with his canons of convocation, still prescribing purgatives rather than ointment for the fevered Church. It may be that if coat and conduct money had not brought about its collapse, a more formidable opposition to ship money would have developed in any case as its permanence became recognised. Professor Barnes has argued that in Somerset opposition was developing constitutional overtones by 1638–39, and a parallel might be drawn with the gradual shift from administrative to principled opposition to patentees in Elizabethan Norfolk.[65] But I must say that there is little evidence that this shift had in fact already occurred. This is surprising, but not more so than the fact that so little fuss had been made of the extension of ship money to the inland counties. Indeed complaints about this appear to have diminished with time. Initially, it was used as a subsidiary ground of complaint (especially by the towns), but little is heard of it after 1637.[66]

61. Ibid., p. 487.   62. *CSPD, 1639*, p. 113.

63. A.M. Everitt, *The Community of Kent and the Great Rebellion* (1966), p. 66; E. Broxap, *The Great Civil War in Lancashire* (reprinted 1974), p. 9.

64. For example *CSPD, 1640*, pp. 314–16 and *passim.*

65. Barnes, *Somerset*; A. Hassell Smith, *County and Court: Government and Politics in Norfolk, 1558–1603* (1974), p. 334 and *passim.*

66. Compare A.H. Lewis, *A Study of Elizabethan Ship Money* (1928), p. 70.

Small wonder that both elections in 1640 were so fiercely contested and witnessed the rout of the Courtiers.[67] But it is equally clear that even opposition magnates had difficulty in securing the election of clients 'foreign' to the seats. As John Gruenfelder says: 'national issues played an important role . . . these issues added to the growing spirit of localism a desire to elect men of reputation and connection within the county or borough'.[68] Of course the elections of 1640 were about ship money, religious innovations and other royal policies. But this does not mean that the elections were about the opposition leaders' constitutional case against those policies. They were against the *effects* of royal policy on the local community. Each county reacted differently according to the particular local burden of particular policies. Paul Slack, correcting Gruenfelder's thesis in a study of the Salisbury elections of 1640, shows how concern with national political issues arose out of local controversies.[69]

The petitions which the communities sent up with their members (local factions frequently sinking their differences for this, if not for the elections themselves) were a curious blend of national and local issues. For example, a Berkshire grand jury petition from Midsummer 1640 spoke of 'sundry grievances of divers natures', headed by ship money and coat and conduct money, but then moved on to deal with the report that many – threatened by impressment – had forsaken their places of habitation and taken to the woods, leaving their families 'to bee maintained by the parrish, and harvest worke undone for wante of labourers'; while a Herefordshire grand jury petition of January 1641 was concerned first with wears erected on the River Wye (blocking navigation, and not 'putt downe according to the statute of Magna Carta'), then with the dumping of Spanish wool on the English market to the detriment of English sheep farmers, then with the jurisdiction of the Council in the Marches, then with ship money and coat and conduct money, and finally with the damage to woodland occasioned by new iron mills.[70] In many counties, local factions contended to portray themselves as the men best able to demand a restoration of good government. The electorate listened gratefully to those pushed forward by great men who seemed to speak knowledgeably and

67. J.K. Gruenfelder, 'The Elections to the Short Parliament' in H.S. Reinmuth (ed.), *Early Stuart Studies* (1970); Keeler, *Long Parliament*, pp. 33–80.

68. Gruenfelder, 'Elections to the Short Parliament', p. 224.

69. P. Slack, 'An Election to the Short Parliament', *BIHR*, Vol. 113 (1973).

70. PRO, SP 16, Vol. 468/42. See also Webb, *Herefordshire*, Vol. 2, pp. 335–6 (*RP* doc. 5b).

authoritatively about the grounds of misrule. The voters put their trust in men whose religious, even political, radicalism did not emerge until later; either it was hardly mentioned or the electors were deafened by the talk of an end to the past innovations. Only later did the implications emerge. In Cheshire, for example, the conservative gentry backed Sir William Brereton, a puritan with 'official' Country connections through the Massachusetts Bay Company and known to be popular with the freeholders. They had no doubt that he was really 'their' man. They cheered the early measures of the Long Parliament but grew alarmed when Brereton took up the cause of presbyterianism and the ideal of the godly commonwealth. By the middle of 1641 his erstwhile backers had turned against him. One of them said that he 'loved Sir Wm Brereton well, but yet . . . loved decency, order and good discipline better'. Brereton represents the articulate minority swept in by the spring tide of fear and confusion of 1640.[71] When the panic receded, they were left far more prominently placed in the political landscape than would have seemed possible in terms of their actual numbers and representativeness at other times. By mid-1641 the Long Parliament had ceased to represent the views of the English provinces.

In 1640 Charles I had no party. He was faced by a national tax strike and a parliament containing men who sought power for themselves as the prelude to a radical shift of policy. He was also faced by massive desertions from the Court, both by men who shared the principles of the opposition groups, and by those prepared to ally with the opposition in order to dump Strafford and advance themselves. What is remarkable about the outbreak of the civil war is not why the Crown was confronted by an organised opposition: it is how the Crown gained a party of its own.

Reactions to Crisis, 1640–42

The leaders of the various groups within the Long Parliament maintained an uneasy alliance for almost twelve months. There was agreement about the need to destroy the institutional instruments of royal misrule, the prerogative courts (Star Chamber, High Commission, the Councils in the North and the Marches), and the need for regular parliaments for the presentation and redress of the grievances of the subject (achieved in a Triennial Act which included

71. Morrill, *Cheshire*, pp. 29–34 and *passim*.

machinery for elections to be held even if the King failed to issue writs). For the immediate future the King agreed to a Bill which allowed the Long Parliament to sit until it agreed to its own dissolution. The advocates of Thorough were removed from power (Strafford by attainder, the judges and Laudian bishops by impeachment), or fled abroad; but there was less agreement about the solution to other problems. Foremost amongst them was the reform of the Church, for although the machinery of Laudian innovation was broken, there were considerable and growing disagreements about what should take its place. The question of further sanctions to limit the Crown had barely been raised, since it was widely imagined that Charles would be forced to take leaders of the opposition into his government. This presumption was based partly on the belief that Charles had no political choice. But it was also thought that there were insufficient alternative men able enough to fill the increasing number of vacancies. Indeed, a start had been made in the spring of 1641 by the swearing of four leading lords on to the Privy Council and by the offer of the Solicitorship to Oliver St John, Hampden's principal counsel in the ship money case. It was widely expected that Bedford would come in as the new Lord Treasurer and Pym as Chancellor of the Exchequer.

But by the autumn a fresh crisis had arisen. Bedford was dead, and the King seemed determined to abandon the policy of conciliation. He had found new advisers from unforeseen sources, Hamilton from Scotland and Digby, a former oppositionist recently returned from Spain. The Scots army, sympathetic to (indeed its leaders in close communication with) leading parliamentarians, had gone home and was disbanding, just as the rebellion in Ireland created the need for a fresh army which might later become available for use in England. As the unity of the Parliament crumbled, those who had hitherto seen their possession of office as an essential safeguard against a royal coup, had little choice but to seek fresh guarantees to preserve their own safety and to maintain the administrative revolution of the past year.

Meanwhile, the King's credibility had collapsed. Many of the parliamentary leaders had been in close touch with the Covenanters in Scotland since 1638 (it was fear that Strafford would publicise these treasonable designs which prompted the precipitous attack on him in the first week of the parliament), and they were fully aware that the King had adopted tactics towards the Covenanters which were entirely governed by deceit and double-dealing. As Henry Parker said in 1642: 'there was no difference . . . betwixt that case of the Scots and this of ours.'[72] The exact extent of royal involvement in the Army Plots of 1641 to get rid of Parliament and its leaders was dangerously unclear.

Any remaining doubts about the King's ill-faith were removed by the attempt on the Five Members in January 1642. All hope of a *rapprochement* had vanished, and out of the atmosphere of suspicion and distrust a new policy had to be forged. At last there emerged an issue on which no compromise was possible. Parliamentary control first of the London militia, then of the provincial trained bands, and finally of the army became the cornerstone of Pym's demand for a radical, though essentially pragmatic, redistribution of executive power. A justification of these claims, newly generated by the crisis of 1641–42, couched in the language of mixed monarchy, was evolved only after the event.[73]

But in the process, the kaleidoscope of power had been shaken and a new pattern formed. The moderate, pragmatic reformers around Pym allied themselves to all those who were determined to achieve an immediate and radical revolution in the Church. These religious radicals included political conservatives like Sir Simonds d'Ewes and also that group around Lords Say and Brooke whom we have already seen as the visionaries of the 1630s. But meanwhile the Great Tew group, those men like Falkland and Hyde who had retained a narrowly constitutionalist and conservative interpretation of the crisis of 1640, were rapidly moving away from those whom they now believed to be challenging the traditional constitution. After working secretly for Charles in the two Houses for several months, they were taken into the government and accepted important posts in the spring of 1642.

Splits in the unity of the opposition had begun to appear midway through 1641. Although the Commons had passed the attainder of Strafford with little opposition, the debates on religion – particularly between the advocates of presbyterianism and of limited episcopacy – had become so heated that the issue had to be temporarily shelved. But it was the debates on the Grand Remonstrance (November 1641), that catalogue of royal misdeeds which adumbrated parliamentary demands for control of royal appointments, which really revealed the divisions within the Commons. The tendentious and

---

72. Quoted by M.J. Mendle, 'Politics and Political Thought' in Russell (ed.), *Origins*, p. 231.
73. For the essentially pragmatic nature of the Militia Ordinance, see L.W. Schwoerer, 'The Fittest Subject for a King's Quarrel; An Essay on the Militia Controversy, 1642', *JBS*, Vol. II (1971).

aggressive content of the Remonstrance itself led 148 members to
vote against it; but the decision to publish it, to appeal directly
to the people without offering it to King or House of Lords, led to
unprecedented scenes of fury in the Commons. It was concern for
proper parliamentary procedure which Hyde stressed in his speech
against the Remonstrance. This was the great turning-point in the
history of the Long Parliament. Pym's decision to press forward
with it at all costs was both cause and effect of the breakdown in the
unity of the opposition to Charles. Aware of the disappearance of
a majority for further change in the Lords, and conscious of the
erosion of support in the Commons, he was forced to appeal to
forces outside the parliament, just as he was forced to further the
aims of those radicals seeking to overthrow the oligarchy in the
government of London and to maintain popular pressure around
the doors of the Houses of Parliament. Angry, anxious pickets had
earlier lobbied the Lords to secure the attainder of Strafford. They
were called on again to ensure the passage of the Bill depriving the
bishops of their votes in the Upper House and to complete the
revolution in city government.

Yet this calculated appeal to the populace could only result in
the further alienation of those who saw in such tactics the continuation of the very threats to order and hierarchy which had made
them so desperately opposed to the Crown in 1640. The royalist
party was born out of the same concern for adherence to law and
constitutional propriety which had been the hallmark of the speeches
of Hyde, Colepepper, Falkland, Dering and their allies throughout.
These men now came to see that it was time to close with the
King; and when he offered them the positions within the government which had earlier seemed to be the right of the Bedford–Pym
group, they could accept without any change in their principles.
Throughout 1642 they represented the King's publicly declared
policy. They advocated on his behalf a theory of mixed monarchy
which was consistent with their earlier views. It was the other Country party leaders and the King who had shifted their ground. Pym,
in the Nineteen Propositions, put forward a ·parliamentary programme which articulated the case for fresh controls to preserve
the revolution of 1640–41. Colepepper's Answer to the Nineteen
Propositions was a defence of that revolution as it stood; but it also
pointed to the dangerous social implications of Pym's tactical and
ideological shift. The appeal to the people, he wrote, would soon
awaken them to an awareness of their latent power: they would
realise

that all this was done by them, but not for them and grow weary of journey-work, and set up for themselves, call parity and independence liberty, devour that estate which had devoured the rest; destroy all rights and proprieties, all distinctions of families and merit, and by this means this splendid and excellently distinguished form of government end in a dark, equal chaos of confusion, and the long line of our many noble ancestors in a Jack Cade or a Wat Tyler.[74]

The situation in the provinces was rather different. Men at Westminster were acutely aware of the interplay of personality and politics, had lived through and corporately experienced the great debates and the traumas of 1640–41, above all were subject to forces which tended to polarise and divide. In the counties, on the other hand, the pressures tended to unite the ruling groups and to make them increasingly confused about the nature, and unsure of the importance, of events at Westminster and Whitehall. The central reality for them was the increasing evidence of the collapse of order. It is unclear whether rioting and violence were more extensive than hitherto, but most gentlemen certainly *believed* that they were. Disruption, often with an overt class basis, was certainly widespread. The King's army marching to Scotland had sacked churches or attacked their conductors in at least twenty counties; preachers, unmuzzled and vengeful, had instigated attacks on Laudian ornaments in the churches (altar rails and stained glass windows were prime targets); disruption of religious services and the settling of old scores were widespread. Enclosure riots spread across the country, particularly in the midlands and north; in some cases not only the fences but the houses of the gentry were attacked. I have found evidence of enclosure rioting in twenty-six English counties in the years 1640–44. Apprentices, affected by the dislocation of the cloth trade, rioted in many towns, and these riots often extended to attacks on the homes of respectable catholics; there was widespread opposition to the payment of tithes, with tithebarns and manorial records being burned (for example at the Buckinghamshire home of Sir Richard Minshall in August 1642). Some instances showed a high level of organisation. The enclosures of Gillingham forest were thrown down by men operating a shift system; and during the

74. For the Hyde–Colepepper group see Wormald, *Clarendon*; Mendle, in Russell (ed.), *Origins*; J.T. Pickles, 'Studies in Royalism in the English Civil War', University of Manchester MA thesis (1968), ch. 1. For the Grand Remonstrance, see S.R. Gardiner, *The Fall of the Monarchy of Charles I* (1882), Vol. 2, pp. 303–27 and J. Bruce (ed.), 'The Verney Papers', *Camden Society* (1845), pp. 120–8. For the Nineteen Propositions and the King's Reply, see C.C. Weston, *English Constitutional Theory and the House of Lords, 1558–1832* (1965), ch. 1.

Countess of Sussex's confrontation with oyster fishermen in the
Essex marshes, her opponents established a common defence fund
to pay for their disruption and to help the families of those killed
or injured in the ensuing violence.[75]

A wave of rumours about popish plots and about the intention
of the Irish rebels to carry their campaign into England, also led
to fresh rioting.[76] The gentry were aware that many rioters had
asserted that 'if we take not advantage of this time, we shall never
have the opportunity again'.[77]

Whether or not these riots were more serious than those earlier
in the century, they profoundly shocked the gentry whose overwhelming response was to assert that at such a time the political
differences between King and Parliament could not be allowed to
continue. The great majority yearned for settlement.

Furthermore, they were confused. It is true that the years 1641
and 1642 saw an astonishing increase in the volume of news and
propaganda: the first English newspapers devoted to English affairs,
the publication of many important speeches by leaders of all parties, the concoction of didactic pamphlets appealing to particular
interest groups such as the London artisans or the provincial gentry.
In a period of indecision men scrambled to read everything they
could. Many letters from the capital not only gave the latest news
but referred to the enclosure of newsletters and pamphlets, often
representing the views of different opinions or parties. But in general the content of the propaganda would only serve to confuse.
Both sides were aiming at the middle ground: 'I will, to the utmost
of my power, defend and maintain the true reformed protestant
religion established in the Church of England . . . govern by the
known lawe of the land, and that the liberty and property of the
subject may be by them preserved . . . and I do solemnly and faithfully

75. See C. Hill, 'The Many-Headed Monster in Later Tudor and Early Stuart
Political Thinking' in C.H. Carter (ed.), *From the Renaissance to the Counter Reformation*
(1966), pp. 296–324; B.S. Manning, 'The Outbreak of the English Civil War' in R.H.
Parry (ed.), *The English Civil War and Afterwards* (1970), pp. 8–19; R. Yarlott, 'The
Long Parliament and Fear of Popular Pressure, 1640–1646', University of Leeds MA
thesis (1963), chs 1 and 4. For a case study of the riots of 1642, see D.E. Underdown,
Somerset in the Civil Wars and Interregnum (1973), pp. 25–30. Such organisation was
not entirely new. A 'common purse' had been created by rioters in the west in the
late 1620s and the Fens in the mid-1630s.

76. R. Clifton, 'Fear of Popery' in Russell (ed.), *Origins*, pp. 144–67; also his 'Fear
of Catholicism during the First Civil War', *P. and P.* (1971); K.J. Lindley, 'The
Impact of the 1641 Rebellion upon England and Wales, 1641–1645', *Irish History
Studies* (1970).

77. Hill, 'Many-Headed Monster', p. 309.

promise, in the sight of God, to maintain the just privileges and freedom of parliament.' This is from Charles I's protestation at Shrewsbury.[78] Earlier in the same month, Parliament commissioned Essex with the words: 'we, the lords and commons assembled in parliament, have . . . for the just and necessary defence of the protestant religion, of your majesty's person, crown, and dignity, of the laws and liberties of the kingdom, and the privileges of parliaments, taken up arms . . .'.[79]

Both sides emphasised their own moderation and caricatured their opponents as 'schismaticks and atheists' or 'papists and malignants'. No wonder the provincial gentry were confused: Lady Sussex wrote that 'both sides promise so fair, that I cannot see what it is they should fight for'.[80] William Pleydell said, 'we have to steer the bark of state betwixt Scylla and Charybdis, popery on the one side, and I know not what to call it on the other';[81] having read the propaganda of both sides, over eight thousand signatories to a Cheshire Remonstrance could only conclude that 'the joynt actes of a good kinge and a faithfull councell, have so apparantly concurred to the generall good, that wee cannot but looke upon all such as unworthy of future happiness, who doe admitt for currant, that dangerous and disloyall distinction . . . vizt, For the Kinge or for the Parliament'.[82]

With no county (except Middlesex) having all its MPs committed to one party, every community was briefed in moderation by the two sides. The great majority of letters back to the counties throughout the first nine months of 1642 stressed the hopes of a peaceful settlement. Only those in London or with the King knew the extent of the breach, and very few were prepared to admit it.[83] Every communication between the two sides was treated as an olive branch, and the provinces were left unclear as to why no settlement was concluded. And all the time the threat of the collapse of order and local government loomed closer. Incomprehension of the scale of the crisis is exemplified by the comment of Mistress Eure in a letter to Ralph Verney: 'I wish all were well ended, for things stand in soe ill a condition here as we can make noe money of our co[a]lpits.'[84] Lady Sussex too was afraid her rents would not be

78. E. Hyde, Earl of Clarendon, *History of the Great Rebellion* (6 vols, 1887), Book 6, paras 26–7.
79. Quoted in T. May, *The History of the Parliament of England* (1844), p. 247.
80. Verney, *Memoirs*, Vol. 2, p. 90. See *RP* doc. 3a.
81. Quoted by Yarlott, 'Long Parliament', ch. 4.   82. BL Harl. MS 2107 fo. 6.
83. For example, *RP* docs 1–3.
84. Verney, *Memoirs*, Vol. 2, p. 90. See *RP* docs 3b–d.

paid unless a settlement was reached.[85] Most people saw much worse consequences if there was no agreement. Lord Savile wrote: 'I would not have the king trample on the parliament, or the parliament lessen him so much as to make a way for the people to rule us all.'[86] One pamphleteer added: 'most nobility and gentry stickle in their counties for subscription for peace and accommodation, seriously considering that this war would produce a parity in the laity as well as the clergy'.[87] These sentiments were the stuff of royalist propaganda as we have seen, but parliamentarians were equally sensitive. Pembroke probably permitted the publication of a speech he never actually made, but was said to have made in the Lords on 19 December. In it, Pembroke's ghost writer, calling for peace, said: 'we hear every base fellow say in the street as we pass by in our coaches, That they hope to see us a foot shortly and to be as good men as the Lords; and I think they will be as good as their words, if we take this course.'[88]

Fear drove some men into royalism; it drove far more into neutralism. Faced by the threat of social disintegration and incomprehension of the course of events at the centre, most counties closed ranks behind county barriers, determined (as they had been in the 1630s) to protect the administrative integrity of their shires as the first line of defence against disorder. Attempts to neutralise whole areas of the country were set in motion which have never received adequate attention from historians.[89] Indeed, I have found evidence of attempted neutrality pacts in twenty-two English counties and in many boroughs. They can be divided into two broad groups: the totally committed efforts of moderate men – usually representing the leading county governors – to raise a third force to put down both sides and keep out all 'foreigners'; and the demilitarisation pacts made between the royalist commissioners of array and the parliamentarian militia commissioners in an attempt to prevent bloodshed. The first type were more stable and were grounded

85. Verney, *Memoirs*, Vol. 2, p. 83.
86. Quoted by Hill, 'Many-Headed Monster', p. 310.
87. BM, Thomason Tracts, E 93/12.
88. Quoted in C.M. Thomas, 'The First Civil War in Glamorganshire', University of Wales MA thesis (1963), p. 74.
89. The pioneering work in this field is B.S. Manning, 'Neutrals and Neutralism in the English Civil War', University of Oxford D.Phil. thesis (1957); I cannot accept Dr Manning's starting-point that neutralism was 'a temporary stopping place for men of moderate views', and must record that his almost total dependence on printed sources has led him to confuse different types of neutralism. It is still an original and important work. See also the section on neutralism in Holmes, thesis, ch. 2 (omitted in the subsequent book).

more clearly on carefully articulated principles. Thus a group consisting of almost all the active Cheshire justices drew up in August a declaration in which they claimed that both King and Parliament had pledged themselves to the same aims and objectives, that Cheshire men would not submit to either the commission or array or the Militia Ordinance but would call for a cessation of arms and for 'some moderate persons' to act as mediators in the remaining disputes. The copy of this declaration in the papers of Elias Ashmole is conjoined to a copy of the articles agreed by the justices of the West Riding, in which it was agreed to suspend both the Militia Ordinance and the commission of array while 'some moderate person' sought to mediate locally. Meanwhile, they would prevent any outside forces from entering the county. They also sought to suspend both parliamentary and royal commissions 'without disputing the legality or illegality of either, but as finding neither of them soe necessary at this tyme as for setting them on foot to involve this county in blood'. Above all, everything was to be done by and through the 'legall officers and their assistancs onely'.[90] In neighbouring Staffordshire, a specially convened sessions of the peace, held three weeks after the battle of Edgehill, attended by future royalists and parliamentarians, resulted in a declaration against the activities of both sides in neighbouring counties and warned them both to keep out. The justices and grand jury together decided to raise an independent force of eight hundred foot and two hundred horse which would act simply in the name of the county. It was the determined incursions of outsiders, notably from Shropshire, and a rising of the Moorlanders against new fiscal and economic hardships which toppled the majority into the royalist camp; but for many the aim was to quiet the county with royalist help, not to provide a base for royalist attacks on parliamentarians elsewhere.[91]

In Lincolnshire, the gentry declared that they would fight neither for nor against the King, and they raised a troop of horse 'only for the preservation of peace within themselves, in that they resolve (having thus discharged their duties both to the King and the two Houses of Parliament) not to embark further by sending any forces

90. BL Ashmole MS 830 fos 280–4. In *RP* I assumed that the articles of agreement were part of the Cheshire agreement. I am grateful to Anthony Fletcher for pointing out this error to me.
91. Pickles, 'Studies in Royalism', ch. 2; D.H. Pennington, 'County and Country: Staffordshire in Civil War Politics', *N. Staffordshire Journal of Field Studies*, Vol. 6 (1966); D.H. Pennington and I.A. Roots, *The Committee at Stafford, 1643–1645* (1957), p. xx.

out of the county, to aid either side, but as much as in them lies, to endeavour accommodation'.[92]

The crisis of 1642, far from demonstrating the limitations of provincialism, marked its triumph. Nottinghamshire gentry remonstrated with their knights for exceeding their commission and for involving them in the arbitrary orders of the parliament. The petitioners suggested that it was no part of the representatives' function to tell the county what to do.[93]

The same point is made by the conciliators in those counties where the neutrality moves were initiated by the leaders of the two parties. In Yorkshire, for example, where the leading commissioners of array and Deputy Lieutenants attempted a demilitarisation, the aim, according to a local critic, was 'to put the county in a mere neutrality; that is to estate themselves in a civil independency; this is to make every county a free estate . . . to set up an interpretive court above a legislative, and to call the conclusions of England to the Bar of Yorkshire'.[94] Similar attempts by the leaders of both sides achieved success briefly in Cheshire, Cornwall, Devon and Wiltshire,[95] and were attempted in several other counties.[96]

Clive Holmes has drawn attention to the very widespread neutralism in all the counties of East Anglia, heartland of parliamentarianism and puritanism.[97] In Suffolk, for example, a group of gentlemen attempted to gain the support of the grand jury at assizes for a petition which proclaimed neutralist ends.[98] Both the Militia Ordinance and the collection of Propositions were left unenforced until Sir Nathaniel Barnardiston arrived from Westminster. Holmes has argued that Suffolk was particularly hard hit by popular riots with a hard edge of social conflict, and that most gentry were prepared to support any movement which would put down the riots and maintain order. Initially they supported the neutralist group, but once the Militia Ordinance had been implemented they backed the local parliamentarians as the most likely way to prevent further violence. Local parliamentarian propaganda

---

92. BL, Thomason Tracts, E 113/7.   93. Quoted by Hirst, 'Defection', p. 194.
94. BL, Thomason Tracts, E 240/30.
95. For Cheshire, see Morrill, *Cheshire*, pp. 66–9 (see also Manning, 'Neutrals', pp. 66–102, but compare W. Phillips (ed.), 'The Ottley Papers', *Trans. Salop. Arch. and Nat. Hist. Soc.*, 2nd ser., Vol. 6, pp. 40–2). For Devon and Cornwall, see E. Andriette, *Devon and Exeter in the Civil War* (1972), pp. 82–4; M. Coate, *Cornwall in the Great Civil War and Interregnum* (1930), pp. 36–7, 54–6; Manning, 'Neutrals', pp. 103 ff. For Wiltshire, see G.A. Harrison, 'Royalist Organisation in Wiltshire, 1642–1646', University of London Ph.D. thesis (1963), ch. 2.
96. For example Lancashire, Dorset, Leicestershire.
97. Holmes, *Eastern Association*, pp. 31–62.   98. BL Tanner MS 63 fo. 110.

stressed that volunteers were sought solely for local defence and because 'at this present, there are disorders and distempers in this county . . . and evill affected persons who hunger after Rapines and spoylings and plunder of men's houses'.[99] Holmes has also drawn attention to neutralist movements in Essex, Cambridgeshire, Hertfordshire and Norfolk.[100]

Neutralism was just as prevalent in the towns, particularly where ancient walls offered corporations the opportunity of keeping out trouble. Towns like Chester, Worcester and Sandwich initially refused to implement the instruction of either side, while elsewhere city militias were called up to exclude all 'foreigners'. As members of the corporation of Chester wrote to the County commissioners of array, in refusing to submit to their authority:

> That as it is a sacred Truth that a kingdome divided cannot stand, so it is a legall principle that his Royall Majesty and the Parliament [are] the representative body of the kingdome and that in the cordiall union of his Majesty and his Parliament consists the safety, glory and hope thereof.
>
> And they for their parts heartily wish they may be accursed as Corah and his accomplices that doe or shall purposely occasion or foment any difference betwixt his Majesty and his Parliament: and therefore they further doe declare their readines with their lives and fortunes to obey his Majesty as their most deare and dread soveraigne according to their due allegiance, and their resolution to defend the priviledges of Parliament according to their free and just Protestation and that as God and the fundamentall lawes of this kingdome have joyned his Majesty and the Parliament together so they cannot agree upon a disioynted obedience but declare themselves enemies to all such as shall goe about to put his Majesty and the Parliament asunder.[101]

The ruling groups, far from identifying oligarchy with royalism, identified civil war with economic disaster. They were keenly aware of the danger that the requirements of war would lead to the invasion of borough rights, especially by county interests (several Kentish boroughs afford good examples of this).[102] Furthermore, local

99. Holmes, *Eastern Association*, pp. 48–52. 100. Ibid., pp. 34–62.

101. 'The humble petition A divers of His Majesty's loyall subjects within the city of Chester' (Aug. 1642). See *RP* doc. 12. For Worcester, see J.W. Willis-Bund (ed.), 'The Diary of Henry Townshend of Elmley Lovett, 1640–1663', 3 vols, *Worcs. Historical Society* (1915–20), Vol. 1, p. xxvii, Vol. 2, p. 87; for Sandwich, see M.V. Jones, 'The Political History of the Parliamentary Boroughs of Kent, 1642–1662', University of London Ph.D. thesis (1967), ch. 1, particularly pp. 63–4.

102. Ibid., pp. 71–96.

studies do not in general bear out the assertion that 'progressive' towns like those in the clothing areas, or the 'middling sort' elsewhere, declared for Parliament. All the citizens of a town like Newcastle-upon-Tyne were afraid of economic dislocation and the prospect of losing the coal trade monopoly to Sunderland. Professor Howell concludes: 'the inhabitants of the town were anxious to see which side would win in the field before they committed themselves too strongly.' Although Howell found 'some evidence of an economic cleavage in the town corresponding to the division into royalist and parliamentarian', he concludes that this only occurred in the later stages of the war, and then amongst a minority; the town as a whole 'was not moved by the great issues after the period of anti-Straffordian reform, and was again embroiled in its own particular and local problems'.[103]

In many towns members of the corporation remained in office after serving throughout a royalist occupation. This was not primarily because Parliament could find no one else, but because it was quite clear that the majority were time-servers ready to obey any government that safeguarded local rights and charters. When, later, the regime wanted enthusiasm, it would have to purge the boroughs; so long as it was satisfied with obedience, it could rely on the traditional governors.[104] Many remained in office under several different wartime occupations; towns like Wells and Stafford, reluctant to obey, but determined not to disobey anyone who promised to respect their rights, represent the essential urban passivity.[105] Leaders on both sides soon learned that towns like Gloucester and Winchester were loyal only as far as self-interest and the terms of their charters allowed.[106]

There were exceptions, above all London where a social revolution in 1641–42 made possible the creation of a parliamentarian army, the financing of a rebellion, and the continued pursuit of a godly reformation. The concentration of puritan preachers in such towns as Manchester no doubt made others zealous for the cause,

103. Howell, *Newcastle*, pp. 147–50, 159, 162–5.

104. For example A.M. Johnson, 'Politics in Chester during the Civil Wars and Interregnum' in P. Clark and P. Slack (eds), *Crisis and Order in English Towns, 1500–1700* (1972); Howell, *Newcastle*, ch. 5; Jones, 'Political History', pp. 71–2 and ch. 5.

105. Pennington, 'County and Country', pp. 12–25; D. Underdown, 'A Case Concerning Bishop's Lands: Cornelius Burges and the Corporation of Wells', *EHR*, Vol. 78 (1963), pp. 18 ff.

106. G.N. Godwin, *The Civil War in Hampshire* (1882), p. 13; J.K.G. Taylor, 'The Civil Government of Gloucester, 1640–1646', *Transactions of the Bristol and Gloucestershire Archaeological Society*, Vol. 67 (1947–48), p. 75 and *passim*.

but they were not the norm.[107] Equally, there were counties where the neutralist current hardly existed, such as Lancashire, long divided bitterly between puritans and papists, or Shropshire where the zephyrs of peace from Cheshire were contemptuously ignored.[108] But generally the parties formed behind, or were restrained by, a barrier of fear and indecision.

The moment of decision was delayed, for most men, until they received commissions from either (or both) King or Parliament. The instruments each chose are revealing. Parliament's Militia Ordinance had no real constitutional base other than expediency, but despite its theoretical novelty, it granted powers and employed machinery very similar to those of the traditional Lieutenancy. Some might see it as 'a somewhat desperate course',[109] but most accepted it as normal enough in practical terms. The King, on the other hand, consulted the judges and came up with the commission of array. This had been devised by Edward I, hallowed by statute in 1405, employed widely up to the Wars of the Roses, and then abandoned in favour of the Lieutenancy. Its great advantage from Charles's point of view was that the soldiers raised by the array could be legally moved from one part of the country to another (not possible under the Lieutenancy) and also that the commissioners could be granted much wider general powers. But it was a dreadful blunder, and one Charles could have foreseen, for he had already employed it in the West Country during the Bishops' Wars and had been told in no uncertain terms by a Devon grand jury that the statute on which it was based had lapsed and that its terms were ambiguous.[110] Indeed Clarendon later acknowledged that it was a serious error: 'many did believe, that if the king had resorted to the old known way of lords lieutenant and deputy lieutenants, his service would have been better carried on; the commission of array was a thing we had not before heard of ... and so was received with jealousy, and easily discredited by the glosses and suggestions of the houses.'[111] It was a typically Caroline act, a resort to

107. V. Pearl, *London and the Outbreak of the Puritan Revolution* (1961).

108. Blackwood, 'Lancashire Gentry', ch. 4; Broxap, *Lancashire*, ch. 2; R.C. Richardson, *Puritanism in North-West England* (1972), chs 1 and 5. For evidence of the fear of popular revolt in Lancashire, see also A.J. Hawkes, 'Wigan's Part in the Civil War', *Trans. Lancs. and Cheshire Antiq. Soc.* (1930–31), pp. 119–20. For Shropshire, see for example H. Beaumont, 'Events in Shropshire at the Commencement of the Civil War', *Trans. Salop. Arch. Soc.*, Vol. 51 (1941–43); 'Ottley Papers', Vol. 6, pp. 60–2.

109. D. Gardiner (ed.), *The Oxinden Letters, 1607–1642* (1933), p. 295.

110. *CSPD, 1640–1641*, pp. 148–9. *RP* doc. 7a.

111. Clarendon, *History*, Book 5, para. 364.

narrow and moribund legality, an act lacking imagination and fore-
sight, not least because it was issued in Latin which allowed the
parliamentarians to translate it 'into what English they pleased',
persuading the poorer sort that it empowered the commissioners
to impose crippling taxes and labour services. The Marquis of Hertford, for example, felt the need to repudiate 'false and scandalous
suggestions' that it was intended to 'enthrall the people' and to
allow the commissioners 'to take what they pleased of any man's
estate'.[112] No wonder several grand juries, even in subsequently
royalist counties, petitioned forcefully against it. As Sir Robert
Foster CJ, riding the Western Circuit in August 1642 reported to
the King: 'The trewet is, the countries are mutch possessed with
the illegalities of the commissioners of array, and the unlimited
power (as is alledged) in the commissioners, and by reason thereof
infinitely avers ther unto', and he went on to call for both it and
the Militia Ordinance to be set aside and 'some waye to be established by Act of Parliament for the quiet settlinge of the militia of
the Kingdom'.[113] In the circumstances many moderate men may
have felt that the Militia Ordinance had more of a customary feel
to it.

Nevertheless, it was the arrival of the two commissions which
forced most prominent men to take a stand. For the moderate who
wanted to delay the moment of choice, indeed who prayed that war
could still be avoided, the ensuing weeks were nerve-racking. Henry
Oxinden wrote: 'Methinks my condition betwixt the commission of
Array and ordinance of parliament is like his that is between Silla
and Carybdis, and nothing but Omnipotencie can bring mee clearely
and reputably off.'[114] Thomas Knyvett, the Norfolk moderate, told
his wife that he had been handed a commission under the Militia
Ordinance:

> Twas no place to dispute, so I tooke it and desired sometime to
> Advize upon it. I had not received this meny howers, but I met with
> a declaration point Blanck against it by the King. This distraction
> made me Advise with some understanding men what condition I
> stand in, wch is no other than a great many men of Quallity are.
> What further commands we shall receive to put this ordinance in
> execution; if they runn in a way that trenches upon my obedience

---

112. Underdown, *Somerset*, pp. 31–2; see also Andriette, *Devon and Exeter*, p. 57.
113. For Worcestershire, see Willis-Bund (ed.), 'Townshend', Vol. 1, p. xix, Vol. 2,
p. 65; for Somerset, see J.S. Cockburn (ed.), 'Somerset Assize Orders, 1640–1659',
Somerset Rec. Soc., Vol. 71 (1971), pp. 53–5. *RP* doc. 7e.
114. Gardiner (ed.), *Oxinden Letters*, pp. 311–12. *RP* doc. 2c.

against the Kinge, I shall doe according to my conscience, And this is the resolution of All honest men that I can speake with.[115]

In a letter later in the same month (31 May 1642) he showed similar suspicions of the King's acts and a rising desperation:

I am nowe resolved the next weeke shall bring me home, althoughe the susspence & doubts of these times are as greate as ever, as you may see by these point blanck commands opposite to each other; but both tends to the keeping of the Peace, so as we hope we shall not fighte yet. The King hath a mighty greate court at Yorke, And a great concourse of people every day. Towe dayes since heer weare fayer hopes of propositions of Accommodation, but the Spirit of contradiction have brought a clowed vpon that glimse of sunshinie, And the demands on both sides so vngrantable as thers little hope of any loving Accordance. Yet both strives for the maintenance of the Lawes, And the Question is not so much howe to be governd by them, as who shalbe Master and Judge of them; A Lamentable condition to consume the wealth & treasuer of such a kingdome, perhapps the bloode to[o], vpon a feawe nice willfull Quibbles. Out of these prints you may feele howe the Pulse of the King & Kindome beates, both highely distempered, And if God doth not please to raise vp skillfull Phisitions that may Apply Lenatives & cooling Julipps, Phlebothomye wilbe a dessperate cuer to Abate this heat.[116]

Those less prominent in their communities could escape the worst of these anxieties – at a price. If they were asked not to take commissions but to obey the commissioners they could always accommodate both. Thus William Davenport of Bramhall sent men and horse to a royalist muster and lent £100 on the parliamentarian propositions.[117] Their predicament is also demonstrated by that of Edmund Jodrell of Yeardsley, another minor Cheshire gentleman. He lent £20 on the propositions to Parliament and sent a man to a royalist muster of the trained bands, only to find that the two sides thought this insufficient. The royalist request for further aid was peremptory and stern, but less coarse-grained than that of the parliamentary council of war, who demanded a further £100: 'otherwise that course wilbe used wch will not any way tend to your good', and signed themselves 'your loving friends'.[118] No wonder moderate opinion fragmented. Alan Everitt has traced three groups

---

115. Schofield (ed.), *Knyvett*, pp. 102–3. *RP* doc. 1c.
116. Schofield (ed.), *Knyvett*, pp. 105, 107. *RP* doc. 1d.
117. Morrill, 'William Davenport', pp. 124–9.
118. H. Malbon, 'Memorials of the Civil Wars in Cheshire', *Lancs. and Cheshire Rec. Soc.*, Vol. 19 (1889), Appendix C.

of Kentish moderates who illustrate what happened. One group, faced by personal summonses from the King, moved off unhappily north to join him. Thus Sir Edward Dering, who 'did not like one side or the other so well as to join myself with either. A composing third way was my wish and my prayer', felt obliged to accept the King's order, going 'out of my own house and from my own country the most unwilling man that ever went'. Similarly, another group abandoned accommodation in the face of express orders from Parliament. For the hallmark of the moderate was that he wanted to obey *both* sides, not *neither*, and when one side issued a direct and personal order, he acquiesced. Those not directly charged by either side could and did continue to sit on the fence. In Kent they were too disorganised to create a third force, but they continued to delay declaring themselves.[119]

A similar split in moderate opinion occurred in Norfolk. The leading justices (men like Sir John Holland and Sir John Potts), instructed to implement the Militia Ordinance, reconciled this with the overriding need to preserve order by declaring that the main object of the Ordinance was to repress popular disturbances and to keep 'foreign' forces from the county. 'Potts' ideal seems to have been that Norfolk should accept nominal control of Parliament but with the two factions within the county providing supply for neither side and dedicated to neutrality.'[120] Thomas Knyvett represents a second strand: dedicated to peace, prepared neither to resign his post in the militia nor to exercise it in the name of the King and Parliament, but resolved to await an opportunity to act for the good of the whole local community.[121] A third group, headed by Sir John Spelman, attempted to dissuade both sides from raising forces, arguing that if either did so it 'would bring the warre into the county which . . . I shall seeke to diverte, & were that endeavour as well pursued on the one side as I persuade myselfe it has been and yet is on the other, I am confident of our country as it is Privileged above all others in scituation, so it would have enioyed that priviledg in immunity from the comon calamity.'[122]

Thus in 1642 men desperately wished to avoid a conflict or, at least, to let it pass them by. The war began despite, yet also because of, the longing for peace. For while the moderates, as always, talked and agonised, extremists seized the initiative. The indecisiveness

119. Everitt, *Kent*, pp. 119–24.
120. Holmes, *Eastern Association*, pp. 57–61; see also BL Tanner MS 63 fos 117, 121.
121. Schofield (ed.), *Knyvett, passim.*
122. BL Tanner MS 64 fo. 145. *RP* doc. 11c.

of the moderates is perfectly captured in the Devon petitions of July 1642. They wrote to the King in the most abject terms:

> Most Gracious and Dread Sovereign,
> Your poor dejected Suppliants cannot so far neglect our own Duties and Affections, as to be silent, either in our incessant Prayers to GOD, for the Augmentation of Your Majesty's Honour, Your own and Your Kingdom's Preservation, which are inseperably bound up together; or, in these Times of public Calamity, in our Petitions to Your Majesty: The lamentable Distractions and Convulsions, whereby each member is drawn from the other, and each loyal Heart rent within itself, makes us fly to Your Majesty as a Physician to cure us, and Fall at Your Feet as a Compassionate Father to relieve us; being confident that Your Majesty owns as well a Will as an Ability to help. The Debt we owe, our Joy and Gratitude, through Your Majesty's Bounty and Goodness, commands to acknowledge, in the highest Pitch of Thankfulness which either Love or Duty can present, Our Obligation to Your Majesty, for passing so many good Laws, for Your and Your Kingdom's Benefit; and yet the unhappy Differences between Your Majesty and Both Houses of Parliament have, to our unexpressible Grief, bereaved us of the Fruit which we were ready to reap, and left us nothing but Complaints, Tears and Prayers, to feed on. Your Majesty commands our Obedience to the Commission of Array; whilst both Houses of Parliament adjudgeth us Betrayers of our Liberty and Property if we do so. They persuade submission to the Militia; whilst Your Majesty proclaims it unlawful, and derogatory to your Prerogative. How unhappy are we here, made Judges in apparent Contraries! In how hard a Condition are we, whilst a Two-fold Obedience, like Twins in the Womb, strives to be borne to both! We cannot choose but look upon the Privileges of Parliament with a natural Affection; from our Father's Loins, we desire a Touch that leads thither, as the Needle to the Load-stone; we desire to preserve them, because the Death of Liberty, without the Support, is inevitable ... This Petition was read and published in open Court, and unanimously consented unto, *nemine contradicente.*

But they also wrote to the two Houses in very similar terms, making a similar plea for a peaceful settlement and reconciliation: 'distractions are amongst us, through various commands, hardly to be reconciled but by the unity of King and Parliament. Unity in Religion, Unity in Loyal affections to His Majesty, will, according to our Protestation, by God's Mercy keep us still in Peace and Charity.' The leading men of Devon went heavy-heartedly to war.[123]

123. *LJ* Vol. 5, p. 295, printed in Andriette, *Devon and Exeter*, p. 54. *RP* doc. 9a.

The Choice of Sides

At times of crisis men look to known patterns of political and social behaviour. Passivity is the simplest way out, the line of least resistance. To obey an order is less of a political act than to reject it. Anyone who claims to stand for the protection of traditional values and the maintenance of order will be widely supported. In this context, localism meant not an indifference to the great issues agitating Church and State, but a preoccupation with the way these issues could be harmonised with the restoration of normality. The pre-existent power groupings within each county buckled under the pressures and tensions of national events, but each county retained a distinctive pattern.

In Leicestershire, two implacably opposed gentry factions – both traditionally puritan – had long struggled for local dominance. Both the leading families, the Greys and the Hastings, had connections with the Court and with the leading members of the opposition. The original cause of their feud had long been forgotten. When civil war broke out, both groups tried to prevent the involvement of Leicestershire. Only haltingly was the county forced into the war. Then the line-up followed the traditional one; the families who had always been attached to the Hastings' interests declared for the King, those who had always supported the Greys declared for Parliament. Yet the county remained largely apart from the war, with very little military activity until 1645; the royalists dominated the north and west, Parliament the south and east.[124]

A similar situation prevailed in Wiltshire. The two ancient factions were headed by the Marquis of Hertford and the Earl of Pembroke, and the rivalry of their families had been worked out for generations in struggles to control the Lieutenancy and the commissions of the peace. In 1640 Pembroke was a Courtier; despite his distinguished lineage the Earl was a profligate who had run through the family fortune and was only semi-literate. His religious views were confused, combining a vindictive puritan hatred of catholicism and support for a preaching ministry, with a staunch liking for the Prayer Book (he was later to oppose the Presbyterian Directory of Public Worship). In 1640, Hertford was in self-imposed exile from the Court. By inclination and family ties (for example to Essex) he was one of the inner circle of Country leaders (and his

124. A.M. Everitt, 'The Local Community and the Great Rebellion', *Historical Association Pamphlet*, G. 70 (1969), pp. 10–18.

brother, Francis Seymour, had been a leading opponent of ship money). He was one of the hard-line peers who demanded in a petition of August 1640 that Charles call Parliament to redress the ills of the nation. In the elections of 1640 Pembroke used his influence on behalf of Court candidates, but his position was an ambivalent one for he was bitterly opposed to other Courtier groups, being a long-standing supporter of the pro-French party, along with the Earls of Northumberland and Holland. He thus allied himself with the opposition over the attainder of Strafford in the hope of strengthening his position. The plan misfired, and he was shortly afterwards dismissed from his office as Lord Chamberlain. This was disastrous for a man dependent on the profits of office to remain financially afloat. He was forced into an ever-closer liaison with the opposition as the only way back to office. Almost simultaneously Hertford (who had used his electoral influence for the opposition) was brought into the government as part of Charles's policy of conciliation. He became a Privy Councillor and, a month after Pembroke's disgrace, governor to the Prince of Wales. By the spring of 1642 the change of roles was complete. Hertford voted against the Militia Ordinance and set out to join the King, while Pembroke voted for the Ordinance and became a leading figure on parliamentary committees. But as late as June an upset to the new alignment seemed possible. Hertford reappeared at Westminster and asked that charges of delinquency against him be dropped; immediately Pembroke entered into correspondence with Hyde and tried to rebuild his bridges with the King; but both sets of negotiations broke down, and Hertford returned to York. Shortly afterwards he was appointed Charles's Lieutenant General in the West, while Pembroke was granted a similar commission by Parliament. Both were largely motivated by personal rivalry and self-interest, although a measure of wider concern is evident in Hertford. However, both soon got cold feet, fearful that they were becoming over-committed. The rivalry of their families over the years had never before taken on such a winner-take-all air. Although both set their commissioners to work to call out the militia, their concern with the outcome is shown by the petition drawn up by their representatives three weeks after the battle of Edgehill, in which they called for a cessation of hostilities. Eight future royalist leaders and nine future parliamentarians were amongst the twenty-five signatories. Subsequently they went separate ways, Hertford remaining an active royalist (though prone to costly disagreements with rival commanders), Pembroke retreating as governor to the Isle of Wight where he could, if necessary, bargain himself out of trouble. Only when the war was won did he once again appear prominently at London, swimming with the strongest currents (he was one of the few peers to take his seat in the Rump when the House of Lords was abolished in 1649). Yet the local gentry continued to support whichever of the two great families they had been traditionally allied with. Neither group wanted a civil war, but throughout the period and notwithstanding the political gyrations of the leaders, membership of the two great Wiltshire interests remained stable. The ancient Seymour (Hertford) and Herbert (Pembroke) rivalry remained the unchangeable basis of local politics.[125]

In Cheshire, a rather different pattern prevailed. The élite there had been divided for some years over issues of local precedence. Faced by the political crisis of 1640–41 and by the emergence of a radical puritan group amongst the lesser gentry and freeholders, one of these groups gradually moved into an alliance with the Court, prompted largely by their determination to protect a modified episcopacy. The other group attempted to remain neutral, using its influence to keep the peace. In the autumn of 1642 this group petitioned for a national settlement and tried to raise a third force to keep both sides out of the county. After the failure of this scheme, the group divided, its leaders working for a pacification from within the ranks of the royalist and parliamentarian parties.[126]

Where there were no traditional and deeply felt divisions within a county, the élite might act together throughout. Thus in Buckinghamshire, despite the clear preference of men below the highest ranks for keeping out of the conflict, almost all the leading families co-operated closely with John Hampden.[127] In Shropshire, opposition to the solidly royalist front presented by the justices was soon suppressed, and here commitment to the King did mean more than the use of his name and commission for essentially local peace-keeping aims.[128]

The situation in many other counties was more deeply confused. In Devon the royalists were the first to appear but the commissioners of array were deeply distrusted. In July many leading gentry had sent petitions to both King and Parliament seeking a peaceful settlement, and the execution of royalist commissions in August

125. Harrison, 'Royalist . . . Wiltshire', pp. 1–157 *passim*; Crummett, 'Lay Peers in Parliament', *passim*.
126. Morrill, *Cheshire*, chs 1 and 2, *passim*.
127. A.M. Johnson, 'Buckinghamshire, 1640–1660', University of Wales MA thesis (1963), pp. 70–8.
128. Beaumont, 'Events in Shropshire'.

led to further demonstrations, for 'the Arraymen ... are look'd upon as the first instigators of a breach of the peace'. Although a great many of the gentry were later to appear for the King, the overwhelming feeling in the autumn of 1642 was a desire to procrastinate. The majority opposed the commission of array as they were shortly to oppose the militia commission: it was the same spirit which led them to oppose ship money and coat and conduct money.[129] Similarly in Kent, men who were later, in 1643 and 1648 (in response to parliamentary attempts to destroy local autonomy), to fight in the name of the King, stayed at home in 1642. At Westminster in later 1642 any action was a positive one; to stay was to identify with the parliament, to leave was seen as a declaration of royalism. In the shires, a dogged stay-at-home policy could still be construed as loyalty to both sides.

Just as pre-existent alignments played distinctive roles in determining allegiance in many counties (Somerset[130] and Lancashire affording two more clear-cut examples),[131] so every town reacted in its own way. The city of Chester, torn by disputes over local trading rights, recently compounded by religious differences, split along the lines laid down in these essentially local divisions;[132] so did Newcastle, despite the fact that the warring factions had made common cause in the crisis of 1640–41.[133] In Ludlow a long-standing local dispute only took on national dimensions in the course of 1641–42,[134] in Lincoln there had long been an anglican and a puritan dimension to a broader local conflict which bequeathed the royalist and parliamentarian factions to the days of the civil war.[135] But in the main urban centres the initial response was a desire for conciliation and non-commitment. The Chester corporation drew up a neutrality petition; the Bristol common councillors appointed a committee of Ten which spent two months trying to draw up a petition in favour of reconciliation which could be addressed severally to King and Parliament; Brian Manning has drawn attention to

129. Andriette, *Devon and Exeter*, pp. 55–65.

130. Underdown, *Somerset*, pp. 23–48.

131. Broxap, *Lancashire*, ch. 4; Blackwood, 'Lancashire Gentry', ch. 4.

132. Johnson, 'Politics in Chester' in Clark and Slack (eds), *Crisis and Order*; but see also 'The humble petition of divers of his Majesty's loyall subjects within the city of Chester' (July 1642), *RP* doc. 12. The only copy of this known to me is in Chester city library.

133. Howell, *Newcastle*, chs 2, 3, 4, 8, *passim*.

134. P. Williams, 'Government and Politics at Ludlow, 1590–1642', *Trans. Salop. Arch. Soc.*, Vol. 56 (1957–60).

135. For the pre-war factions and religion, see J.W.F. Hill, *Tudor and Stuart Lincoln* (1956), pp. 109–27.

neutralist sentiment in Hull, Salisbury and the Cornish boroughs.[136]
Sandwich reflects the passivity of the smaller towns, publishing propaganda letters from both sides until late in 1642 (for example the
council posted up copies of the Militia Ordinance but did not
command its execution).[137] Tewkesbury submitted passively to both
sides in turn.[138]

The lesson is the same as that for the counties. Side-taking for
the great majority was largely contingent. Men delayed declaring
themselves until forced to do so by the appearance of activist groups
on one or both sides. Polarisation then usually followed the lines of
purely local groupings and although many families were divided,
and many friends parted, the prior sub-political divisions within
each shire or borough were reflected in the line-up of forces by
early 1643. It was not always obvious which group would support each side: it was frequently determined by the attitude of the
leaders or simply by the accident of events. Since indecision sprang
from a loyalty to both sides, an express command from one of
them would often lead to reluctant acquiescence in that command
and only thus to commitment; in the case of Chester, for example,
it was probably the arrival of royalist commands and commanders
which swung the corporation away from neutralism into acquiescent
royalism; the arrival of Sir George Booth or Sir Richard Wilbraham
at that juncture could easily have swung the city into acquiescent
parliamentarianism.

All this emphasis on neutralism and pacifism begs the question:
Why did civil war break out? Who were the activists and how did
they break down the pacifism of the majority?

Although the final breakdown between King and Parliament
concerned control of the militia, the provincial significance of this
issue should not be overrated. Few petitions from the provinces
referred to it, or to the constitutional amendments called for by
Pym in the Nineteen Propositions, or to the general question of
trust. All petitions, royalist and parliamentarian, assumed that the
political and constitutional differences were negotiable. The concept of mixed monarchy was universally acclaimed in the counties.
What emerges quite clearly from a study of the activists in the
summer of 1642 (those who pushed themselves forward) is that, for
them, religion was the crucial issue. Quite simply, in most counties

136. Summarised with references in Howell, *Newcastle*, pp. 338–42.
137. Jones, 'Boroughs of Kent', pp. 63–4.
138. J. Corbet, *An Historical Relation of the Military Government of Gloucester* (1645),
pp. 25–35.

the active royalists are the defenders of episcopacy who saw in puritanism a fundamental challenge to all society and order, and the parliamentarians are those determined to introduce a godly reformation which might, for a few of them, leave room for bishops, but in most cases did not. What the puritan activists did agree on, however, was the need to go beyond a restoration of traditional pre-Laudian Erastian anglicanism to create a new, militant evangelical Church. It may well be that amongst the peerage and ancient gentry, the tug of honour, indoctrination into the values of a patriarchal society, a reflex obedience to the anointed King, were finally decisive in committing them to fighting with their monarch, but the great majority of royalists in 1642 are more likely to have agreed with Thomas Holles, the ex-puritan ('truly I love religion as well as any man, but I do not understand the religion of rebellion'), than with the Earl of Cumberland ('the same loyal blood of my ancestors runs still in my veins which they were never sparing of when their sovereign commanded them to fight').[139]

I have argued that Charles I broke the old rule by which the political and cultural views of educated society had always been found within the government and the Court; important currents of thoughts had been excluded. This is even more the case with religion. The Elizabethan settlement had been severely tested by a puritan movement whose aims were to change the liturgy and ecclesiastical structure of the Church, but which remained firmly attached to the notion of a national Church under the royal supremacy exercised through Parliament, and which showed no significant doctrinal shift away from the orthodox calvinism of the bishops. The movement was broken partly because of the gentry backlash against the extreme language with which some puritans advocated their cause in the face of royal intransigence. One lesson of the 1580s was that the gentry would sympathise with puritans while the corruption and inefficiency of the Church were perpetuated, but that their support would evaporate once the puritans demonstrated a wider political and social radicalism. So it was again in the 1630s. The easy-going policy of James and Archbishop Abbot which afforded *de facto* comprehension of ceremonial and liturgical nonconformity was acceptable to most of the leading gentry who, by controlling most of the advowsons, could appoint ministers who would remodel their services to suit their patrons. Under the

---

139. See J.G. Marston, 'Gentry Honour and Royalism in Early Stuart England', *JBS*, Vol. 13 (1973), pp. 21–43.

circumstances, most moderate anglicans would feel little sympathy
for the puritans themselves who sought to introduce modifications
in the Prayer Book which would bring England into line with continental protestants and then impose these changes on all. Most
anglicans in the 1620s preferred the *de facto* toleration. But the rise
of Arminianism, first evident in the 1610s, increasingly prominent
in the 1620s (though still described as a 'sect' in 1629), and tri-
umphant in the 1630s thanks almost entirely to royal sponsorship,
pushed the moderates firmly into the arms of the radicals. For the
first time the Church was divided over doctrine, and it was the
bishops who were heterodox; for the first time for decades there
was a serious drive to enforce conformity in matters of ceremonial, liturgy and practice, and it was conformity in the Arminian
non-conformity to tradition; for the first time the English Church's
relationship to the protestant communion was reassessed and the
independence of the Anglican Church proclaimed. It seemed that,
despite the bishops' increased meddling in local and central government, the links between Church and State were being severed
and that the Church was demanding an autonomous existence, a *de
iure* priesthood. Laud's beauty of holiness, his concern to refurbish
Church revenues and Church control over the appointments to
livings, were all breaks with tradition and posed a threat to the
gentry's effective control over the Church. In 1640 the country was
as completely united against Laud as it was against ship money.[140]
There was a national movement for ecclesiastical reform and the
anger of even the most moderate men led them to make immoderate speeches. The desperation of 1640 was well expressed by
Benjamin Rudyerd in a speech quoted above [p. 32], just as by
1641 he was ready to defend the deans and chapters (whom he had
earlier called 'drones') since 'I am as much for reformation, for
purging and maintaining religion as any man . . . but I am not for
innovation, demolition nor abolition'.[141]

Many made this adjustment of perspective between 1640 and
1642, and it turned them into active royalists. In October 1640 Sir
Thomas Aston was one of those appointed to summarise Cheshire's
grievances to be presented to the Long Parliament; in this exercise

140. The above is a synthesis of a great many works. Clearly the most important
is N. Tyacke, 'Puritanism, Arminianism and Counter-Revolution' in Russell (ed.),
Outbreak; for a recent case study of the Laudian Church militant, see Richardson,
Puritanism; for the reaction of moderates and radicals to this onslaught in the
north-west, see also J.S. Morrill, 'Puritanism and the Church in the Diocese of Chester', *Northern History*, Vol. 8 (1973).
141. BL Tanner MS 65 fo. 178; BL Tanner MS 66 fo. 184. See also *RP* docs 6a–c.

he was closely allied to Sir William Brereton, the county puritan leader. Yet by the middle of 1641 he had been disgusted and alienated by the social and economic radicalism of the Cheshire puritans. In his *Remonstrance against Presbytery*, he reprinted a Cheshire puritan pamphlet which had linked the redress of ecclesiastical grievances with changes in civil government (including a call for the abolition of tithes, for the reform of the courts, particularly the county courts and manorial courts, and for a reduction in entry fines and other dues owed to landlords). The petition ended with a call for godly reformation of the Church: 'This would replant our conscionable ministers, and supplant our Lordly Prelacy: This would take away extorted heriots, excessive fines and unlimited boones, for it would learn landlords more compassion and tenants due submission . . .'. Aston still had nothing but contempt for Laudians: 'wee have had our swarme of flies to destroy our fruits; wee have felt the storme of a distempered fate, as well as they'; but he had a different solution to the new crisis: 'we had rather with prayer and patience wait and hope for the reunion of our distructed peace than rend the breaches wider . . .'. He was terrified of the general aims of the puritans: 'under pretext of reforming the Church, the true aime of such spirits is to shake off the yoke of all obedience, either to ecclesiastical, civill, common, statute or customarie lawes of the kingdome and to introduce a mere arbitrary government'. His comparison with Scotland is revealing. There, he argued, presbyterianism worked because 'their nobility and gentrie (having absolute power over the tenants) shall ever beare sway in the Church. But it will not be so with us, the inferior sort of people once finding their power in popular election of elders will rather exclude both nobility and gentry.'[142] By the summer of 1641, Aston and his supporters were in touch with the Court and they later formed a formidable royalist party in Cheshire, harking back in all their public and private letters to the link between religious radicalism and the disintegration of all traditional rights and beliefs.[143]

The Hereford royalists put the King's defence of the protestant religion as the first and foremost reason for supporting him. Parliament had been called after 'the Kingdome for many yeares past both groaned under Taxes of Loanes, ship money and the like dismall effects of an Arbitrary government, and a high stretcht Prerogative . . .'. But these grievances had been settled and now for

142. Sir Thomas Aston, *A Remonstrance Against Presbytery* (1641) (from the introduction 'to a Reader', from the preface, and from sections Al, A17). See *RP* docs 5e, 5f.

143. See Morrill, *Cheshire*, ch. 2.

the protestant Religion; we cannot but with griefe of heart remember how it hath beene assaulted in the In-workes and skirtes of it, the Liturgie and decent ceremonies established by law; yea in the very body of it the 39 Articles. In what danger this Church of England hath beene, to be overrunne with Brownisme and Anabaptisme . . .[144]

Similarly those Worcestershire leaders shortly to declare for the King instigated a Remonstrance in the summer of 1642 which represented

as a great grievance that of late there have sprung up diverse sects and schisms and many dangerous doctrines are publicly vented and the Government of the church by Bishops under those Religious princes of ever Blessed memory Queen Elizabeth and King James traduced as Antichristian, the liturgy depraved . . .[145]

This reaction in favour of a controlled and limited episcopacy can be found in the correspondence between Henry Oxinden of Deane and his cousin Henry Oxinden of Barham. The former, although rattled by the activities of the sects and their call for the separation of the godly from the national Church, remained in late 1641 equally horrified by the 'con-formalists [that] risort most to this place, preists which must needs have a specious pompous religion, al glorious without; bishops [who] must continue their dignities least despised and brought into contempt'. But as events unfolded, his cousin urged a fall-back on tradition:

Little did I once dream that there would arise out of the ashes of the Bishops a precize ofspring, outwardly pious and zealous, seemingly humble and lowly, but inwardly wicked and profane, secretly proud and ambitious, more medling, more temperalizing then those they condemned. By which itt is now too apparant that whatsoever they of this stamp pretended, their end in weakening of Regall power and absolutlie demolishing Episcopall, was thereby to reigne like Lords and Kings themselves in their owne Circuits, & there to gentelize over their flocke not comitted unto them by their Lord & Maister for that intent. I thinke it therefore high time for all gentleman to cast about with themselves, and endeavour rather to maintaine Episcopall government in itts former state, with some diminution in temporalities, then to introduce I know not what presbiteriall government; which will uppon the matter equalize men of meane condition with the gentrie; at leastwise set up a teacher greater than a Bishop in

144. J. Webb, *Memorials of the Civil War . . . as it affected Herefordshire and Adjacent Counties* (2 vols, 1879), Vol. 2, pp. 343–4; see also Herefordshire petition in favour of episcopacy, May 1642, ibid., Vol. 2, pp. 337–8.
145. Willis-Bund (ed.), 'Townshend', Vol. 2, p. 45. Note that it was the pre-Laudian Church which was being defended. See also *RP* docs 2a, 2d.

everie parish who, like Mr John Swan, will studie more to inslave his parishioners then to save their soules . . .[146]

On the parliamentarian side, Sir Simonds d'Ewes is simply an extreme example of those men whose religious views in the end required them to stand out against the King. In every other respect a deeply conservative figure, he made austere adherence to a primitive reformed Church a prerequisite for settlement. But out in the shires it was the puritan activists like William Brereton in Cheshire, John Pyne in Somerset, John Hutchinson in Nottinghamshire who launched the parliamentarian movement. As moderate men abandoned their opposition to the Laudian Church in 1640–41, the hard core of real root-and-branch men emerged in many counties. Their aims were not always, or usually, as socially radical as Aston and the rest believed them to be. But they saw the achievement of a reorganised, forceful Church striving to create a moral and godly commonwealth as possible only if the King were made to accept it. While the great majority of men dithered or wrote petitions and talked of raising a third force for peace, it was the men who felt most strongly about religion who began the war.

This is a point made recently with great force by Brian Manning.[147] In the same article he goes on to argue that the godly were closely identified with the 'middling sort of people', thus adapting the old argument that the English revolution was essentially a conflict between different social groups. Brian Manning uses only printed sources, most of it propaganda material and much of it (particularly his extensive use of the memoirs of Richard Baxter and John Corbet) coming from the Welsh border counties. Coincidentally, David Underdown has argued that in Somerset it was the 'sub-political' social groups, the minor gentry, yeomen and craftsmen who declared for Parliament and temporarily swept aside a majority of the greater gentry who had tentatively and unenthusiastically declared for the King.[148] But it must be said that Brian Manning's main point is not satisfactorily demonstrated. He has shown that much propaganda of the civil war years was intended to prove that Parliament had the support of the middling sort. He has also shown that this propaganda was widely believed. But he has not shown that it was *true*. There was also a mountain of propaganda purporting

---

146. Gardiner (ed.), *Oxinden Letters*, pp. 257–8; Gardiner, *Oxinden and Peyton Letters*, pp. 36–7.
147. Manning (ed.), *Politics, Religion*, pp. 83–126.
148. Underdown, *Somerset*, pp. 31–41.

to show that the catholics flocked to the royalist colours and gained a major foothold at every level of the royalist party. There is also plenty of evidence to show that all parliamentarians and many royalists (however reluctantly) accepted the truth of these allegations. Yet Keith Lindley has convincingly demonstrated that the story was unfounded.[149]

We need many more local studies before we can accept Brian Manning's revision of the old argument. Meanwhile, the evidence seems on balance against it. It needs to be shown that puritanism really was strongest amongst the middling sort in the countryside; it needs to be shown why local studies have failed to find numerically significant differences in the number of yeomen and other freeholders amongst the known activists on each side; it needs to be shown why before, and even more during, the war so much of the neutralism arose from precisely these middling sort.[150] It is true, however, that the gentry feared an imminent social revolution, and certainly this strongly affected their actions and responses to successive crises. Above all it increased their paralysis and indecision and allowed the activists to seize control.

Broadly speaking, in the south and east puritan minorities (usually led by the most prominent gentry families) were strong enough to seize power as the majority prevaricated and then, temporarily at least, acquiesced; in the north and in Wales the great territorial magnates chose the King, and the majority, again after toying with neutralism, gave muted support to ensure a quiet life and a minimum of local dislocation. Yet the will to contain the war, to prevent it getting out of hand, remained. By the end of 1642, the political nation was at war, but not reconciled to it. Provincialism, and provincial conservatism, had received a severe setback, only to assume new forms and disguises in the years to come. The battles which were fought in the inns and secluded manor houses of rural England were to prove more decisive in deciding the outcome of the civil war than were most of the events on the battlefield.

149. K.J. Lindley, 'The Part played by Catholics' in Manning (ed.), *Politics, Religion*, pp. 127–78.
150. See below, ch. 3.

CHAPTER TWO

The Progress of War

Introduction

In the middle of a debate during the summer of 1643 in which
some members of the House of Lords expressed concern at the
seizure and deployment of royal land revenues, Lord Wharton said
that 'they were not tied to a law for these were times of necessity
and imminent danger'.[1]

The administrative history of the civil war can be written around
that remark. The desperate need to avert defeat quite overcame
those principles and convictions which had brought a majority of
the Commons and a minority of the Lords to take up arms against
the King. In the course of 1643 almost every clause of the Petition
of Right was ignored: imprisonment without trial or appeal, the
suspension of courts of law, the imposition of arbitrary taxes and
the subordination of property rights were all endorsed by parliamentary ordinance. This improbable revolution was the greatest
achievement of John Pym, and the story of his tactical triumphs
(the application of pragmatic methods to attain pragmatic ends)
has been unfolded by Jack Hexter.[2] Every setback on the battlefield
or in the rounds of negotiations with the King was used to push a
fresh drastic measure through a demoralised House of Commons.

None of this was achieved without protest. One Lancashire committee-man said that the weekly assessment was 'illegal, and the
Earle of Strafford lost his life for the like act',[3] while Sir Roger
Twysden, a man who initially respected both sides, came to liken
the Kent sequestration committee to Star Chamber.[4] Some MPs,

1. Quoted in Crummett, 'Lay Peers in Parliament', Part 2, p. 412.
2. J.H. Hexter, *The Reign of King Pym* (1941), pp. 13–32.
3. PRO, SP 16, Vol. 507/115.   4. Jessup, *Twysolen*, p. 78.

like Sir John Holland and Sir Ralph Verney, withdrew from the
House and went into exile in protest against specific issues which
contravened their sense of natural justice. Holland left the House
in November 1643 after telling his fellow MPs that he would not
observe the order sending him into Norfolk to sequester the estates
of Sir William Paston, 'my cousin Knyvett &c . . . Sir, I could never
prevayle with myself to be active in what is against my own heart
and judgment & this is some part of my condition.' He cannot
bring himself to act against those engaged in neutralist and anti-
war activity, nor those 'to whom I have the neerest relations of
Blood and obligations of freindship'. Sir Ralph Verney left England
in the summer of 1643 at the time of Parliament's Vow and Covenant, telling his friend the parliamentarian pamphleteer that:

> The truth is when I saw the covenant pressed with such severity, that
> your kinnesman meerly for refusal was not only suspended and soe
> made uncapable to serve his country, but reserved for greater pun-
> ishment . . . I thought it might be lesse offensive to the House and
> more convenient for my selfe to retreate for a while till the fury of
> that flame were over then to doe that, whereof I soe much doubted,
> or trouble them to invent punishments (where the law appointed
> non), for such an unfortunate creature, for soe I have just cause to
> stile myself, being I heare the King hath already sequestered my
> estate, and the Parliament dayly threatens to doe that and more . . .
> rather than make a solemne vow and covenant wherein I am not
> satisfied I must chuse to suffer and content myselfe with the testimoney
> that my owne conscience will ever afford mee that whilst there was a
> probability that I might serve them there I did it faithfully.[5]

But the majority in and out of Parliament were swept along by
the momentum of events, no single specific issue proving too great
a burden to their consciences. There must have been many like Sir
Simonds d'Ewes, who, in Hexter's words, 'derives a sort of morbid
pleasure from recording in his diary the successive outrages perpetrated . . . on the body of his beloved mistress, the common law',[6]
but at any given moment the immediate necessity of a proposal
then at hand precluded a stand on principle.

This chapter is largely concerned with the development and
nature of parliamentarian tyranny. It will examine the complexity
and imbalance of the machinery created to fight the war. It will
concern itself with the outrages committed to custom, tradition
and the common law; also with the battle between national and

5. BL Tanner MS 321 fo. 8; Verney, *Memoirs*, Vol. 2, pp. 212–13; *RP* docs 21a, 21b.
6. Hexter, *King Pym*, p. 31.

local priorities, and with the continuing vitality of provincialism. Only then can we turn, in the third chapter, to discuss reactions against the war, different forms of provincialism which opposed and sometimes defeated the new bureaucracy. Here we shall be almost exclusively concerned with the machinery of war and how the lofty idealism of 1642 shrivelled to the bitter cry of a Devon grand jury in 1647 that the fruit of victory 'after so large Expence of Blood and Treasure, is only the Exchange of Men in places, but not of Manners; old Burdens with new Names, and new Men with old corruptions'.[7]

The Structures of Wartime Government

Both King and Parliament scrambled structures for raising, supplying and deploying several field armies and dozens of local garrisons; and indeed for waging war not only in the kingdom of England but in the kingdoms of Ireland and Scotland. New layers were laid on top of or cut across existing ones, causing friction that led not only to inefficiency but also to internal arguments that could become bloody and catch hapless civilians in the crossfire within as well as between the competing sides. The structures of war not only put military effectiveness about civil liberties; they also put the population at large at the mercy of men (both on different sides and within the same side) desperately trying to fund a war that cost perhaps ten times as much in real terms as any war that England had ever experienced. This section will look at the creation of those untidy bureaucracies of war.

The very fact that the King retained in his person supreme authority and command in matters civil and military gave him an enormous advantage over Parliament. The latter, essentially a legislative body with rather vague judicial powers, was ill-suited in every way to acting as an executive. Since it was unprepared to delegate supreme power to an individual or small council, its task of creating and supervising a military and administrative structure was far less simple than Charles I's and involved the gradual and piecemeal erection of a flimsy system of checks and balances. It will, however, be the argument of this chapter that Parliament's war machine was more ruthless, more arbitrary but ultimately more successful, and more firmly under central control than the King's.

7. J. Rushworth, *Historical Collections* (8 vols, 1659–1701), Vol. 7, pp. 742–3.

Royalist organisation was a curious blend of the traditional and the expedient.[8] The King's advisers quickly realised that the Privy Council was ill-suited to wartime conditions, and they established a Council of War in which the King's leading civil servants and military commanders sat side by side, a Council which possessed overall military, logistic and fiscal responsibilities. The field officers and heads of the main finance departments, who had all moved with their offices from London to Oxford (Lord Treasurer, Chancellor of the Exchequer, etc.), all sat *ex officio*. Other specialists like the Muster-Master-General attended as occasion and opportunity afforded. The military structure, with Charles himself as supreme commander, involved a main field army and regional commanders (colonels-general), whose relationship to one another and to the main army was never adequately clarified. County forces and the whole local apparatus of fiscal and civil support were generally operated by commissions of array in each county, but the commissioners were expected to work with and through the normal parochial, divisional and county officers (constables, sheriffs, JPs, borough corporations). In general, the King was also concerned that most important matters (certainly fiscal ones) were formally discussed or approved in every shire, either by the grand jury as 'the body of the county' or by general meetings of freeholders. The commissioners answered directly to the Council of War.

The system was more successful at co-ordinating military and civilian administration at central and county than at regional levels. The relationship of the colonels-general to the commissioners of array themselves was very uncertain, but no formal body existed to co-ordinate the endeavours of all the counties within each Association. The several groups of commissioners seem to have met together only in order to defend local interests against the demands of the Oxford High Command, or in order to confront a local commander.

This is necessarily an oversimplified account of the system. It never operated smoothly and there was much desperate expediency (the increasing use of a special treasury of war – which virtually 'recreated the old Tudor Chamber–Exchequer conflict' – is a simple example).[9] But it does reveal something of Charles's respect for local autonomy, of his desire to secure consent for his fiscal

8. For a fuller discussion of royalist organisation, see below pp. 111–18 and the references given there.

9. J. Engberg, 'Royalist Finances During the English Civil War', *Scand. Ec.HR*, Vol. 14 (1966), p. 85.

innovations, and of his preference for a relatively uncomplicated administrative pattern.

On the parliamentarian side, the structure was necessarily more complex. An executive had to be created from scratch, and it had to be flexible and capable of acting quickly and effectively. Yet ultimate power and authority had to remain in Parliament itself, a large, politically divided body which had always hitherto seen its role as essentially legislative and judicial. In having both to raise and maintain an army, Parliament had to take care to keep military and civilian functions distinct and yet not in conflict. Furthermore, it had to try to create a structure which would allow national priorities to be asserted, for from the outset centrifugal tendencies predominated. In Norfolk, for example, Parliament's first attempt to finance and supply the war, the Propositions (a system of voluntary loans), was compromised by strong localism on the part of the contributors. Sir John Palgrave pointedly asked that his contribution of cash and horses be employed 'for the defence of the county', and Sir William Paston went even further, stipulating that they were 'for the defence of the county, not to be sent out'.[10] In order to win the war, Parliament had to overcome this strong sense of localism. Somehow, resources had to be generated in the areas of parliamentarian supremacy and transferred to those areas where its administrative control was weak or its commitments were particularly heavy.

The military structure was divided into two distinct parts. The local trained bands remained under the control of the Lords Lieutenant and Deputy Lieutenants, were required to concentrate on local defence, and were directly answerable to the Houses. The field armies (initially consisting entirely of volunteers) were placed under the command of the Earl of Essex, whose commission was modelled on such precedents as those issued to royal commanders for the Bishops' Wars. This conferred on Essex extensive powers to commission officers, issue codes of discipline, and proceed by martial law.[11]

This plan was sensible enough so long as a short, decisive war was envisaged. The militia would keep order in the counties, Essex would engage and defeat the King's marching army. But once the reasoning behind this plan had proved faulty, nothing was done to rethink basic organisation. As other volunteer forces were raised in the provinces, it was decided to subject them to the authority of the

10. BL Tanner MS 64 fos 8–9. See also ibid. fos 30–2, 50–1, 88.
11. See, for example, V. Snow, *Essex the Rebel* (1970), pp. 307–18.

Lord General, while the militia was still left distinct and answerable, via the Lieutenancy, to Parliament itself. Although Parliament created Associations of counties[12] as the basis for new regional armies and *nominated* a major general for each, all appointments, including those of the major generals, were formally made by Essex, and no regional commander could commission his own officers, choose garrison commanders or exercise discipline except on licence from Essex. Although the Houses retained the right, either directly or through a committee,[13] to consult with the Lord General over strategy, it was never made clear quite who held ultimate responsibility in this respect. This liaison committee, however, was empowered to direct the activities of the Deputy Lieutenants, so a degree of unity was imposed.

The structures of civil government were much more complex.[14] Parliament established a series of new taxes and rates some administered by the Houses themselves, others by central committees, made up of MPs or of senior London business men. Almost all of these central committees worked through bodies of commissioners named by Parliament for each county (and for a small number of major cities). The major exception to this was the Excise, handled locally by men chosen by the central committee made up of London merchants. Membership of the various county committees was overlapping and in some cases one body of men were responsible for all taxes (except the Excise), but in other cases not.

The main sources of war finance were a whole series of separate *assessments, the fifth and twentieth part, sequestrations* and *compositions,* and *excise.* The *assessment* grew out of the 'weekly contribution' first approved by the Houses in the spring of 1643. It was the Houses that set a target figure for each county and left it to the local commissioners to divide their quota up between the hundreds, lathes, wapentakes or other administrative subdivisions of their counties; these in turn were divided up between the parishes, and parish targets were then divided between householders by the constables. It was the system used for innumerable local purposes with increasing frequency throughout the sixteenth century and for national purposes for the first time in the collection of ship money in the

---

12. See below, pp. 102–4.   13. See below, pp. 83–5.
14. For what follows, see in general G.E. Aylmer, *The State's Servants* (1973), pp. 8–29, and then *passim*; also the introduction by M.A.E. Green in the *Cal. of the Comm. for the Advance of Money*, Vol. 3, and the *Cal. Comm. Compg.*, Vols 1 and 5, and other works cited in this section. I have also included material from some unpublished lectures given at Oxford in Hilary term 1966 by Donald Pennington.

1630s. There was a national assessment to fund the national war effort, but also a host of special ordinances that provided for particular needs, many of which applied to single counties or regions (e.g. for the Scots, for the relief of protestant refugees from Ireland, for particular garrisons). Constables in the worst-affected counties might find themselves trying to raise money for six or seven different purposes every month at the height of the war. In addition to the various assessments, the other direct levy was the *fifth and twentieth part*. This was a compulsory levy made on all householders who had not lent money (*sine die*) to the Parliament in 1642. Their failure to commit themselves at the appropriate time was to cost them a compulsory levy equivalent to one fifth of what a local committee judged to be their annual income or else one twentieth of the capital value of their moveable goods. Needless to say, the problems of concealment by those liable to pay, and of arbitrary decision-making by those responsible for the assessments, were endless and the result was frustration and bitterness. Perhaps the most contentious and resented of all was the process of *sequestration*. Committees in every county were made responsible for identifying all those who had voluntarily contributed to the royalist war effort and certifying their names and known estates to a central committee that then ordered the confiscation of all their property, the sale of their moveable goods and the appropriation of any revenues or debts owed to the sequestered royalists. In due course this led on a second phase in which those whose royalism was deemed to be mild ('delinquency') and who were willing to swear oaths of loyalty to Parliament and to its projected Church settlement were allowed to pay a substantial fine ('*compositions*') and to regain their estates (although this process was denied to 'papists in arms' and others adjudged to be guilty of war crimes ('malignants')).[15] Finally, Parliament imposed a sales tax or internal customs duty on a wide range of basic commodities such as beer, salt and meat, entrusting the levying of these supremely unpopular excises to a national committee of London merchants who were empowered to appoint their own sub-commissioners in every county.[16]

Parliament granted considerable autonomy to these national and local committees, although it usually retained the right to hear appeals from the county committees and from their victims. In the case of compositions, it also retained final authority to release the

15. See also below, pp. 93–7.
16. *A. and O.*, Vol. 1, pp. 202 ff. and *passim*, for the many later Excise ordinances. For extracts from an Excise ordinance, see *RP* doc. 14a.

estates of the delinquents after the size of their fines and the extent of their contrition had been determined. Where either the local or central committees assumed additional powers in the course of the war, they did so in defiance both of the ordinances and of the Houses.

The arrangements for receiving and disbursing revenue once more reveal the desire to diversify authority. No revenue-raising committee had full control over the final destination of the money it raised. Instead each source was diverted into a separate treasury, so that there were almost as many treasuries as funds. In some cases, the treasuries were totally distinct (in location, staffing, etc.) from the body which raised the money. Decentralisation was again the hallmark of the system, the purpose being to prevent the growth of powerful interests capable of weakening the ultimate control of the two Houses.[17] In practice, the separation of funds came to have a different significance. As Parliament met most of its immediate financial commitments by raising loans from the city of London or its merchants (negotiated by yet another standing committee), each fund was used mainly as security against particular loans.

This careful fragmentation of authority was not the main weakness of this system. For Parliament, like the King, never really reconciled two conflicting principles: one demanding that the main fiscal or civil unit of administration should be the county, the other requiring that the only feasible military unit should be the region or Association. In an effort to overcome this incompatibility, Parliament attempted to create co-ordinating committees in each Association. But these seem usually to have been toothless bodies consisting of delegates from the various county committees, denied the power to ensure effective co-operation between the counties and with the local major general. Only the Eastern Association, which set up a central treasury and a permanent secretariat, really got off the ground, and the complete failure of even this association to fulfil its obligations to maintain Newport Pagnell (a crucial garrison on the Great North Road), and its failure to survive the revolt of individual committees against the absorption of its army into the New Model in early 1645, show its limitations.[18]

In an effort to forge links between the military and civilian organisations, Parliament adopted two further expedients. First, they tried wherever possible to ensure that the Deputy Lieutenancy and the county committees consisted of the same men, thus easing friction

17. For this paragraph, see the main finance ordinances in *A. and O.*, Vol. 1; also Aylmer, *State's Servants*.
18. See below, pp. 111–18.

at a county level.[19] Secondly, they extended the remit of the Committee of Safety and later the Committee of Both Kingdoms (those committees charged with advising with the Lord General) to include correspondence with county committees on questions of general security and on the deployment of county forces. Neither was, however, empowered to interfere with the functions of the revenue-raising committees. Above all, they, rather than the Houses, were expected to mediate or settle disputes within and between committees, or between committees and soldiers.

The powers of the Committee of Safety[20] had been enlarged piecemeal during 1643 with the result that their exact extent was frequently vague or unclear. In addition, its authority was often undermined by the creation of special committees to deal with matters within its jurisdiction (for example one to grant 'protections', guarantees of immunity from plunder and sequestration, to royalists living quietly in Parliament-controlled areas). Furthermore, in practice it failed to establish regular contact with, and did not receive regular reports from, the county committees; and it had signally failed in its main task of maintaining a flow of cash and provisions to Essex's army. Politically, it was too closely connected with the supporters of the Earl of Essex to survive the reshaping of political alignments at the end of 1643. The alliance with the Scots brought fresh political and administrative complications: the Scots army was independent of Essex, yet a joint strategy had to be devised; the English were its paymasters and the Scots wanted their fiscal demands related to those of other claimants. Such administrative and political changes required that the committee be restructured and that a new lynchpin connecting the military and civilian structures should be forged. The result was the Committee of Both Kingdoms,[21] a body a majority of whose members were from the House of Commons but with others drawn from the House of Lords and with several Scottish nobles. After a long parliamentary battle,

19. See below pp. 96–8.
20. L. Glow, 'The Committee of Safety', *EHR*, Vol. 80 (1965).
21. W. Notestein, 'The Establishment of the Committee of Both Kingdoms', *Am.HR*, Vol. 17 (1911–12); L. Mulligan (also Glow), 'Peace Negotiation, Politics and the Committee of Both Kingdoms', *HJ*, Vol. 12 (1969) is arbitrary in her assessment of members' political affiliations and unfair to the Scots; the most persuasive writer on political groupings between 1644 and 1647 is V. Pearl (see particularly 'Oliver St John and the "Middle Group" in the Long Parliament, August 1643–May 1646', *EHR*, Vol. 81 (1966)). But see also M.P. Mahony, 'The Presbyterian Party in the Long Parliament, 2 July 1644 to 3 June 1647', University of Oxford D.Phil. thesis (1973). J.R. MacCormack, *Revolutionary Politics in the Long Parliament* (1974), is unreliable and unconvincing.

the Committee was specifically empowered to 'advise, consult, order and direct, concerning the carrying on and managing the war for the best advantage . . .'. As a consequence, it directed strategy, allocated resources, settled local disputes and involved itself in open and clandestine negotiations with the King.

It established a broad independence of Parliament, not simply withdrawing much information, but enforcing from its members an oath to maintain the secrecy of its proceedings (denounced by the Lords as unconstitutional). Bulstrode Whitlocke, as usual torn between political realism and an instinctive sense of legal propriety, compared the committee to schemes envisaged by the Provisions of Oxford (1258) and during the reign of Richard II, neither of which he thought had conferred powers so unlimited.[22]

The Committee's relations with local committees were complex: it was certainly responsible for resolving many local disputes and preventing the fragmentation of the parliamentary party in many areas. On the other hand, its orders were just as frequently ignored.[23] Nonetheless, it was far more successful than the Committee of Safety had been in maintaining fluent communications with county committees. Many of the latter became accustomed to treating the despatch of regular reports on the military, political and fiscal situation as natural and even useful. It is revealing, however, that when really significant divisions between committee-men and others did occur, petitions were more often addressed to the Speakers of the two Houses than to the Committee.[24]

A reading of the ordinances makes it clear that Parliament intended the structure to be firmly under central control. The local committees were seen simply as the agents of the central committees, and the ordinances rigorously excluded any possibility of local consent or consultation of the local community. There were no concessions to local traditions: the ordinances were to be the last word, completely overriding custom. There was not even provision for open sessions or trial by jury. Committees were to consult in private and make decisions on the basis of instructions from the centre. Such is the tone. But the ordinances failed to give adequate guidance on many issues and county committees, still consisting largely of JPs with vast experience of tactfully ignoring Privy Council injunctions, had little difficulty in adapting such orders to suit local conditions or their own prejudices. The first Assessments

22. Cited in Notestein, 'Establishment'.   23. *CSPD, 1645–1647, passim.*
24. BL Tanner MSS 59–62, *passim.*

Ordinance (February 1643) provides a good example of this. It named committees in every county and instructed them to nominate assessors and collectors in each hundred or division. It gave powers of arrest and the right to distrain and fine obstructors; it listed what income and what property was liable to be taxed and what was to be excluded (for example church ornaments and servants' yearly wages were not to be assessed); it fixed the total sum to be levied in each county; but it was otherwise completely silent about the principles by which the committees were to proceed in making assessments. Were they to use traditional rates or to make new ones? How were they to relate rates on personal property to rates on income? Could payment be made in kind and at what rates? All these questions, many of them highly contentious, were left unanswered. The ordinance did state that where lands were rack-rented the landlord should pay, and that otherwise the rate should be 'apportioned' between lord and tenant.[25] But no guidance was offered on how this apportionment should be calculated. Only in later years, between 1649 and 1653, was any effort made to ensure that the assessment was directly related to income and only then were uniform rules administered within each county. But the attempt to turn the assessment into an income tax at a standard rate was soon abandoned. Probably the coyness of the early ordinances reflected acute embarrassment at the paternity of the assessment: it was a direct descendant of ship money. But in practice the coyness led to wide differences in the approach of each county.[26]

Similarly the Sequestration Ordinance which set up central and local committees to confiscate and administer the estates of delinquents (royalists and catholics) was quite clear in laying down the administrative relationships of the various agents to one another; it was less precise about the principles upon which decisions in actual

---

25. *A. and O.*, Vol. 1, pp. 85–100. To make matters even more complicated, when additional assessments for local purposes were later added, and sub-committees empowered to raise these additional sums, they were given freedom to develop their own criteria. Here, for example, is the Ordinance of 26 May 1645 empowering Sir John Gell to raise special rates for his Derbyshire forces: 'there shall be Monethly Charged, Rated, Taxed and Levied upon the several Hundreds, Towns, Persons, Commodities and places of, and in the said County, in an equal, indifferent and proportionable way, according to their Estates, and according to the ancient and most usual and indifferent Rates, such a Monethly Sum as the Committee herein named shall think fit for the Service aforesaid, not exceeding the Sum of Sixteen hundred pounds, over and besides the Rates formerly set for the New Model, the Scots Army, and for Ireland, to continue from the first of May, 1645, until the first of December following, if the War shall so long continue' (*A. and O.*, Vol. 1, pp. 686–8).

26. See below, pp. 109–10, also W. Kennedy, *English Taxation, 1640–1799* (1913), pp. 38–42.

cases were to be reached. The central committee can be found for
some months pouring out memoranda for the use of local committees; many of these (which had little legal validity) extended
or distorted the terms of the original ordinance. For example, the
Committee of Kent wrote to a number of gentlemen who had made
no effort to support the war saying that if they began regularly to
pay sums to them, they would not proceed to sequestration (the
revenues from which would be syphoned off by central committees
for national rather than local use).[27] The accounts committees set
up to examine the financial activities of the revenue committees
were frequently involved in conflicts precisely because they criticised these unauthorised practices.[28]

An air of improvisation continued to prevail even in the ordinances themselves. In July 1645 the Houses admitted that the committee in Surrey had been hamstrung for two years by ambiguities
in the special ordinances for that county.[29] The committee at Gold-
smith's Hall is a fine example of expediency at work. This was first
created to supervise the allocation of financial resources for the
Scots army. To this end, it was later granted access to the money
raised through composition fines. Next it was instructed to handle
negotiations with the compounding delinquents, ensuring that reliable estimates of their incomes were returned and that fines were
commensurate with their status and delinquency. It then ceased to
handle other funds for payment of the Scots, and as Parliament
turned increasingly to compositions for a great many other purposes,
it ceased to concern itself with the Scots altogether. Combining the
characteristics of a chameleon and a boa-constrictor, the committee
transformed itself and then crushed and finally consumed the old
committees for sequestration and the advance of money to form a
new super-committee during the Commonwealth period.[30]

In the summer of 1642, Parliament devised a military structure
which made sense only so long as the war was expected to be short-
lived and decisive. Commissioners in every county were instructed

27. For example, PRO, SP 20, Vol. 1, *passim*; BL Harl. MSS 5494, 5497, *passim*.
Also below, pp. 91–2. A simple example was the growing claim of both local
and central committees to the right to grant protections against anti-royalist legislation. The Kent example comes from H.F. Abell, *Kent in the Great Civil War* (1901),
p. 155n. See also *RP* doc. 17c.

28. See D.H. Pennington, 'The Accounts of the Kingdom' in F.J. Fisher (ed.),
Essays in the Economic and Social History of Tudor and Stuart England (1961), and also
below, pp. 95–9.

29. *A. and O.*, Vol. 1, pp. 726–31.

30. See the introductions to the Calendars of the committee, as in n. 14; also
Aylmer, *State's Servants*.

to deploy the militia to pacify their own area; and they were made solely responsible to the Houses and their committees. Meanwhile, a grand army of 20,000 foot and 5,000 horse was to be raised to confront the King, and control of volunteers throughout the country was handed over to a single Captain General, the Earl of Essex. Volunteer forces not enrolled directly into his field army were still subject to his authority. This was a perfectly sensible arrangement in the context of a single campaign in 1642. It was totally inadequate to cope with the complexities of war in 1643–44. On the one hand, militia and volunteer/conscript forces were left too independent of one another. On the other hand, the concentration of authority in the hands of Essex over the several field armies that had now evolved led to conflict between him and the commanders of the regional armies, as well as between all of them and the committees empowered by the Houses to have general oversight of the conduct of war. A much more flexible system could have been devised. The attempt to adapt the 1642 model to a totally different situation was unwise.

In fact Essex retained a stranglehold on appointments and the power to restrict the strategic freedom of others when he himself had an army of insignificant size. For example, in July 1643 he directly commanded only 3,000 foot and 2,500 horse. Even after a sustained recruitment campaign in the spring of 1643, the total never again exceeded 11,000, and for long periods Lord Fairfax (in Yorkshire), the Earl of Manchester (in the Eastern Association) and Sir William Waller (in the South Eastern Association) each had a larger army.[31] Others like the Earl of Denbigh (west midlands), Sir William Brereton (Cheshire), and even Sir Thomas Myddleton (North Wales), all had virtually independent armies, yet all were hampered at times by the Lord General's interference. The Committee of Both Kingdoms spent much time arbitrating disputes over precedence, particularly where militia forces (technically independent, but increasingly integrated into the regional forces) were concerned.

In December 1643 the Earl of Denbigh wrote to the Earl of Essex complaining that several Staffordshire officers, whose commissions predated his, had refused to obey his orders saying that they had received their commissions from Essex and were answerable only to him. Another colonel claimed that he owed a prior

31. Furthermore, for most of 1644 the Scots provided the largest single army on the parliamentary side (except when several independent English armies came together, as at the second battle of Newbury).

obedience to Philip Skippon, Sergeant-Major-General under Essex, then in service in Nottinghamshire and Lincolnshire. A few weeks later the Staffordshire militia denied Denbigh's authority over them as Major General of the association and claimed that the Deputy Lieutenants held sole responsibility for them. Sir William Brereton, General of the Cheshire forces, regularly received help from Shropshire and Staffordshire forces without Denbigh's advice or permission being sought.[32]

In Lincolnshire, the Lord Lieutenant, Lord Willoughby of Parham, had quickly established himself as the principal military and civilian leader in the county. But in September 1643 he found his authority ignored by Parliament when it empowered the Earl of Manchester to appoint a governor of Boston. Shortly afterwards Lincolnshire was made part of the Eastern Association. The aim of the Houses was a good one: Manchester's forces were needed to buttress Parliament's cause in Lincolnshire but they were renowned for not wanting to serve outside the Association. Yet the ruling over Boston was a clear breach of Willoughby's commission which had unambiguously empowered him to make all appointments in the county under 'licence' from Essex. By failing to foresee or to correct this conflict of interests, Parliament inaugurated a long and bitter struggle which raged both in the county and at Westminster.[33]

In Wiltshire, the royalist ascendancy may actually have resulted from the conflict between rival commanders on the parliamentarian side. While the Deputy Lieutenants exercised the militia (though they also sought an agreement with the commissioners of array to keep the county out of the war), Parliament appointed the truculent, unpopular Sir Edward Baynton (a former energetic ship-money sheriff) as commander of the county's volunteers. Shortly afterwards, a royalist leader reported that 'Sir Edward Baynton lorded it with such an exquisite tyranny that he hath converted more to the King's side by persecution than I have been able to win either by my rhetoric or my reason'. Parliament continued to give contradictory orders to the Deputy Lieutenants (now headed by Sir Edward Hungerford) and to Baynton. Early in January, the latter's patience ran out and he imprisoned Hungerford at Cirencester, only to find himself under arrest a few days later and on his way to Gloucester gaol. Parliament continued for some time to back both sides, but

---

32. See Morrill, *Cheshire*, pp. 139–45, and Pennington and Roots, *Committee at Stafford*, pp. lxxiv–lxxxiii.

33. C. Holmes, 'Colonel King and Lincolnshire Politics, 1642–1646', *HJ*, Vol. 16 (1973).

was finally forced to issue a fresh, enlarged list of commissioners which excluded Baynton. By then it was too late; the royalists had had time to prepare a pre-emptive strike which gave them effective control over Wiltshire for two and a half years.[34]

The conflict between the Houses in the autumn of 1643 over the intended creation of a new army under Sir William Waller, independent of both the Earl of Essex and the Committee of Safety, thus raised fundamental jurisdictional questions, quite apart from the political calculation of the radicals that the army would reverse the damage caused by Essex's reluctance to push for outright victory. Essex's own claim that such a move would weaken his own army and hinder its recruitment is implausible in view of his willingness to allow the Earl of Manchester to create a new army for the Eastern Association. The latter was not to be granted a completely independent command, however.[35]

None of these problems was much affected by the creation of the New Model Army. The direction of strategy and overall military authority was still divided between the new Lord General (Sir Thomas Fairfax) and the Committee of Both Kingdoms, and their relationship remained ill-defined. Nor did the New Model stand in a different relation to the other regional armies, whose degree of subordination to the Lord General remained ambiguous until the summer of 1647 (in this respect Fairfax's authority over Massey's western army[36] and Poyntz's northern army was particularly ambiguous). The New Model was little more than a merger of the armies of Essex, Manchester and Waller, with the officers reshuffled, possibly in order to achieve a balance of the various political and religious views. The New Model was no more a 'national' army than Essex's had been.[37] Nor, in the early stages, was it any less mutinous. It can be argued that its success in 1645 was the result less of its own professionalism, discipline or puritan conviction, than of royalist miscalculation and regular pay. It is true that for the first time an effective single force was kept together over a long period, but this is the consequence of the strategic situation prevailing in

34. This sorry tale is told at length by G.A. Harrison, 'Royalist Organisation in Wiltshire, 1642–1646', University of London Ph.D. thesis (1963), pp. 104–57.

35. Snow, *Essex the Rebel*, pp. 375–9, 395–6, 411–12; Hexter, *King Pym*, pp. 111–41; J. Adair, *Roundhead General* (1970), pp. 98–110.

36. For Massey's commission, see BL Tanner MS 60 fo. 160.

37. For this startling revision of the traditional view, readers are asked to await the completion of fundamental and persuasive research by Mark Kishlansky. [This was later published as *The Rise of the New Model Army* (Cambridge, 1979).] For the traditional view, see C.H. Firth, *Cromwell's Army* (1962 edition).

late 1644 and only remained possible because of Naseby. Had the King evaded a confrontation in June the New Model would almost certainly have divided, half remaining to protect London while the rest joined Massey for a campaign in the west. The King did not attack the New Model in April, preferring to move north to relieve Chester, largely because he saw the New Model as no more than an amalgam of old forces whose union would simply perpetuate the old bickering. The forces from the Eastern Association in particular deeply resented being placed under new officers and being required to serve outside the Association; they were actively supported in this by the county committees. For example, local committees protected those officers like Richard Browne who refused to take their men to rendezvous. Committees such as that of Norfolk carried on a campaign of passive resistance to the ordinance for several months.[38] Nonetheless, as a consequence of the remodelling, Parliament did gain a mobile, flexible army with a noticeably lower rate of desertion than earlier armies. It did hold together after Naseby and did subdue the south-west. But the reason lies more in the maintenance of regular pay, and in the committee rooms of London, than in any professionalism, nationalism, godliness or political consciousness engendered by the iron will and pure mind of Oliver Cromwell.

Arbitrary Power

Thus far, we have looked only at the system as envisaged by the two Houses. The practice was, however, far more complex. Even the main premise that a series of parallel but autonomous central committees, answerable to Parliament, should administer through a single multi-purpose committee in each county, was compromised by Parliament itself. For in those areas where the military situation made effective local government difficult, regional committees were established, comprising local MPs and sometimes other members, who were given wide powers to oversee the workings of county committees. Typical were the committee for the Northern Counties set up late in 1643[39] and the Committee of the West which in 1645 restructured the military and civilian government of Wiltshire.[40]

---

38. See Holmes, *Eastern Association*, pp. 195–224.
39. L. Glow, 'The Methods of Moderation: Pym and Parliament', *JMH*, Vol. 36 (1964).
40. *A. and O.*, Vol. 1, pp. 489–96; also BL Add. MS 22084 fo. 25.

Some local commanders (Sir Thomas Myddleton in North Wales, Sir William Brereton in Cheshire) were also granted powers which cut across those of the main central committees.[41] Other committees were empowered to raise unspecified sums (up to a maximum) for local defence.[42] In 1645 the Committee of Kent were empowered to compound with those on the fringes of the recent insurrection in the county.[43] The Earl of Manchester's commission gave him an authority over assessments and sequestrations in the Eastern Association largely independent of local and central committees.[44] There was even a special central committee responsible for receiving and preserving valuable collections of papers and books, a committee which thus labelled the sequestrators as philistines.[45]

The consequences could only be a heightening of the endemic confusion and a decline in executive efficiency, as many committees looked to different authorities on the same questions. Only briefly, in the autumn of 1644, was the trend towards administrative fragmentation reversed. For several months Parliament strove to rationalise the Associations, to refresh and restructure county committees, and to make sensible arrangements to supply and deploy local forces. But after the passage of the New Model Ordinance,[46] the march towards chaos was resumed.

The other major characteristic of the system was its essential arbitrariness. The naked tyranny of the ordinances was often mitigated by local custom, but it was never successfully disguised. I have consistently used the term 'administration' to describe the committee structure of the 1640s; it would have been just as accurate to describe it as a structure of prerogative courts whose judgements reflected the commissioners' sense of equity rather than the precedents of common law or local custom. The sequestration procedure is typical. Agents of the county committee would present a case against a man charged with delinquency, largely made up of written interrogatories (another borrowing from civil law). The suspected royalist would respond (with the help of counsel if he wished), and the committee would then rule whether, in their opinion, the man's actions brought him within the terms of the ordinances. The man could then appeal to the central committee (meanwhile his estates

---

41. *A. and O.*, Vol. 1, pp. 179–83, 378–81, 409–12.
42. For example ibid., pp. 273, 662, 686–8.   43. Ibid., pp. 247–8.
44. Ibid., p. 309.   45. Ibid., pp. 343–5.
46. Indeed, the New Model Ordinance, whatever its political provenance, should also be seen as the culmination of a long process of rationalisation, as the military tip of an administrative iceberg designed to crush the royalist cause.

would be confiscated, rents withheld, and personal estates inventoried ready for sale) where a similar procedure took place. Once the central committee had confirmed the sequestration order, the personal estate was supposed to be sold, the real estate leased out, and there was no way that the delinquent could recover his lands without a direct order of both Houses. To defy the local committee in this or anything else was useless: it could impose fines of up to £20 and could imprison without trial or charge until the fine was paid. The central committee had powers to imprison indefinitely without redress. The system was completely self-contained; once trapped in its vindictive claws, its victims had no remedy at law. All the finance ordinances expressly indemnified both local and central committees and forbade appeals to the courts.[47]

The powers of the committee were in many ways as arbitrary as those possessed by the old prerogative courts; their jurisdiction was as open-ended, particularly in respect to sequestrations. In the original ordinance of March 1643, delinquency was clearly defined as positive and freely undertaken acts designed to help the royalist cause. But from August 1643 onwards, the definition was greatly extended, partly in the ordinances, partly by the glosses periodically issued by the central and local committees. By late 1644 almost any act of omission, any criticism of the parliamentarian cause, could be construed as delinquency. Indeed, the ordinances ordered that anyone who declined to act as a sequestrator should himself be sequestered. For example, the Assessment Ordinance laid down that anyone concealing goods from the eyes of the assessors should be treated as a delinquent. In the fevered minds of the former champions of fundamental law, simple dishonesty had become a major political crime.[48]

Other ordinances constantly overthrew those very liberties of the subject which had been the stuff of opposition complaint against the monarchy in 1640 and of parliamentarian propaganda in 1642: powers of distraint and of arrest without trial; the right to impose oaths on defendants; the seizure of men's goods for the public service.

The Excise Ordinance probably represents the erosion of values most clearly. For in addition to being granted powers to fine, arrest and detain without trial (with the accompanying indemnity and immunity from action in the courts), the Excise commissioners

47. For example *A. and O.*, Vol. 1, pp. 106–17.
48. Ibid., pp. 254–5, 352–4; PRO, SP 20, Vol. 1, *passim*; BL Harl. MS 5494, for example fos 29–33.

were granted power to enter and search the premises of 'every person that selleth, Buyeth or spendeth any of the said Commodities'. The right of unlimited access had been one of the most frequent complaints made against the monopolists.[49]

A curious example of the cynical denial of rights occurs in the Assessment Ordinance where the individual's right to appeal to Parliament against an excessive rate was accepted in general but specifically withheld from those who had failed to lend money on the Propositions or who had not yet paid their fifth and twentieth part (assessment payable to the Committee for the Advance of Money).[50]

Parliament had quite deliberately established a system which was apart from the common law, yet which exercised quasi-judicial powers as of right. Quite unlike the King, Parliament seemed determined to impose its priorities at the expense of traditional institutions and rights. Symbolically, Parliament passed an ordinance which forbade the holding of assizes and denounced the holding of them as illegal.[51] By 1645 all sense of tradition had gone. Following a rebellion at Dover in June, Parliament set up a Council of War empowered to proceed by martial law against the rebels. It would have been just as convenient, in a basically stable county, to call a special sessions of the peace; it would certainly have been as simple and more traditional to issue a commission of oyer and terminer. The trial of civilians by martial law was as flagrant a breach of the Petition of Right as could be imagined; it was an action as damaging to the fundamental rights of the subject as anything done by Charles I. It was a total denial of the conventional political wisdoms for which Parliament claimed to be fighting.[52]

Regional Variations

I argued in the previous chapter that the administrative pattern in each county was distinctively its own; each had a separate pattern for the meetings of quarter sessions; each used grand jurors in its own way; each developed its own precedents for dealing with a range of social evils.[53] The government of Charles I had posed a threat to the integrity of such local customs, but it had not destroyed them.

49. *A. and O.*, Vol. 1, pp. 202 ff. See *RP* doc. 14a.
50. *A. and O.*, Vol. 1, pp. 98–100.   51. Ibid., pp. 191–2.   52. Ibid., pp. 692–4.
53. For further notes on this, see J.S. Morrill, *The Cheshire Grand Jury, 1625–1659: A Social and Administrative Study* (1976).

Similarly, every county developed its own distinctive administrative structure during the war. The piecemeal fashion in which the system was established, the vagueness of many of the instructions, simply encouraged more local self-expression than Parliament had anticipated. But there were times when diversification was actually promoted by Westminster. Sir William Brereton's commission as commander-in-chief in Cheshire in May 1644, for example, gave him wide powers to name various groups of commissioners, but did not restrict his choice to those already serving as Deputy Lieutenants and assessment commissioners. In fact, he chose different men to perform each major task.[54]

The duties of local committees can be divided into at least eight distinct areas: the first was control of the militia and the second responsibility for general security (duties arising from the Militia Ordinance and from the traditional concerns of the Lieutenancy). Four others were concerned with the implementation of distinct finance ordinances (for Assessments, the Advance of Money, Sequestrations and the Excise). A further duty touched the auditing of local accounts. Finally, local committees were also responsible for ejecting scandalous ministers (royalists) and giving succour to plundered ministers (those expelled from their livings in royalist areas). Parliament itself appointed local commissioners for all these functions except accounts and the Excise, for which sub-committees were nominated by the relevant central committee. In practice, Parliament appears normally to have wanted to consolidate the membership of the various committees in each county in order to create a single, all-purpose county committee. And so it often turned out. In Staffordshire, each new duty was automatically entrusted to the existing committee which had grown out of the Lieutenancy in 1642.[55] Similarly in Cornwall, Somerset, Buckinghamshire and Suffolk, counties with very different backgrounds and civil war experience, there evolved a single county committee with a single secretariat which integrated its duties under the various ordinances and exercised an indivisible jurisdiction.[56] In Kent, too, the Deputy Lieutenancy developed into a general purposes committee which administered the assessment, advance of money and ecclesiastical ordinances as part of its daily duties alongside problems of military organisation

54. *A. and O.*, Vol. 1, pp. 409–13. Morrill, *Cheshire*, ch. 3 *passim*.

55. Pennington and Roots, *Committee at Stafford*, pp. xv–xvii.

56. Coate, *Cornwall*, pp. 221 ff; Underdown, *Somerset*, pp. 122 ff; A.M. Johnson, 'Buckinghamshire, 1640–1660', University of Wales MA thesis (1963), pp. 92–102; A.M. Everitt, 'Suffolk and the Great Rebellion', *Suffolk Rec. Soc.*, Vol. 8 (1960), pp. 22–8.

and general security. But when the same men came to implement the Sequestration Ordinance, they chose to hold separate meetings, work through a different secretariat, and keep separate records.[57]

One curious feature, even in some of these 'mainstream' counties, was that the actual membership of the committee was not necessarily that nominated by Parliament. Several county committees found it expedient to recruit additional numbers to help them in their work, although there was no provision for any such recruitment in any of the ordinances. In the early days of the war, the need for such local freedom was clear enough; many of those named in the militia commissions refused to serve and the burden on the others was too great. When they came to hold meetings about raising money and supplies on the Propositions (voluntary loans) and to discuss general problems of county security, the Deputy Lieutenants often requested others to help, normally either JPs or men who had served earlier in the year as commissioners for the parliamentary assessment levied for the defeat of the Irish rebels. In some counties, such general meetings of the gentry had a long history. In Suffolk, for example, a quite formal system of meetings (with its own detailed code of forms and precedents) had been evolving since the Elizabethan period and was adapted to meet the new situation.[58] At any rate, it is clear that many counties treated parliamentary nominations as advisory only: in Cheshire, Cumberland, Staffordshire and probably elsewhere men were co-opted locally to the county committees and were never officially approved by Parliament (or at least not until some time after they had begun to act).[59] This assertion of a local right to influence the membership of committees was just as well in view of the fallibility of the Houses, or their clerks, in drawing up the committee lists. At one point Yorkshire had no formally approved committees at all;[60] in June 1643 the Houses nominated to the committee of Berkshire a man they had already expelled from the Commons as a royalist;[61] the ordinance establishing the Committees for the Advancement of Money (May 1643) included a list of names for Essex copied by a clerk from the wrong document and was nonsense in view of other recent committee lists for the county.[62]

---

57. Everitt, *Kent*, pp. 126–32.   58. Ibid., p. 126.

59. Morrill, *Cheshire*, pp. 82–3; C.B. Phillips, 'County Committees and Local Government in Cumberland and Westmoreland, 1642–1660', *Northern History*, Vol. 5 (1970), p. 36; Pennington and Roots, *Committee at Stafford*, pp. xvi–xvii.

60. *CJ*, Vol. 5, p. 85.   61. *A. and O.*, Vol. 1, p. 170.

62. B. Quintrell, 'The Divisional Committee of Southern Essex During the Civil Wars', University of Manchester MA thesis (1962), pp. 22–3.

In many counties, however, there was far greater diversification of duties. In Cumberland and Westmorland, the committees for ejecting scandalous ministers were quite distinct from the general committees.[63] In Yorkshire, sequestrations were entrusted to special committees in each Riding rather than to the county committee.[64] In Cambridgeshire, the general committee was saddled with extra commissioners only in the execution of the Sequestration Ordinance, a source of much confusion and tension.[65] In Lancashire, the Deputy Lieutenants retained a separate identity and distinct responsibilities,[66] and there and elsewhere were given additional status as representing the quorum for meetings of the county committees.[67] Cheshire, with its militia, assessment, sequestration and ecclesiastical duties all performed by quite different committees (and with special 'general' committees at one point usurping these functions in two of the seven hundreds), was, however, exceptional.[68]

Committee practice, as well as committee membership, often defied the letter of the ordinances. For example, a special ordinance for the western counties had laid down that the nominees were to meet on a rota system, no member serving for more than a fortnight at a time. Such a system was inimical to the interests of John Pyne and his faction in Somerset, and they simply ignored the relevant clause.[69] In Dorset, the system was adapted, six or seven being on duty at any time, but some men serving several 'terms' on the run.[70] Although other ordinances laid down a quorum, such provisions were widely ignored.[71]

Just as striking was the tendency for the committees in many counties to subdivide themselves into hundredal or lathal sub-committees, or at least to delegate power to divisional committees under their control. Thus in Cheshire and Yorkshire, sequestration business was administered by committees in the hundreds and Ridings answerable directly to the central committee at Westminster.[72] In Kent, both the general and the sequestration committees divided themselves into lathal groups, while delegates for each lathe

63. Phillips, *Civil War in Wales*, p. 35n.

64. P.G. Holiday, 'Royalist Composition Fines and Land Sales in Yorkshire, 1645–1665', University of Leeds Ph.D. thesis (1966).

65. PRO, SP 20, Vol. 1, *passim* (for example pp. 158–9, 300, 326, 349).

66. For example HMC *10th Report*, Appendix IV (Captain Stewart's MS), pp. 66–8.

67. For example *A. and O.*, Vol. 1, p. 297 (Eastern Association), p. 726 (Surrey).

68. Morrill, *Cheshire*, pp. 79–94.   69. Underdown, *Somerset*, pp. 125–7.

70. C.H. Mayo (ed.), *The Minutes of the Dorset Standing Committee* (1902), *passim.*

71. For example Pennington and Roots, *Committee at Stafford*, p. xxv; Morrill, *Cheshire*, p. 89 and n.

72. Above, pp. 85–6.

constituted a standing committee whose powers became increasingly vestigial.[73] In Dorset, the county committee appointed not only its own agents and collectors for sequestrations, but also sub-committees (distinct in membership from themselves) in each hundred to draw up reports on delinquents. But they retained most effective power in themselves.[74] In Essex, as in Kent, the county committee carried out much of its work at regular sub-committee meetings in each of the three old divisions of the county; but there the county committee itself enjoyed a fair degree of responsibility and retained its own secretariat.[75] Many of these developments reflect well-established county traditions. In Essex and Kent, for example, the divisions and the lathes had long been the crucial units of self-government. Indeed Alan Everitt sees the committee structure of Kent as the logical continuation of the old duties of quarter and petty sessions and emphasises other traditional aspects in the procedure of the lathal committees.[76]

The creation of quite separate sub-committees of accounts in each county in 1644–45 created enormous difficulties. The central committee (meeting at Cornhill) was, as Donald Pennington has pointed out, independent of Parliament at every level:

> It was not to be a parliamentary committee or even a combination of MPs and outsiders. In an early self-denying clause, Lords and Commons excluded themselves from membership. . . . At the centre the Committee for Taking the Accounts of the Kingdom consisted mainly of merchants below the level of the leading Aldermen.[77]

This committee, whose duties were to check and pass the accounts of all creditors and debtors of the state, was given the right to appoint its own sub-committees in every county. It had been ruled that the sub-commissioners, like the central committee, must not be men already holding military or civil offices under the parliament, and in some cases the county committees were not consulted by the commissioners at Cornhill before they made their nominations. This in itself caused a lot of ill-feeling.

The history of these sub-committees reveals more clearly than anything else the extent to which it is impossible to generalise about administrative developments in the 1640s. Dominated at Westminster by the political 'presbyterians', headed by the anti-radical zealot, William Prynne, and necessarily drawn from those not previously

---

73. Everitt, *Kent,* pp. 126 ff.   74. Mayo, *Standing Committee of Dorset, passim.*
75. Quintrell, 'Committee of S. Essex', *passim.*   76. Everitt, *Kent,* pp. 131–2.
77. Pennington, 'Accounts of the Kingdom', p. 187.

active for Parliament (and therefore crypto-royalist or neutralist?),
these local sub-committees have commonly been assumed to have
represented a conservative influence. Yet there is no doubt that
they were mainly men of middling status (including many townsmen), and this ought conventionally to have made historians look
at them as part of the radical middling sort swept to power by the
civil war.[78]

In fact, each county was once more a law unto itself. In Suffolk
and Norfolk, the county committee sent up lists of nominees which
were happily accepted at Cornhill; the sub-committees in these counties soon became the trusted allies of the main committees, taking
over the job of collecting arrears.[79] Indeed, the Lancashire accounts
committee wrote in November 1646 to the central committee urg-
ing that it would be more appropriate for the accounts of county
forces to be taken by the standing committee.[80]

In other counties, the sub-committee quickly allied itself to an
existing faction and became involved in local feuds. Staffordshire
and Montgomeryshire afford clear examples of this.[81] Elsewhere the
arrival of the accounts committee introduced an element of conflict where none had existed before. In Kent the county committee
told Cornhill whom to appoint as the sub-committee of accounts
and then found the latter's investigation of itself too probing;[82] in
Warwickshire, two separate accounts committees at Warwick and
Coventry came to blows with one another and with the two corresponding general committees, as well as imprisoning and bullying
officials of the old Midlands Association.[83] In Cumberland, the
accounts committees complained that the sequestrators were all
former royalists who 'now protect papists & delinquents in there
persons and estates',[84] while in South Wales the county committee
refused to administer the oath to the nominees of Cornhill, whom
they described as 'ambidexters' and crypto-royalists.[85]

In Montgomery, the accounts committee were allied to county
radicals, in Somerset and Lincoln to those moderate elements

78. For this identification in relation to the committees, see, for example, D.E.
Underdown, *Pride's Purge* (1971), pp. 24–39; Manning (ed.), *Religion and Politics*,
pp. 83–127. For the composition of the committees, see Pennington, 'Accounts of
the Kingdom', pp. 192–4.
    79. Ibid., p. 193; Everitt, *Suffolk*, p. 23.   80. *CSPD, 1645–1647*, p. 485.
    81. See PRO, SP 28, Vol. 256, many unfoliated letters.
    82. Everitt, *Kent*, pp. 172–84.
    83. Pennington, 'Accounts of the Kingdom', pp. 195–8; for much additional
evidence see the letter book of the Warwickshire accounts committee (PRO, SP 28/
254); also PRO, SP 20, Vol. 1, p. 656.
    84. PRO, SP 28/208, unfoliated.   85. PRO, SP 28/256, unfoliated.

seeking to end the arbitrary jurisdiction of the general committee caucus.[86]

In some counties, finally, the separation of the personnel and functions imposed by the ordinance was ignored. In Cheshire, the Deputy Lieutenants dominated the accounts committee and co-opted men of their own views (opposed to the policies of Sir William Brereton),[87] while in Essex at least two members of the county committee were active on the accounts committee.[88] While d'Ewes inveighed against them for exercising arbitrary powers,[89] other men used them to expose the arbitrary activities of the main committees. The most dramatic account of the conflict between standing committees and sub-committees comes in a report from the Committee for Taking the Accounts of the Kingdom to the House of Commons on 10 October 1646. Six charges are levelled by the Committee, each illustrated by examples from several counties. The first was that in many counties the request by the sub-commissioners to view accounts was ignored. The second was that 'divers of their members who have been most active in your service and some of their Chairmen have bin iniustly imprisoned upon frivolus or false surmises' (as in Lincolnshire, in Montgomeryshire [where a habeas corpus secured by the imprisoned Chairman had been ignored], in Rutland, and in Derbyshire). In Leicestershire and Sussex, sub-commissioners had had their estates sequestered as though they were delinquents; others had been arrested and called up on specious suits to attend other central committees; others again had been sued for theft after they had secured the papers of those whose accounts they were vetting; and finally others had been massively over-assessed for taxation. It was a tale of bitter fiscal trench-warfare.[90]

It is often said, and rarely contradicted, that Parliament's cause was particularly strongly taken up by the towns: not by the oligarchs, necessarily, but certainly by the middling sort. This case may eventually be proven, but at present such statements are based on presumption rather than evidence. Furthermore, there is some circumstantial evidence which suggests otherwise.[91]

86. Ibid.; also Underdown, *Somerset*, pp. 141–2; Holmes, 'Colonel King'.

87. Morrill, *Cheshire*, pp. 90–2.

88. Quintrell, 'Committee of S. Essex', pp. 78–82.

89. Quoted by Pennington, 'Accounts of the Kingdom', p. 190.

90. PRO, SP 28, Vol. 256, unfoliated. For fuller extracts, see *RP* doc. 18. For a spectacular row in Montgomeryshire, see PRO, SP 28/253, *passim*; for Lincolnshire, see Holmes, 'Colonel King'.

91. See also above, pp. 57–8, 66–8.

All the main administrative ordinances, whether they were setting up general or specific committees in each county, allowed for
distinct committees to exist in the major boroughs. But only in the
major boroughs: in Somerset, for example, only Bristol was left
administratively distinct, while all the other boroughs, whatever their
traditional jurisdictional independence, were made integral parts
of county government (this was not offset by the presence of a few
townsmen on the committees – a fact much vaunted and over-
played by historians). Canterbury was the only Kentish town to
remain distinct; the privileges of the Cinque Ports were swept aside.
During the earlier part of the civil war, only nineteen towns were
given assessments separate from the counties (this was increased to
twenty-five by the ordinance of October 1644). Ship money writs
had included separate assessments for 189 towns.[92] Most towns –
even (indeed particularly) those loyal to Parliament – found their
traditional fiscal independence destroyed.

Many of the ordinances establishing Association committees pointedly excluded representatives of the boroughs.[93] And even where
committees of local aldermen were established, their role was often
an uneasy one; they frequently had to share their authority with a
military governor imposed from outside, or even (where the town
was an enclave in a largely royalist area) with leading gentlemen –
refugees from the countryside. In either case, borough committees
appear usually to have been even more intensely localist and preoccupied with the traditional rights of the town than the county
commissioners were with shire traditions. We urgently need more
studies of urban communities (particularly of some which were
consistently parliamentarian), but the signs are that most of the
inhabitants (and not just the oligarchs) quickly reacted against
parliamentarian disregard for local rights. The so-called 'royalist'
risings of the Norfolk and Kentish towns in 1643[94] may well simply
be evidence of a localist backlash against enforced integration into
wider administrative units.

The evidence from Gloucester points to a similar conclusion.
There the governor, Edward Massey (himself a conservative figure
in national politics), found his defence of the city constantly challenged by the local committee, consisting of members of the pre-
war corporation. The city raised large sums of money and many

92. Gordon, 'Collection of Ship Money'.
93. *A. and O.*, Vol. 1, pp. 230, 338, 540.   94. See below, pp. 127–32.

recruits without causing a fuss, but then fought resolutely against any breach of the city's royal charter. Thus they insisted on naming all the militia officers and even the officers of the regiment which was recruited in the town to serve with Sir William Waller. They complained bitterly when Parliament tried to reduce tension by creating a special committee consisting of representatives of the garrison, gentry refugees and city aldermen. Again and again the charter was invoked to hinder Massey's plans.[95]

The letters from the committee of Hull show the same determination to preserve their traditions of self-government. In July 1643, for example, they complained of the 'tyrannical government . . . [by which] all the libertyes of this poore Incorporacon have been trampled underfoot'.[96]

The best-documented examples are the Kentish boroughs. Both Alan Everitt and Madeleine Jones have described the invasion of borough rights during the war and the unpleasantness that this caused. As Alan Everitt has written: 'the friction was not political, for the senior port and ringleader, boastful Sandwich, was noisily, though emptily, parliamentarian'. Despite their policy of non-cooperation, all the Cinque Ports were eventually integrated into the county machine. Even the oligarchy of Canterbury, nominally with its own committees, succumbed to county pressure, and accepted seats on the general committee in exchange for abandoning their separateness.[97]

Similarly in Nottingham, the committees of city and county acted as one, although Parliament continued to nominate them separately. However, town–country tensions were amongst the major causes of the divisions within the committees.[98]

Studies of the gradual erosion of urban independence after the war in erstwhile royalist towns like Chester make the same point. Indeed Chester represents the essential continuity of urban thought; the corporation spent much of the war seeking to preserve city rights against the claims of successive governors and county commissioners of array. It spent the next fifteen years fighting off the encroachments of the county committees.[99]

---

95. J.K.G. Taylor, 'The Civil Government of Gloucester, 1640–1666', *Trans. Bristol and Gloucs. Arch. Soc.*, Vol. 67 (1947–48), pp. 59–118.

96. BL Tanner MS 62 fo. 155; see also ibid., 58 fo. 261.

97. Everitt, *Kent*, pp. 135–7; Jones, 'Boroughs of Kent', pp. 68–73.

98. Wood, *Nottinghamshire*, pp. 124–8; C.H. Firth (ed.), *The Memoirs of Colonel Hutchinson, passim*.

99. Morrill, *Cheshire*, p. 189.

Conflict of Centre and Locality

Meanwhile the integrity of county government was threatened by the growth of the Associations. It soon became obvious to everyone that while the county might be the natural unit for civil government, it was useless as a military base. In the winter of 1642–43, the counties were busy associating themselves for common defence and then asking either King or Parliament to bless their union.[100] Even the neutralists in the south-west hoped to establish an Association with a common defence fund to repel 'foreigners'.[101]

By December 1642, both sides were busy formalising these Associations; some covered enormous areas – such as the parliamentarian East Midlands Association stretching from Derbyshire and Nottinghamshire in the north to Bedfordshire and Buckinghamshire in the south (though curiously excluding Lincolnshire);[102] others were very simple, such as the Association of Warwickshire and Staffordshire.[103]

Each Association was given different, though vague powers. The East Midlands Association was given a general committee of defence for each county, and empowered to raise money 'upon the Propositions formally agreed by both Houses of Parliament, or by any way that they shall judge convenient'.[104] The Association of Norfolk, Norwich, Suffolk, Essex, Cambridge, Hertfordshire and the Isle of Ely (formed five days later) was not given new committees; rather everything was left to the discretion of the 'Lords Lieutenant, Deputy-Lieutenants, Colonels, Captains and other Officers', in each shire.[105] Within a week, another Association, this time in the west, was established, but power there was established in a committee of MPs who were to direct the affairs of the Association from Westminster.[106]

And so it continued. Throughout 1643 new Associations were being established which either never functioned or were soon replaced. Many of the ordinances were never repealed so that some counties were technically part of several quite separate associations. Shropshire was included in five such parliamentarian Associations in less than six months, but this was exceptional.[107]

---

100. For example J.W. Willis-Bund (ed.), 'The Diary of Henry Townshend', *Worcs. Hist. Soc.* (3 vols, 1915–20), Vol. 2, pp. 96–9, and *passim*; Holmes, *Eastern Association*, pp. 62–8.
101. See above, pp. 66–7.   102. *A. and O.*, Vol. 1, pp. 49–51.
103. Ibid., pp. 53–8.   104. Ibid., pp. 49–51.   105. Ibid., pp. 51–2.
106. Ibid., pp. 52–3.   107. Ibid., pp. 79, 124–7, 177; *LJ*, Vol. 6, p. 92.

Many of the changes were rational enough. The original East Midlands Association was a geographical nonsense. It was gradually dismantled; Huntingdon, for example, being engrossed by a revamped Eastern Association (along with Lincolnshire). The most important new Association of the year was, however, that formed in the south-east and comprising Kent, Surrey, Sussex and Hampshire.

Much more progress was made in 1644 with a whole series of new Associations in areas hitherto dominated by the royalists (the Northern Association, the South Wales Association, a new Western Association) and also an additional South Midlands Association (Oxford, Berkshire, Buckinghamshire).[108]

Yet each Association was given a distinctive organisation. Some had joint committees made up of representatives of each county (South Eastern Association, Eastern Association), some set up county committees answerable to a general Association committee of MPs sitting at Westminster (Western Association, Northern Association), and some had no co-ordinating committee at all (Midlands Association). In some the committees firmly controlled the local military operations, in others the commander-in-chief was granted a broad independence of the committees. In none did the work of assessments and other revenues pass out of the hands of the county committees; but in a few, central treasuries under the control of Association committees were established.[109]

The underlying trend was towards Associations self-sufficient militarily (though it was hoped that some of them would raise additional revenues to maintain the armies in still-disputed areas). As Parliament strengthened its grip on southern, eastern and northern England in 1644, a definite pattern emerged. The wording of the ordinances underlined the primary purpose of the Associations – the mutual assistance, defence and preservation of the constituent counties. Several ordinances (for the South Eastern Association (March 1644) or the west (August 1644)) specifically required that the forces to be raised were not to leave the Association without the consent of the local committee or of the Committee of Both Kingdoms.[110] These developments cleared the way for the emergence of a single 'marching army' which would be capable of moving to help any Association 'invaded' from without or else able to march into royalist-held territory (as after Naseby). Either way, the need to unite those three 'marching armies' which in 1644 had operated

108. *A. and O.*, *passim.* For extracts from this last ordinance, see *RP* doc. 14c.
109. *A. and O.*, *passim.* 110. *A. and O.*, Vol. 1, pp. 417, 493.

semi-independently was made all the clearer by the new Associations which predated it. But it also explains the rage of the Eastern Association's committees; every other Association had its primarily local interests confirmed by the ordinances of 1644. The Eastern Association (most secure of all from invasion, of course) was expected to abandon its own army and act as paymaster for the New Model.[111]

'From the Power of a Committee, Libera Nos Domine'

In July 1646 Humphrey Willis, a minor gentleman and a former Clubman leader,[112] wrote a pamphlet entitled *The Power of the Committee of Somerset*. At its head stands a biblical motto, 'It seems to mee unreasonable to send a Prisoner, and not with all to signifie the crimes laid against him' (Acts 25: 27), beneath which is written 'contrary to the scripture, Magna Carta and the Petition [of Right]'.[113]

Commenting on Willis's activities, David Underdown has written: 'Ideas, like protecting "the ancient and fundamental laws of the kingdom" may seem conventional enough in name, but they were held strongly enough to inspire the great bulk of parliamentarian sympathisers.'[114] He could have added that as the power of county committees grew, an increasing number of these sympathisers became restless, even openly hostile. We have already seen how what men thought of as 'the ancient and fundamental laws' were eroded in the ordinances themselves.[115] What may yet require emphasis is the extent to which men of all social backgrounds in the provinces were less concerned with the deepest questions of sovereignty and of the ruler's answerability to the nation and to legal institutions than with their own prescriptive rights, local traditions and customs. The idea of inalienable rights was already present in the Petition of Right: when the Levellers in their proposed constitutions declared that Parliament could not legislate in matters concerning the subject's native rights, they were being less radical than they sometimes appear. The history of Magna Carta in the seventeenth century is an attempt to erect an inviolable charter

---

111. Holmes, *Eastern Association*, pp. 195–220.
112. Underdown, *Somerset*, pp. 107–8.
113. BL Thomason Tracts, E/345/3. For a discussion of Willis's pamphlets, see Underdown, *Somerset*, pp. 133–7.
114. Ibid., p. 118.   115. Above, pp. 75–6.

that bound ruler and people and by which the ruler accepted the inalienable rights of the subject: the limitations imposed on all authority, elective, contractual or absolute, that it must work within the context not simply of law, but of that of which law was the imperfect expression, the birthright of the people. The Petition of Right of 1628, curiously (for a work of such limited specific claims) exalted to the pantheon of parliamentarian mythology, adamantly denounced the use of martial law as contrary to statute and Magna Carta. Here Magna Carta can have only a rhetorical and symbolic importance. There is no reference to martial law within it; rather the men of 1628 are invoking their conception of its spirit, the invocation of due process of law which included the notion of trial by one's peers.

The Petition was drawn up in the days of Parliament's self-confident constitutionalism. By 1643, hard necessity had blunted those principles. With some reluctance, powers of martial law were granted first to the Earl of Essex, then to the regional commanders, finally to civilians, and the jurisdiction of these commissions was broadened to include the trial of civilians. Although as late as 1645 the Commons refused to pass a Bill granting county committees general power of martial law to punish deserters (this was during the first great wave of army mutinies of which I have written elsewhere),[116] they were increasingly forced in practice to accede to the clamour from regional commanders and committees who said that they could not hope to restrain their men from desertion or plunder without constant recourse to martial law.

Both King and Parliament similarly delayed – and remained uncomfortable about – the introduction of impressment. Essex complained at the Houses' constant denial of it (it was finally introduced not for him but for Manchester's Eastern Association army). Both sides significantly appear to have used impressment only to strengthen existing units, not to create new ones.[117] Although the traditional freedom from forcible enlistment was destroyed, both sides carefully regulated the system of impressment. They insisted that the traditional civilian machinery be employed; that the number to be raised should be divided by local commissioners between the hundreds, and by the head constables between the parishes. The petty

---

116. J.S. Morrill, 'Mutiny and Discontent in English Provincial Armies 1645–1647', *P. and P.* (1972). See also *CJ*, Vol. 4, pp. 135, 257, and MacCormack, *Revolutionary Politics*, pp. 36, 74.

117. I. Roy, 'The Royalist Army in the First Civil War', University of Oxford, D.Phil. thesis (1963), ch. 4.

constables were to choose the actual men to be enlisted, and if they needed assistance to get recruits to the rendezvous they were to summon the militia, not the Army in which the men were to serve. In every way, this parallels the nearest precedents available, for the recruitment of the trained bands. To reduce the unpopularity of the measure, priority in selection was to go to unmarried men and those whose departure would cause least hardship to others (for example the servant of a royalist barber was spared by parliamentarian commissioners on the grounds that the wife 'hath noe other to keepe her shoppe'). The system was open to corruption but was designed to conceal the basic break with legality.[118]

The betrayal of earlier principles was also involved in the ordinances of indemnity, demanded by officers and men of the Army throughout 1646–47. The reluctance of the Houses to pass the ordinance was a major source of conflict between Parliament and the Army in April and May 1647, but eventually the Commons gave way. The indemnity committee, established on 21 May, had power to halt and require the annulment of proceedings in other courts. As a consequence, the rights of both the government and of the individual to seek redress for personal injuries or criminal acts at common law were stayed. No King had ever claimed such wide powers to set aside the law.[119] A rather different principle was involved in the claims of the generals to issue protections to individual royalists, exempting them from the effect of parliamentary ordinances, and in the controversial clauses of the surrender articles of

118. There are interesting remarks on this system in Holmes, *Eastern Association*, pp. 164–8, and Quintrell, 'Committee of S. Essex', pp. 113–19. See also R.W. Ketton-Cremer, *Norfolk in the Civil War* (1969), pp. 266–8. For some royalist impressment regulations, *RP* doc. 15c. The royalists in Wiltshire produced a succinct guide to impressment, as used by both sides:

First. The persons you are to impress for this service, you shall make choice of such as are of able bodies.
Secondly. Such as are for their quality fit to be common soldiers.
Thirdly. Such as are fit for their age.
Fourthly. Such as are single men rather than married men.
Fifthly. Such as being married men, are not housekeepers.
Sixthly. Such as not being housekeepers, are out of service rather than such as are in service.
Seventhly. Such as are mechanics, tradesmen, or others, rather than husbandmen: but no mariners.
Eightly. Next you shall take care that they be conveniently apparelled either of their own or by the assistance of the parish where they are impressed.
(J. Waylen, *History of Marlborough* (1854), p. 22)

119. *A. and O.*, Vol. 1, pp. 936–8, 953–4. For the para-legal nature of this committee, see Aylmer, *State's Servants*, pp. 13–14. Also *RP* doc. 15e.

many royalist-held towns by which the delinquents were offered preferential terms of composition or other benefits.[120] The Yorkshire committee were not alone in thinking that such precedents 'will beget an opinion that the sword hath a power above the Lawe, which will utterly destroy the authority of Parliament'.[121] The events of the 1640s threw both enacted and common law into limbo.

But the litany of the oppressed centred more on the activities of the committees than of the armies:

> From extempore prayer and the godly ditty
> From the churlish government of a city
> From the power of a county committee
> Libera Nos Domine.[122]

Most recent writers who have weighed the charges of corruption, self-interest and tyranny, have tended to give the committees the benefit of the doubt.[123] But there is no doubt that the secrecy which surrounded their proceedings, the absence of traditional safeguards and the neglect of normal judicial channels, all tended to encourage speculation about the probity of their decisions. It is true that a majority of commissioners (at least until 1645–46) were JPs, but it is simply not the case that they proceeded *qua* their role of justices. Men were often committed to prison by men who were not justices and by means other than by due process; that is they were not committed to the charge of the sheriff and his agents, but to the care of agents of the committee itself. In counties where quarter sessions continued to sit, those imprisoned by the committee were not brought before the court except in special circumstances.[124]

Perhaps most important – and this is the crucial difference between the royalist and parliamentarian organisation – Parliament's wartime administration found no room for juries – either grand juries of presentment and indictment, or petty juries of trial and inquiry. One of the normative administrative and judicial experiences of the English system was the evolution of the jury which advised and formally empowered those in authority to order, direct

120. For example R. Bell (ed.), *Memorials of the Fairfax Family* (2 vols, 1849), BL Vol. 1, p. 203; Add. MS 5497 fo. 57; Snow, *Essex the Rebel*, p. 352; BL Tanner MS 60 fo. 125. Coate, *Cornwall*, pp. 226 ff. See also *RP* doc. 15d.

121. BL Tanner MS 60 fos 119–20.

122. Quoted by D.H. Pennington, 'The Cost of the English Civil War', *History Today* (February 1958), p. 128.

123. For example Holmes, 'Colonel King', pp. 133–7; Everitt, *Kent*, pp. 176–85; Underdown, *Somerset*, pp. 121–37.

124. Compare below, pp. 116–17.

or judge. Much of the Tudor and Stuart social legislation could
only be activated by a jury presentment; even the most minor commission or court was assisted by a jury of freeholders. Representing
'the body of the county', local opinion, the jury – far more than
Parliament – was the democratic element in seventeenth-century
government. Selected by the sheriff, and readily 'fixed' (more even
than elections) though they were, juries were a uniquely English
and thoroughly persistent feature of all local government.[125] No
ordinance between 1642 and 1646 required the impanelling of
juries, and county committees acted as prosecution, judge and jury
in their own cases, with the defendant having little or no right of
appeal. Indeed, where the regular courts did sit, grand juries spent
much time petitioning against or presenting the committees for
abuse of power. Sometimes, the sessions juries were responding to
political pressure from local factions hostile to the ruling juntas, as
when the Lincolnshire jury responded to a charge by Edward King
against his political enemies by indicting the Excisemen,[126] or when
the Staffordshire grand jury denounced the county committee for
inequitable and unjust practices, possibly at the instigation of the
ousted supporters of the Earl of Denbigh.[127] But even in these cases
the political animus may have contained an element of outrage at
the ways of the committee-men. Elsewhere grand jury attacks may
have been spontaneous (for example the activities of the Cheshire
grand juries between 1645 and 1652).[128] It is extraordinary how
infrequently the committees made use of grand juries to further
their ends at Westminster, particularly in view of the way both sides
had fought to gain grand jury support in 1642. Royalist commissioners continued to look to them for support. The only example
on the parliamentarian side comes from Somerset in 1648, where
the jury had to be rigged from top to bottom.[129] Perhaps before we
rush to support those historians who see the middling sort (the
yeomen and freeholders) as a predominantly radical group pushing their way inexorably to power in the 1640s, we ought to reflect
that such men, whenever they sat on grand juries, seem to have

125. There is an obvious risk of overstatement here, but the point needs making
boldly in view of its total neglect by historians. In *The Cheshire Grand Jury, 1625–1659*
(1976), I have developed this argument more soberly but at length. See particularly
the final section for some comparative material.

126. Holmes, 'Colonel King', pp. 472–80. This is the only weak section in an
excellent article. How had King got the job of delivering the charge? Why were the
Excisemen in no way answerable to the county committee?

127. Pennington and Roots, *Committee at Stafford*, pp. 342–4.

128. Morrill, *Cheshire Grand Jury, passim.*   129. Underdown, *Somerset*, pp. 150–1.

opposed the county committee system and to have sought return to pre-war methods and men.[130]

Instead of hearkening to the chorus of concern at the break with tradition, however, committees concentrated on ever increasing their powers and asking for restrictions on their activities to be lifted. The committee at Cambridge, for example, found their power 'too short to carry on such various and weighty business effectually; as not enabling us to imprison or any ways secure dangerous malignants, refractory persons and such as disobey and abuse not only our authority but yours, nor to punish mutinous soldiers'.[131] Similarly the committee at Essex sought 'powers of compulsion' to speed up the assessment and collection of taxes and to compel tradesmen and apprentices to assist them.[132] The committee of Sussex lamented their lack of jurisdiction to enforce the Solemn League and Covenant on all the inhabitants.[133] Clearly the committees were not the reluctant agents of an arbitrary government.

The expedients used by committees to raise money for Parliament reveal further the disregard for precedent and local tradition. As we have already observed, the Assessment ordinances were dark as to the exact method of rating, although the obvious precedents were ship money and the £400,000 assessment for Ireland voted in 1642. In general, sheriffs and commissioners for these had adapted existing local rates (scot and lot, poor rates, etc.). But the weekly assessment, which can be likened to the equivalent of a parliamentary subsidy every fortnight,[134] could only intensify the rating disputes which these earlier expedients had created. Some counties grasped the nettle firmly and set out to establish entirely new valuations. In Kent, the county committee appointed two or more persons in each hundred to ascertain the total county income and to fix a poundage rate necessary to bring in the sum required (initially it was fixed at 1s 5d on real estate, 4d on personal).[135]

This attempt to turn the assessment into a straightforward income tax was unusual however. The Buckinghamshire committee explicitly rejected such a change.[136] Elsewhere, traditional rates were still employed, although some effort was made to correct manifest inequalities and above all to question traditional exemptions.[137] Thus

---

130. For more on this, see below, pp. 169–72.

131. HMC, *Portland MS*, Vol. 1, p. 135.   132. BL Tanner MS 60 fo. 225.

133. Ibid., fo. 493.   134. Pennington, 'The Cost', p. 128.

135. Everitt, *Kent*, p. 187.   136. Johnson, 'Buckinghamshire', pp. 126–32.

137. Holmes, *Eastern Association*, pp. 133–41; Morrill, *Cheshire*, pp. 95–8; Pennington and Roots, *Committee at Stafford*, p. xxx.

hundreds, parishes, or even individuals within a parish, could ask the committee to revise their assessment. The ruling that while rates on rack-rented lands should be paid by the landlord, those on copyholds or other lands held 'at any easie or small rant or undervalue . . . [should] be apportioned between the party or parties . . . as the Taxers should think meete', proved a fruitful source of chaos.[138]

In most counties, the committee employed the head constables to divide the sums between the parishes, and used the petty constables to *collect* the money. But the actual distribution of the rate within the parish or village was left to assessors, two or more 'substantial' inhabitants. It is far from certain how these were chosen. It seems likely that in most counties they were directly nominated by the committee; in Derbyshire this was specifically the case.[139] But elsewhere they were elected by the parishes themselves; this appears to have been the case occasionally in Staffordshire and Essex.[140]

Once again, Kent is different. The head constables and petty constables were bypassed, and both assessments and collections were carried out by minor gentry nominated by the committee, each issued with special accounts books, collecting bags and boxes, and even pen and ink.[141] In any case, the dislocation of war had made it impossible for new petty or head constables to be chosen (at the courts' leet or at petty sessions) and in Wiltshire at any rate, the justices resisted attempts to nominate them by alternative methods.[142]

Greater mystery surrounds the collection of the fifth and twentieth part (forced loans). These assessments (from those who had failed to contribute adequately on the Propositions) have often been said to have been left to the constables, but direct evidence that this was so is lacking. In East Anglia, the assessments were initially undertaken by officers seconded from the army, and later the whole Association was divided into areas which did not correspond to county or divisional boundaries, each under a 'foreign' commissioner.[143] In Staffordshire, at least one captain was empowered to assess and collect the money 'from such persons as he thinks fit

138. *A. and O.*, Vol. 1, p. 237; see Pennington and Roots, *Committee at Stafford*, pp. xxx–xxxiii and references to the order book there given.

139. F. Fisher, 'The Civil War Papers of the Constable of Hope', *Trans. of Derbys. Hist. Soc.*, Vol. 33 (1950).

140. Pennington and Roots, *Committee at Stafford*, p. 235; Quintrell, 'Committee of S. Essex', p. 75.

141. Everitt, *Kent*, pp. 157–8.

142. Harrison, 'Royalist . . . Wiltshire', pp. 467–70.

143. Holmes, *Eastern Association*, pp. 131–2.

to advance the said monies' in a group of adjacent constablewicks.[144] Indeed, in the view of Pennington and Roots, 'no apparent effort was made to extract . . . a once-for-all payment from everyone liable to contribute. . . . The demand was one that could conveniently be held over the heads of people whose good behaviour was in doubt . . .'.[145]

But the greatest break with tradition necessarily came with sequestrations. Here the task of setting the rents on sequestered property (this normally involved collecting rents from settled tenants and leasing the demesne out at annual rack-rents either to the owner's nominee or to consortia of local peasants)[146] was entrusted to agents appointed by the local committees. In Staffordshire, constables sometimes acted as agents in their own parishes, and occasionally the delinquent's own bailiff would act for the committee, but Staffordshire may well not have been typical.[147] In Lancashire, regiments of foot or troops of horse were allocated the receipts from specified sequestrations, and instructed to set and receive the rents, but this was certainly unusual (though in Cheshire one company took over an untenanted field which they sowed with wheat and thus provisioned themselves).[148]

Everywhere, the civil war totally disrupted the pattern and certainties of village life. Increasingly the burden and unpopularity of the work caused agents to risk the wrath of the committee rather than face the retribution of their neighbours. When the Staffordshire committee tried to get the churchwardens to make a collection for the poor protestants in Ireland, only nineteen pounds was contributed in a year.[149] The old ways could not cope and had to be replaced. But the popular reaction was not one of understanding; it was of sullen resentment. Out of the disintegration of the old communal world, movements like those of the Clubmen were born.

Royalist Taxes

Royalist wartime government appears deceptively similar to that of its opponents. There are parallels, of course, and the King directly

144. Pennington and Roots, *Committee at Stafford*, p. 41.
145. Ibid., p. xxxiv. For a similar system of threats in Kent, see Abell, *Kent in the Great Civil War*, p. 155n. (*RP* doc. 17c).
146. Morrill, *Cheshire*, pp. 111–17; Pennington and Roots, *Committee at Stafford*, p. xxxvii.
147. Ibid. 148. Morrill, *Cheshire*, p. 110.
149. Pennington and Roots, *Committee at Stafford*, p. xl. The old processes of collecting for the victims of natural disaster were being employed.

cribbed many fiscal expedients from Parliament. But it was a much more reluctant expediency, and a less successful one. At the heart of the royalist war effort lay a painful paradox: the King urged the more traditional approach, attempted to work closer to and through the known laws and ancient local institutions, respected local autonomy. But he was unable to enforce this more restricted constitutionalist approach on his officers, above all on some of his senior army commanders. In consequence, it was the royalists who gained the reputation for lawlessness.

Royalist fiscal measures clearly demonstrate this. What has emerged from recent studies[150] is the extent to which the old financial institutions survived. Civil servants and records simply moved from London to Oxford. Chancery, Exchequer, Court of Wards, all continued to act. Indeed, in the first year of the war over one-third of the receipts of the treasurers at war came from traditional sources (customs duties, wardships, clerical tenths, etc.). Money was also forthcoming from the sale of new titles: sixty-seven new baronets paid £70,000 between them, vain honours at a cut-down price. Charles even sold honorary Oxford degrees for modest fees. He also received massive contributions from his wealthiest supporters (over £318,000 in cash from the Marquess of Worcester, for example). The Queen negotiated substantial loans in the Netherlands, mostly to buy arms and ammunition abroad.

Thus the King, like Parliament, tried to avoid resorting to taxation. He then adopted all of their major fiscal measures, but only after the Houses had shown the way. However, his administration of these new taxes was quite different from theirs.

The contribution, to be collected weekly or monthly, was Charles's equivalent of the assessment. But he did not demand a fixed sum from every county. Rather, he sought to relate the amount raised to the number of soldiers serving in or for each county and required that the amount should be considered, and assented to, either by a grand jury or by a formal general meeting of freeholders.[151] Traditional rating lists were to be employed, and, to help the poor inhabitants, a proportion (usually up to one-half) was made payable in

150. For what follows, see J. Engberg, 'Royalist Finances During the English Civil War', *Scand. Ec. HR*, Vol. 14 (1966), pp. 73–96. But see also Roy, 'Royalist Army', thesis, *passim*, happily soon to be published. On matters of finance, both rely heavily on the papers of Edward Walker in BL Harl. MSS 6802, 6804, 6851–2.

151. See below, pp. 116–17. The contribution grew out of a regular system of forced loans devised late in 1642 whereby county assemblies agreed to raise a certain sum at fixed rates of interest (for example Radnorshire £200 per month, Gloucestershire £6,000 per month).

provisions rather than in cash; the money equivalent of stock items like corn, cheese or meat was also to be laid down by local agreement.[152] Individual counties agreed to pay up to £7,000 per month.[153] In Worcestershire, for example, the grand jury reviewed and renewed the contribution for three months at a time and ordered the rate to be 'assessed by four or more of the sufficient inhabitants of every parish or village . . . according to the usual rates'. The clerk of the peace was also required to instruct the head constables to follow normal procedures (specifically the precedent of the assessment for Ireland of March 1642). It was the head constables who issued warrants to the parishes. Significantly, complaints and appeals were to be heard not by the commissioners of array, but by the justices of the peace. Furthermore, there was an increasing tendency to attach disabling strings to grants. The concerns of the Grand Inquest in January 1643 were with local control of assessments; by October 1644 they were making it a condition of a renewal of the grant that all soldiers be quartered in the towns and not in the countryside, that

> whensoever any person of this County shall be necessitated to defend their persons or estates from the rapine and plunder of the soldiers or other enemies, they may not therefore be called and tried by a Court of War, but by the common law of this land that being the subjects' inheritance according to a late order of the Parliament at Oxford and his Majesty's gracious proclamation therein, [and] that it may be lawful for all the Inhabitants of this County to deduct out of their monthly contribution all such sums of money which shall hereafter become due for quartering either Horse or Foot. Lastly, we do also agree that the 19th, 20th, and 21st month's contribution shall continue at the rate of £3000 a month the one half in money and the other half in provision.[154]

Precisely the same procedure would have been followed if a county bridge had collapsed. The royalists in some areas did modify the old system in one crucial way, however. The *collection* of the contribution was left to the petty constables, but the right to *receive* the money was granted directly to local military commanders who were empowered to 'assist' (though not replace) the constables in making the collection. Although their rights were limited (they had no power to increase, alter or in any way affect the process

152. For example Willis-Bund (ed.), 'Townshend', Vol. 2, pp. l–lii.
153. For example Oxfordshire £1,600 per *week*; Berkshire £1,400 per week; Worcs. £3,000 per *month*; Gloucs. £4,000 per month.
154. Willis-Bund (ed.), 'Townshend', Vol. 2, pp. 93–101.

of assessment), any devolution of fiscal authority to the Army was likely to prove disastrous, and to allow endless opportunities for interference.[155]

The King delayed the introduction of the Excise until it could be approved by his Oxford parliament. But he need not have bothered. It was everywhere opposed, and local commissioners of array connived in organised resistance to it. At Chester, the mayoralty election in 1644 was won by a man pledged to fight its introduction.[156]

Royalist sequestration policy pursued a middle course between custom and innovation. Wherever possible, Charles wished his opponents to be formally indicted for treason by a jury at common law;[157] where sequestration occurred without formal indictment, the accused was allowed to appeal against sequestration to the next assize.[158]

It has been argued that this system, and particularly the contributions from the south and west midlands counties, just about maintained the Oxford army throughout 1643 and 1644. But as Parliament's forces invaded the royalist heartlands, the Council of War's control over the counties slackened. By the spring of 1645, the royalists were still raising a lot of money; but very little was being despatched to Oxford. The crucial factor in the Naseby campaign was not the emergence of a new mighty parliamentarian army. It was that the New Model was receiving regular and adequate pay from the south and eastern counties and from loans advanced by the city of London. The King had no more credit, no more wealthy backers, and his reliance on provincial goodwill had failed. As the New Model grew in size as soldiers deserted other forces to join an army receiving 'regular pay', the King's army was melting away through death, desertion and illness brought on by hunger and poverty.

The problems of the royalist army were compounded by Charles's weakness in granting contradictory instructions to his generals, involving them in unnecessary jurisdictional disputes. It was unforgivable to grant two commanders authority over the same area, or to fail to clarify the relative powers of commissioners of array and

155. Ibid., pp. 96–101.
156. Engberg, 'Royalist Finances', p. 95; Roy, 'Royalist Army', pp. 244–6; Morrill, *Cheshire*, pp. 135–6; Johnson, 'Chester', pp. 212–14; BL Clarendon MS 23 fos 8–9; BL Harl. MS 6804 fos 285–7.
157. See below, p. 116.
158. BM Harl. MS 6804 fo. 158; BL Harl. MS 6851 fos 157–8.

the colonels-general of the Associations in such matters as the appointment of garrison commanders.[159] Two spectacular examples are the conflict over seniority between several royalist commanders which lost them the initiative in the Marston Moor campaign,[160] and a series of conflicts arising out of the establishment of the Prince of Wales at Bristol early in 1645.[161]

Similarly the King's tendency to replenish his forces by commissioning new regiments rather than by bringing existing regiments up to strength led to the costly maintenance of superfluous officers,[162] and his liberality in granting commissions to gentlemen to garrison their manor houses at the expense of the countryside, greatly weakened royalist effectiveness and royalist resources. In Shropshire alone, twenty-five private houses as well as five towns were held in early 1643. Many of these garrisons spent more time fighting one another to gain access to provisions than they did in holding off the common enemy. Poor record-keeping and central interference only added to the problems. As John Cochrane, governor of Towcester, told Prince Rupert:

> I have rencontred many difficulties in the establishing of this garrison [Towcester], but now I am redacted to gretter perplexitie as before, since those hundreds which were by your highness allotted for the maintenance of this garrison, are by his Majesty's express order withdrawen, and assigned to my Lord of Northampton for the entertainment of the garrison at Banburie, & nothing left to me but the Hundreds of Cleley, Tossetter & Nortoun, the two last whereof are so ruinned by the long abode of the horse amongst them, that they can contributt litle or nothing. Clely is possessed be Sir John Digbie, & nothing can be extacted from thence till he be remooved. And when he is removed, the contributions that can be levyed hier will not pay the half of that which is requisitt. . . . Neither is it to be exspected that souldiers will remain heir, where they are typed to a perpetuall dutie, unles they be duelie paid . . .[163]

He was writing on 16 December 1643. It was downhill from then until the end of the war.

159. See, for example, Philipps, *Civil War in Wales*, Vol. 1, pp. 145–7; BL Tanner MS 303, 'A True Accompt of the Interesse and Demeanour of Fitzwilliam Coningsby esq. . . .'; BL Add. MS 36913 fos 120–6, 'A Representation of the State of the King's Affairs in the County Palatine of Chester . . .'.
160. Roy, 'Royalist Army', *passim*.
161. See Coate, *Cornwall*, pp. 164–79 and the sources there given.
162. C.H. Firth, *Cromwell's Army* (1961 edn), pp. 24–6.
163. Ibid., pp. 27–30; E. Warburton, *Prince Rupert and the Cavaliers* (3 vols, 1849), Vol. 2, p. 335. See also Webb, *Herefordshire*, Vol. 1, pp. 128–30.

Royalist Administration

If Parliament's attitude to the subordination of principle in the face of the realities of war can be summed up in the words of Lord Wharton, 'they were not tied to a Law, for these were times of necessity and imminent danger',[164] the royalist attitude is admirably conveyed by the commissioners of the Marcher counties meeting at Ludlow early in 1645: they prayed 'that during this war your Majesty will order that as near as the necessity of the times can admit, our ancient laws shall be observed in force and reputation'.[165] Theirs was a reluctant pragmatism.

Thus, there is widespread evidence that the King sought local approval for all contributions and forced loans. He preferred this to be given by a grand jury, otherwise by a general meeting of freeholders (such as those held in Cornwall in April, Somerset in July, and Wiltshire in November, 1643, or in North Wales and Shropshire later on).[166] Grand juries are known to have approved the contribution in Oxfordshire, Gloucestershire, Staffordshire, Hampshire and Worcestershire.[167] In this last, the grand jury renewed the grant every three months and regularly seized the opportunity to adjust the conditions of assessment and deployment, or even tacked on to the grant serious presentments relating to the failings of the royalist governors of the county.[168]

Similarly, royalist sequestrations in many areas followed the formal indictment of parliamentarians at the assizes. Examples survive for assizes at Salisbury (December 1643), Wells and Chester (February 1644).[169] However, the aim seems to have been not just to facilitate sequestration but also to initiate a propaganda exercise.

At the heart of the royalist programme came the assumption that wherever possible the normal local courts, above all quarter

164. Above, p. 75.
165. Willis-Bund (ed.), 'Townshend', Vol. 2, p. 91.
166. Warburton, *Prince Rupert*, Vol. 2, p. 334n., Vol. 3, p. 146; Coate, *Cornwall*, p. 58; Underdown, *Somerset*, p. 76; W. Phillips (ed.), 'Ottley Papers', Vol. 8, pp. 267–8.
167. Roy, 'Royalist Army', pp. 227–40; Engberg, 'Royalist Finances', pp. 89–92; Pickles, 'Studies in Royalism', pp. 113 ff.; Willis-Bund (ed.), 'Townshend', Vol. 2, p. 96, etc.
168. The Worcestershire grand jury always had possessed precocious powers; see Morrill, *Cheshire Grand Jury*, final section.
169. Harrison, 'Royalist . . . Wiltshire', pp. 456–9; Underdown, *Somerset*, pp. 69–70; J.S. Morrill and R.N. Dore, 'The Allegiance of the Cheshire Gentry in the Great Civil War', *Trans. Lancs. and Cheshire Antiq. Soc.* (1967), Appendix 1. For a list of those indicated at Wells, BL Egerton MS 2978 fo. 152; at Chester, 'Civil War Tracts of Cheshire', *Chetham Soc.*, Vol. 65 (1909), pp. 150 ff. The full Chester indictment, however, only exists in MS, Birm. Pub. Lib. MS 595611, pp. 121–31.

sessions and assizes, should continue to sit. This is the complete reverse of Parliament's practice, since few quarter sessions were held in any of the counties under their total control, and since the Houses failed to appoint any judges to go out on circuit, even ordaining that the holding of assizes was mischievous.[170] Yet the royalists worked hard to keep sessions sitting, even in disputed counties like Wiltshire, Devon and Somerset, all divided in allegiance. In all these, day-to-day administration was still attempted, albeit rather unevenly. Thus in January 1644, the Wiltshire bench ordered a major effort to restore the decaying county bridges, and in Devon 'although limited by the exigencies of war [the JPs' work] continued to extend over such routine matters as petty criminal offences, illegitimacy, road and bridge repairs, runaway apprentices and broken contracts'.[171] On the parliamentarian side, such efforts as were made to deal with these matters were undertaken by the county committees as part of their general duties.[172]

Like Parliament, the King sought to limit the spread of commissions of martial law. Most civil offences (including violence offered to quartered troops) were to be tried 'by the common law of the land', or by commissioners of oyer and terminer. Deserters too were to be tried by juries at common law. At Worcester, a weekly court martial established to deal with plunderers was soon replaced by 'a weekly court of law as opposed to a court martial'.[173]

Royalist theory was much more traditional and legalistic than Parliament's. But there was a dark side to royalist practice: the cavalier spirit. In the words of Lord Wentworth, 'though we have gotten the king but little by plundering, yet I think we have so much terrified the country that I believe the king's warrants will be much more current now than they were'.[174] The royalist hard men, Rupert and Goring prominent amongst them, had no time for legal niceties. Furthermore, as the war wore on, royalist revenues began to run out and local commanders all too quickly took matters into their own hands. The royalist cause suffered from the lawlessness of its adherents despite itself. Even Hopton, the most conscientious of all royalist commanders (he had himself tried at Truro assizes to vindicate his right to bring outside forces into

170. *A. and O.*, Vol. 1, pp. 191–2.
171. Underdown, *Somerset*, pp. 69–70; Andriette, *Devon and Exeter*, pp. 102–4; Harrison, 'Royalist . . . Wiltshire', ch. 7.
172. For example Pennington and Roots, *Committee at Stafford*, pp. xlvi–li.
173. For example Willis-Bund (ed.), 'Townshend', Vol. 1, p. lxv.
174. Warburton, *Prince Rupert*, Vol. 2, p. 193.

Cornwall to clear the county of traitors), was unable to maintain discipline. But the royalists, unlike the parliamentarians, had commanders who believed in terror, believed in the efficacy of looting to instil obedience or at least acquiescence from the country. When Sir William Brereton's soldiers plundered friend and foe alike in Wales, Brereton denounced their 'insolencies' and expressed concern at them, for he believed that the key to popular support lay in the demeanour of the two armies.[175] Few parliamentarian leaders would have disagreed; but several senior royalist commanders would neither have regretted the insolence, nor concerned themselves with its effects.

The Costs of War

This lengthy chapter has concerned itself almost entirely with the administrative innovations of the 1640s, with the calculated shock delivered to men's assumptions and convictions, particularly to those very premises and prejudices which had produced the united opposition of 1640 and the paralysis of 1642. But the conflict also imposed unparalleled fiscal burdens and hardships, and some indication of that burden is necessary here.

There is no counting the cost of the civil war.[176] The records are too patchy and ambiguous. But some sense of the scale can be offered. Kent was paying more in assessments every month by 1645–46 than it had paid in any one year for ship money;[177] the Weekly Assessment Ordinance of February 1643 was equivalent to a parliamentary subsidy every fortnight; the treasurer of the Eastern Association handled in 1644 a sum equivalent to the annual revenue of the Crown before the war. Alan Everitt believes that the assessment represented an income tax of 2s 6d in the £ by 1644–45, and a rate of 2s 0d in the £ has been suggested for Buckinghamshire.[178] A single village in Cheshire paid £15 6s 8d towards the £400,000 assessment for Ireland of March 1642. The villagers paid out £1,164 in goods and services during the ensuing war.[179]

The assessment was inexorable. It ground on, year in, year out. Arrears were never written off, and although one payment might

175. BL Add. MS 11331 fos 20, 25.
176. On this, see Pennington, 'The Cost', p. 131.
177. Compare Gordon, 'Collection of Ship Money', and Everitt, *Kent*, pp. 157–60.
178. Ibid.; Johnson, 'Buckinghamshire', p. 128.
179. BL Harl. MS 2128 fos 46–50.

be deferred, the collectors would return within days demanding the next instalment.[180] What is more, the Weekly Assessment was only one of several assessments, the greatest but not the only one: the special needs of the Scots Army and of Ireland led to further general rates being levied over long periods. In Essex, for example, in the summer of 1645, the inhabitants were paying £6,750 per month for the New Model, £300 per month for 'local defence', £720 a month for the combined garrisons of the Associated counties, £750 for the relief of Ireland, and a further sum for the Scots.[181]

Assessments were the most persistent, but not the only heavy fiscal burden. All householders were expected to contribute money on the Propositions (a notional loan at 8 per cent interest, never repaid) which probably produced more than a million pounds in the years 1642–45. In some counties, as much was raised from this source as from assessments.[182] All those who failed to contribute voluntarily were subjected to the inefficient attention of the Committee for the Advancement of Money. The Excise, however, generated more anger than cash, and does not appear to have been successfully settled outside London and a few other towns until the late 1640s.[183]

In addition, Parliament sought to seize and administer the estates of all known royalists. 'The mountains laboured and brought forth a fiscal mouse', claims Alan Everitt; a system imperfectly conceived, formulated in haste and operated with indifference, according to Brian Quintrell.[184] Nonetheless, substantial sums were raised in many counties (and retained there), enough, at any rate, to cause howls of protest from county committees when Parliament introduced composition fines as a method of inducing repentant royalists to make a settlement with the central authorities to regain their estates.[185]

180. For some notes on the scale of arrears and the problems of collection, see Everitt, *Kent*, p. 159, Johnson, 'Buckinghamshire', pp. 129–34, Morrill, *Cheshire*, pp. 103–5 and, above all, Holmes, *Eastern Association*, pp. 136–41.

181. Quintrell, 'Committee of S. Essex', pp. 41–78.

182. Morrill, *Cheshire*, p. 107n.; Quintrell, 'Committee of S. Essex', p. 61; Johnson, 'Buckinghamshire', pp. 118–26.

183. Morrill, *Cheshire*, p. 99; Everitt, *Kent*, p. 155n.; Holmes, 'Colonel King', pp. 478–9; B.E. and K. Howells (eds), 'Pembrokeshire Life, 1572–1843', *Pembroke Rec. Soc.* (1972), p. 15 (*RP* doc. 17f).

184. Everitt, *Kent*, p. 160; Quintrell, 'Committee of S. Essex', p. 105.

185. Everitt, *Kent*; Morrill, *Cheshire*, pp. 105–6, 111–17; A.M. Morton-Thorpe, 'The Gentry of Derbyshire, 1640–1660', University of Leicester MA thesis (1971), ch. 5; *Cal. Comm. Compg.*, Vols 1 and 5, introductions; P.H. Hardacre, *The Royalists During the Puritan Revolution* (1956), ch. 2.

It is not enough to examine these official sources of income and add a general note recording the lamentable tendency of soldiers to plunder and requisition goods and livestock. For it is now possible to show that in many areas the incidental costs of war exceeded the formal fiscal burdens. One of the tasks of the sub-committees of accounts was to discover the wartime losses of each village community, and many of the returns to their questionnaires have survived. In Buckinghamshire, for example, the thirty-eight surviving returns reveal an expenditure by the householders of over £17,000 on free quarter up to the middle of 1646. This is equivalent to a total for the county of about £90,000, about three times the amount raised in the same period from assessments.[186] I have suggested elsewhere that free quarter cost the population of Cheshire £120,000 in a similar period, and that this too was far more than the total sum raised by all taxation.[187]

Free quarter was the system by which soldiers were billeted on private householders who were compelled to furnish them with room and board. The soldiers were expected to give tickets to the householders specifying what they had received. At a later date the tickets were to be redeemed and the householders reimbursed. Indeed, a large number of tickets were called in periodically in the Eastern Association, and elsewhere tickets could be handed over in lieu of the assessment.[188] But such arrangements were exceptional. Time and again, Parliament granted a county or an Association a special assessment or other financial grant on condition that free quarter should cease; but as arrears mounted, local officials and army officers had little choice but to defy the ordinances. A good example of this is the plight of Westbury:

> And whereas the parliament and yor Excellencie in goodnesse have afforded us very goode orders and declaracons the benefits whereof wee want *videlicet* that if the country shall pay the 60000 li per mensem they shall be freed from free quarters, Whereof six moneths demandes we have already payde and the other three monethes now questioned wee are ready to pay and yet are constantly burthened with free quartering and that which hath next relation to free quarter as may appeare by our accompte of the charge which the sayde towne

186. Johnson, 'Buckinghamshire', pp. 142–5.
187. Morrill, *Cheshire*, p. 107 n. For specific examples, see PRO, SP 28, Vols 148–51, 171–3, 219–21, *passim* (these are examples for the Eastern Association).
188. On this, see the excellent section in Holmes, *Eastern Association*, pp. 153–7. C.H. Firth, *Cromwell's Army* (1962 rev. edn), pp. 295–6.

and parish have beene at which amounts to above the proporcon of
our rate for the 60000 li per mensem already the continuance of
which your poore peticoners are not able to undergoe. And whereas
the rumor of the souldiers paying for theire quarters may appeare to
the world to be somthing yet wee finde it in effect nothing.[189]

Quartering was bad enough; but it was more often than not
accompanied by the forcible seizure and detention of the posses-
sions of those on whom the soldiers were quartered. An analysis of
the Cheshire parish returns suggest that more goods were seized by
soldiers where they were quartered than from villages through which
they were just passing on the march. Typical of such ingratitude
were those of Fairfax's men who departed from quarters in Church
Lawton with 'two flaxen shirts, five yards of woollen cloathe, two
silke garters, one hatbande, six hand carchasses, two Bondes & one
payre of stockinges' belonging to John Chantler.[190] Cheshire villagers claimed that over £90,000 of goods were forcibly taken from
them or destroyed during the war, although this figure may have
included a tithe for sentimental value.[191] Nonetheless, quartering
and its side effects was disastrous for the village community, and
most of the riots and armed risings which led into the Clubmen
movements began with the arrival of troops seeking quarter, rather
than with the arrival of a tax collector.[192] Some, however, found
other ways of keeping soldiers away, as in North Wales: 'from the
first, the inhabitants in those parts where any were sick denied it
was anything but a fever – unless soldiers came there to quarter'.[193]

The civil war put all men on a fiscal treadmill; but their efforts
were in vain. They could not generate enough resources to supply
the armies, the engines of war. By the spring of 1647, the total
arrears of the armies throughout England and Wales were about
two and a half million pounds.[194] Most of this was owed to the small
provincial armies. Many regiments had received less than half their
total earnings when they were ordered to be disbanded.[195] The New
Model itself was always better paid than any other force, not least
because the Monthly Assessment Ordinance by which it was maintained did actually match its real cost, whereas the older armies had

189. W.A. Day (ed.), *The Pythouse Papers* (1879), pp. 30–1. *RP* doc. 15a.
190. BL Harl. MS 1943 fo. 13.   191. Morrill, *Cheshire*, pp. 106–10.
192. See below, pp. 134, 141–2.
193. B.E. Howells (ed.), *A Calendar of Letters Relating to North Wales* (1967), p. 231.
194. A figure published in an article by I. Gentles 'The Arrears of Pay of the
Parliamentary Army at the end of the First Civil War' in *BIHR* 48 (1975), pp. 52–63.
195. See Morrill, 'Mutiny and Discontent', p. 50 and n.

always been maintained out of assessments which would have been insufficient even if they had been collected in full and on time.[196]

Conclusion

Alan Everitt has argued strongly that in the seventeenth century a backcloth of endemic disaster, harvest failures, fire, flood and disease were 'more serious and more persistent than the tragic but temporary upheaval of the civil war'.[197] His point is a good one, but there is a danger of overstating it. Natural disasters struck with seemingly random fury throughout the century; they struck in the 1640s too. But on top of all these constant threats, the war added several years of violence and disruption; on top of the destructive forces of nature came widespread destruction by man. Some areas suffered far more than others, but in an age without insurance the sacking of one's house just once was catastrophic enough. Throughout the war, the plunder of houses, commandeering of horses or livestock, the trampling of crops, was a daily threat. Fifty-one horses were taken away from one small Cheshire village in the course of the war;[198] a gentleman living nearby was plundered six times, three times by each side;[199] another had his home burnt down so that the enemy could not use it as a cover for siege operations;[200] a single village in Shropshire sent twenty men to the war of whom thirteen were killed;[201] a man who had recently inherited his uncle's house was imprisoned by both sides in turn as he moved north to claim it;[202] even the melting down of the church organ pipes to make bullets for the Army materially affected the life of a village community.[203] Such incidents, many of them trivial enough, made the world a darker and less happy place to live in. Such things could and did either incline men to cling more closely than ever to known structures, known ways, or it could cut them loose, freeing them to seek a happier future through new political eschatologies. In the event, the radical conservatism of the Clubmen was to prove more characteristic of the later 1640s than the iconoclasm of the Levellers.

196. Compare Gentles, 'Arrears of Pay', and Holmes, *Eastern Association*, pp. 158–61 and Appendix 7, pp. 236–7.
   197. Everitt, 'The Local Community', p. 26.
   198. Quoted in Morrill, *Cheshire*, p. 109.
   199. Chester City Record Office, CR 63/2/72, Davenport MSS, *passim*. See below, p. 125.
   200. PRO, SP 28/225, unfoliated.
   201. R. Gough, *Antiquities and Memoirs of Myddle* (1875 edn), p. 39.
   202. *CSPD, 1645*, p. 198.   203. BL Harl. MS 2125 fo. 135.

CHAPTER THREE

Reactions to War, 1643–49

Introduction

In 1642, men had been forced to make up their minds between two parties both of which represented essential elements in their fundamental political cosmology. Conflicting allegiances, further cross-cut by local connection and patronage, had led to commitments entered into without certainty, without conviction. Men took commissions in order to give themselves authority to protect their communities and their conception of the world from external attack and internal disintegration.

But the war had got out of hand. Large armies had been mobilised which could not be restrained, armies which could only be paid by a total transformation of the existing fiscal and civil administration, armies which, if they were not paid, would seize what they needed forcibly. In 1642 both sides had fully and conscientiously declared their support for the 'fundamental laws', 'the liberties of the subject', 'the sovereignty of law'. The meaning of such terms was variously understood, but, by any definition, the actions of both sides in succeeding years clearly contravened such laws and liberties. Both sides abandoned a large part of the common ground they had initially shared. Instead of a nation full of fearful neutrals, undecided which way to turn, there developed a nation full of embittered, desperate neutrals, seeking first to hide from the war and then, driven from their hiding places, determined to stand and fight the implications of war, the betrayal of fundamental rights and liberties. In 1642, the political nation feared the spectre of mob rule. By 1645 it confronted those in power, who had shown themselves to be mindless of shared values and traditional rights.

Amidst the volume of despair and anxiety, a single complacent voice sounds out. A midlands rector, in his parish register too, wrote: 'when an uncivil war was being waged most fiercely between King and Parliament throughout the greater part of England, I lived well because I lay low.'[1] His complacency is unique, but his determination to let the war pass him by is extremely common. It is, however, by its very nature, almost impossible to document.

At its crudest, the desire to *contain* the war can be found in the words of an angry opponent of the Nottinghamshire committee: 'what is the cause to me if my goods be lost?'[2] More subtly, this cynicism (the essential difference between the rector and the rest) or, at least, this basic drive for self-preservation, is expressed in an account of the motives of the rural population around Gloucester in declaring for the King: they

> wished, for their own interests, that the king were quietly possessed of that city. For they conceived (not without reason) that the standing out of Gloucester would be unhappy for that county, because, by the falling downe of a great army, they could not but expect a great destruction of their corne, cattle, and all other provisions. And at the last, if it should so fall out that the king should faile of taking that towne, they must be inforced to stoop perpetually under the two burdens, and be cast into a sadd condition of poverty and misery. Whereas if that army did prevaile they were sure to rest in the heart of the king's country, farre from spoile and plunder, and for an easie contribution, inioy free and ample trade.[3]

In South Wales they employed a special term to describe this prevailing mentality: a majority were said to be 'ambidexters', men prepared to adopt any political stance which would limit the hazards of war.[4] In all the solidly royalist areas, there were many men, prepared quietly to co-operate with the prevailing interest, who saw no dishonesty in transferring their active acquiescence to the parliamentarian party once their county was 'liberated'. Such men (and in few areas did Parliament experience difficulty in finding agents) had not been secret parliamentarians all along. They were men who would act for the controlling group in order to preserve as much local autonomy as possible and to limit the consequences of war. Their loyalty was still, as it had been in 1640 and 1642, to their own community.[5]

1. Quoted in D.R. Guttery, *The Great Civil War in Midlands Parishes* (1950), p. 11.
2. Quoted in A.C. Wood, *Nottinghamshire in the Civil War* (1937), p. 54n.
3. T. May, *The History of the Parliament of England* (1647), Part 3, p. 92.
4. H.A. Lloyd, *The Gentry of South-West Wales, 1540–1640* (1967), pp. 123–9.
5. See, for example, the case of Evan Edwards of Rhual, who appears to have actively assisted both sides as occasion demanded in order to restrain them from

Localism

Those who sought to limit the consequences of the war, however, could suffer even greater hardships. William Davenport, whose 'pure' Country credentials were examined above (pp. 32–4), has left eloquent testimony of the sufferings of a determined non-participant. He adopted the line of least resistance, paying every demand made of him by either side so long as it was backed by a warrant in the traditional form. He only protested when his goods were taken by those without due authority. Despite his compliance with a wide range of demands for cash and provisions, he was plundered several times by the forces of both sides. Nor did Parliament's victory bring him any relief. His payments to the royalists were considered grounds for sequestration and his estates were seized. Eventually, the local sequestration committee quite improperly suggested that if he paid them £500 as an earnest of his good faith, they would 'avoid all rigour and extremity'. He complied only to find that the central committee had discounted the local committee's action as *ultra vires*. They refused, however, to deduct the sum from the formal composition fine which they now imposed. Whoever had won the civil war, Davenport would have lost it: had Charles triumphed, Davenport's payments to the parliamentarians would almost certainly have constituted acts of rebellion and he would have suffered at their hands too. Neutrality was no soft option.[6]

The chance survival of a series of depositions taken by sequestration commissioners in Wiltshire in the summer of 1646 afford a contrasting and less gloomy portrait of the efforts of moderate men to promote the coexistence of politically and religiously divided village communities during the war.

Wiltshire was more unsettled during the war than most counties. It was crossed and recrossed by the main field armies of both sides, and both King and Parliament maintained a number of garrisons in the county. Villages often found themselves expected to act upon contradictory instructions from two or more authorities. The depositions taken in 1646 show clearly how older loyalties and values had been preserved in these adverse circumstances.[7]

---

excesses. B.E. Howells (ed.), *A Calendar of Letters Relating to North Wales* (1967), pp. 230–4; N. Tucker, *North Wales in the Civil War* (1958), pp. 67–9.

   6. See Morrill, 'William Davenport', *passim; Cal. Comm. Compg.*, p. 1660. Full extracts in *RP* doc. 20.

   7. For what follows, see BL Add. MS 22084, foliated from the back.

Despite the constant demands and pressures of war, the social and administrative life of the village community persisted. Every effort was made to accommodate the war, not by defying external authority (for example in the form of royalist or parliamentarian committees) but by placating all such external authority. At times, the instructions of both sides would be obeyed. Yet this did not mean that individuals remained politically agnostic. Within each village, individuals could and did hold distinct preferences. But such differences were allowed to coexist. The village alehouse, the parish church, remained centres of debate where a minister sympathetic to the King and a constable sympathetic to Parliament would not only argue over their differences, but also learn to live with them. The most heinous offence (and one denounced in the depositions) was for individuals to involve 'outsiders' in parish life, as by calling on a neighbouring garrison to help collect contributions. But this had not often happened. Conversely, the whole point about the depositions of 1646 was that no denunciation had hitherto been made against ministers who had throughout the war held the royalist Friday Fast but ignored the parliamentarian Wednesday Fast. These depositions had had to wait until after the end of the fighting and were the result of specific inquiries by commissioners sent into the villages. The case of Dr Thomas Mason neatly illustrates this. His political preferences were clear, for he had continued to receive dean and chapter rents in defiance of a parliamentary prohibition, had refused to deliver up his rent roll, and had preached against Parliament. Significantly, 'it was allwayes observed that when at any time the Parliament's forces were at Salisbury, hee never preached, but kept the church doores allwayes shutt.'[8] In other words, he made sure that outsiders did not discover his proclivities, rightly confident that none of his parishioners would denounce him until required to do so by the commissioners after the war.

The effects of the war were *contained*, restricted wherever possible. There were political debates in many private houses and inns,[9] and in villages like Colston, the royalist minister might obstruct a tything-man who tried to implement parliamentarian warrants, but he would not report the man to the royalist commissioners, nor himself be denounced until after the war.

Equally striking was the way so many ministers remained politically inactive until the spring of 1645. They remained in their pulpits whoever controlled their area, refusing to commit themselves

8. Ibid., fos 21–2.   9. Ibid., fos 13–14.

to either side. Despite the abolition of episcopacy, the suspension
of the Church courts and the prospects of a radical reconstruction
of the Church, they refused to be drawn. They continued to minister to their congregations as they had always done – at least, as long
as they could do so. But as soon as Parliament banned the use of
the Prayer Book they were forced into taking an active stand. In
burning the Prayer Book, they would have been forced to accept
changes in their own duties, in their social role. Consequently, in
the summer of 1645 they went on the march. A few openly declared for the King. More associated themselves with the neutralist
anti-war Clubmen movements. For example, a deposition against
Mr Aylesbury declared

> that the said Mr Aylesbury was very forward in the Clubb busines and
> that at the Randevouse by Meere Beakon which was on James day
> last, where one Mr Younge made a longe speeche unto the people
> and when the said Younge had ended his speeche the said Mr Ayles-
> bury spake sayinge, Mr Younge, Mr Younge, lett not the Booke of
> Comon Prayer bee forgotton, butt lett that bee upheld.[10]

Similarly James White, minister of Boscombe, stayed at his post
throughout the war, only to tell a committee in 1647 that 'hee doth
still make use of [the Book of Common Prayer] as occasion re-
quires, and sayth that hee had rather loose his Liveinge than leave
the Comon prayer'.[11] None of the wider political or religious changes
had moved him to protest.

In Wiltshire, men did not pretend that the war did not exist; nor
did they ignore it. They did not welcome it, nor did they allow
themselves to make immediate sacrifices to uphold wider political
or religious views. Only when they were required to make unmistak-
able public and personal commitments to causes inimical to their
consciences did they make a stand.

Anti-war Protests in 1643

So far, we have looked at the quiescent neutrals, those who continued to minimise the effects of war by swimming with the tide.
However confused and uncertain they may have been about the
issues dividing the parties, they stood by the values of the 'pure'
Country in the 1630s. They sought to uphold the integrity of traditional procedures and the independence of local communities. In

10. Ibid., fo. 8.   11. Ibid., fo. 50.

addition, there were many others who had found themselves forced into accepting active commissions on one side or the other in late 1642 and who then found the consequences intolerable, men like Sir Edward Dering[12] who withdrew from the royalist side sickened by his experiences, or Sir John Holland[13] who went into self-imposed exile rather than implement the parliamentarian Sequestration Ordinance. In Wiltshire, half the commissioners of array gave up their commissions in the autumn of 1644 as a protest against the measures adopted by local military commanders.[14] Others changed sides, often finding that the change brought no less burden to their consciences. Neither side can be said to contain more than a small number of determined partisans, and allegiance within both parties was a shifting, rather than a stable, condition. To call someone a 'royalist' or a 'parliamentarian' may mean no more than that he superficially acquiesced in a series of orders for which he had no stomach. Except for the handful who have left positive records of belief in one or other cause, there is no meaningful way of establishing commitment. This point is important in understanding the origins of several 'royalist' and 'parliamentarian' risings during the war. Men who were frightened of acting simply in their own name might well accept commissions from one side or the other in order to validate their opposition to the war itself. It took a long time, and then a great deal of courage, for men to stand up and fight simply as 'neutrals'. But long before the Clubmen risings of 1645, there had been a series of localist movements whose aims were to limit or halt the war rather than to facilitate the victory of one side or the other. The most important of these were the 1643 rebellions in Norfolk and Kent, both of which represent essentially neutralist reactions against the consequences of the war, leavened by the emergence of small groups of convinced royalists who had remained prudently passive up to this point.

The earliest outbreak in Kent followed Parliament's decision to impose the Presbyterian Covenant on every person of age in the county. When members of the county committee ordered the arrest of the rector of Ightham for refusing the oath, scuffles broke out between soldiers and parishioners, during which one of the latter was killed. News of his 'murder' led to angry gatherings throughout the county and culminated in a widespread revolt under gentry leadership. However, in the words of Alan Everitt: 'the rebels were

---

12. See, for example, Everitt, *Kent*, pp. 205–8.   13. Above p. 76; *RP* doc. 21b.
14. See below, pp. 138–40.

essentially moderates rather than cavaliers, and their grievances were primarily local. . . . In many parishes the rebellion became entangled with local squabbles and long-standing family feuds.' Sir Thomas Knyvett, himself arrested for supposed royalist conspiracy in Norfolk, makes no mention of a royalist connection in his discussion of the Kentish rebellion and saw it as an essentially popular movement. It is true that some of the leaders did appeal to the King for help, but others wished to keep *all* external forces out of the county and indeed made this an important plank in their programme. Their manifesto made no reference to the King; it was entirely concerned with local grievances generated by the war. They asked for the continuation of the Prayer Book, that no new ministers be imposed upon them, and that they should not be compelled to take the Covenant. They also sought an undertaking that their goods would not be distrained nor any taxes imposed on them 'contrary to the liberty of the subject'. No wonder Knyvett failed to discover a royalist connection. Some of its leaders did hold royalist commissions, so that it cannot simply be described as a 'neutralist' movement. However, it was essentially a rejection of the *consequences of the war* rather than a repudiation of the principles for which Parliament had initially gone to war.[15]

The later Kentish rebellion (in 1645) reveals the same characteristics. Again the King's name was invoked by the rebels, and again there was talk of aid from Oxford. But the rebels did not proclaim royalist slogans, nor did they intend to shed any of their blood on any soil but Kent's. Rather they announced that the grounds of their rebellion were 'illegal taxes', the abolition of the Prayer Book, the imposition of the Covenant and the impressment of men forced 'from the plough's handle'. The county committee reacted by calling for wider powers to deal with 'neuters and malignants'. If this was a royalist revolt, it was a rather special kind – an appeal to the King to save Kent from the consequences of parliamentarian misrule, with no overt mention of the virtues of the royalist cause. It is in the tradition of the concealed neutralist movements of 1642.[16]

The unrest in Norfolk in the course of 1643 is even more difficult to interpret.[17] None of the long series of conspiracies or insurrections really got off the ground. In early March, following a purge

15. Everitt, *Kent,* pp. 190–5; Schofield (ed.), *Knyvett,* p. 119.
16. Everitt, *Kent,* pp. 214–17.
17. For what follows, see Ketton-Cremer, *Norfolk,* pp. 172–91, 206–15; Schofield (ed.), *Knyvett,* pp. 33–4, 109–13; A. Kingston, *East Anglia and the Great Civil War* (1897), pp. 92–5, 134–9.

of Norwich corporation, a group of local gentry and townsmen (including at least two men who had been active as Deputy Lieutenants for Parliament in the preceding autumn and winter) were arrested for 'royalist' conspiracy. Later in the same month there was a curious incident at Lowestoft, again involving both gentry and townsmen, again quickly halted after a show of force by a body of parliamentarian horse under Cromwell. 'Distractions' were also reported from King's Lynn in March, followed by a briefly successful *coup-de-main* there in August, speedily put down by the arrival of the Earl of Manchester.

All these plots involved the towns, and it is possible that the invasion of borough rights constituted by parliamentarian finance ordinances (including the Assessments Ordinance passed on 1 March) may have played a significant part in generating the unrest. In Lynn, for example, the 'distractions and divisions' reported on 13 March were said to have been directed against the 'constituted officers and captains' (appointed by the county committee?), and the opposition had been led by the Recorder, the man primarily responsible for safeguarding the borough's liberties.

In May, Parliament ordered the arrest of thirteen named royalists at Lynn, but also called for a search of the town for all catholics, delinquents and such as 'avoid the contributions of King and Parliament'. Further signs of resistance to the assessment can be found in the villages around Aylsham in the early summer. In April there was a violent demonstration against the county committee's levying of assessments. Robert Ketton-Cremer has shown how support for Parliament in the county declined as it became evident that there would be no early end to the war. This is further proof of the argument advanced above[18] that many members of the Norfolk establishment had accepted commissions simply in order to legitimate their neutralism, to allow them to maintain the peace of the county while the issue was settled elsewhere. Once Norfolk was unequivocally required to contribute to the wider conflict, they lapsed into passivity.

This background helps to throw light on the exceedingly obscure affairs at Lowestoft in March and Lynn in August 1643. Early in March a number of royalist gentlemen gathered in Lowestoft, intending, as they subsequently maintained, to cross from there to Holland and self-imposed exile. Such a story cannot be discounted, since many gentlemen – including several from East Anglia – had

18. See above, p. 62.

already done the same thing. Since Lowestoft lacked walls or defence works, it was a singularly inappropriate place from which to
launch a rebellion. Furthermore, we possess the correspondence of
one of those seized in the town, Thomas Knyvett, and his assertion
that he was bound for the Netherlands is supported not only by his
public protestations but also in his private letters to his wife,[19] letters in which he was dangerously outspoken on other matters. What
provoked the crisis was not the presence of the gentry, but the
reaction of the parliamentarians, notably Colonel Oliver Cromwell.
He was at Norwich, but hearing rumours of royalist gatherings at
Lowestoft, he set out with men from Norwich and Yarmouth. Contemporary statements are consistent with the view that it was at this
point that the townsmen attempted to arm themselves, fearful of
being plundered. What increased their anxiety was probably the
inclusion, in Cromwell's party, of men from Yarmouth, a town with
a long record of hostility towards Lowestoft. Indeed Knyvett made
this point quite clearly: 'at that time there being a high contest
between the town of Yarmouth and the poor town of Lowestoft,
which made them stand upon their guard to defend themselves
against the threat of Yarmouth.'

Here is part of the official parliamentarian account of what
occurred:

> the town had blocked themselves up only where they had placed
> their ordnance, which were three pieces, before a chain was drawn
> to keep off the horse. The Colonel summoned the town and de-
> manded if they would deliver up their strangers, the town and their
> arms, promising them their favour; if not, none. They yielded to
> deliver up their strangers, but not the rest.

Again, this appears to signify no deep plot involving the gentry and
leading townsmen, but a peaceful town which had turned a blind
eye to royalist comings-and-goings, and which would readily ditch
its embarrassing visitors in exchange for freedom from plunder. A
simple chain was no sort of defence against Cromwell and once he
had crossed it and seized the ordnance the town threw itself on his
mercy. Neither the King nor the royalist cause were ever referred to
except by the later sequestrators seeking to strengthen their case
against the gentry arrested there.

At Lynn in August, Charles I really was proclaimed and Sir
Harmon l'Estrange, replete with a royal commission, was installed
as governor. Yet the largely 'parliamentarian' townsmen accepted

19. Schofield (ed.), *Knyvett*, particularly letters 51 and 52, pp. 109–11.

the coup without protest, and even continued to attend assembly meetings. Furthermore (after a few cannonades by the parliamentarian army which arrived at the gates), when negotiations were opened it was soon apparent that all the townsmen wanted was a confirmation of their former rights and liberties. The Earl of Manchester's formal reply, that 'if they will deliver the town by Saturday nine in the morning, they shall have privilege and freedom; as for freedom from Ordinances of Parliament, they must expect no such thing', indicates that the 'royalists' of Lynn were mainly concerned to avoid the consequences of war.

The Kent and Norfolk 'royalists' of 1643 should perhaps be seen primarily not as tardy converts to the cause of an outright royalist victory but as men reacting against the war without being able to declare themselves 'neutral'. To declare for the King might legitimate resistance without involving any wider commitment than the restoration of local self-government. It is an approach which was later adopted by the gentry of South Wales, and one which they learned to regret.[20]

The Clubmen

In an important passage in his book on civil war Somerset, David Underdown has written:

> The war had been fought between two minorities, struggling in a sea of neutralism and apathy. And the further down the social scale we penetrate the more neutralism and apathy we encounter. The greater gentry may have been largely royalist but even among them there were many . . . who put local loyalties above national ones. Among the lesser gentry and yeomen, too, the Country outlook enabled men to acquiesce in the rule of each side in turn . . . we should not expect to find widespread political involvement below the yeoman level: the poorer farmer and cottager, like the typical peasant in all ages, tended to regard government as a part of a remote natural order which he was powerless to influence. He might in the end revolt against plundering and oppression but only if there were determined men to lead him, and even then with no distinct ideology to guide him.[21]

There is only one point in this with which I would take issue. There is a tendency throughout Underdown's book to see neutrals

20. See below, pp. 174–6.   21. Underdown, *Somerset*, pp. 117–18.

and 'moderates' as 'apathetic', 'ignorant', 'uninvolved'. In fact the 'Country' mentality both in 1642 and 1645 was very positive, clear-sighted, principled. Further on, Underdown says of the grass-roots parliamentarians that they were concerned to purify the Church and prevent arbitrary power from devouring the state and liberty. He adds: 'ideas like protecting "the ancient and fundamental laws of the kingdom" may seem conventional and naïve, but they were held strongly enough to inspire the great bulk of parliamentarian sympathisers'.[22] I would argue that it was concern with the ancient and fundamental laws, liberties and custom which prevented most men from enthusiastic support for either side in 1642, since war seemed likely to bring these tumbling down. And those concerned to protect those traditional rights and generalised notions of liberty were not likely to be won over by Parliament's wartime expedients. Those who resisted the war, who reacted most violently against it, were not always, and not usually, apathetic, or gullible conservatives, easily exploited by one side or the other. They were radical conservatives who were prepared to articulate programmes and organise men and resources to defend not just their homes, but traditional values and rights which both sides had lost sight of in the fratricidal struggle. The Clubmen emerged as the true champions of a fully developed provincialism and conservatism whose importance and significance have been scandalously ignored.

In the course of 1645, Clubmen Associations were formed in Shropshire, Worcestershire and Herefordshire (January–March), Wiltshire, Dorset and Somerset (May–September), Berkshire, Sussex and Hampshire (September–October), and South Wales and the border (August–November).

The seriousness of the threat was partly based on the geographical extent of the movements. But it derived also from the numerical strength of the Clubmen. Although in the event they did not prove an effective military force, their numbers invariably impressed observers and initially inclined both sides to conciliate them. Neither side seriously questioned the Clubmen's claim to be able to raise 20,000 men in Wiltshire and Dorset at forty-eight hours' notice (3,000–4,000 almost certainly were present at one meeting at Grovely in June to approve a petition). The Berkshire Clubmen claimed 16,000 adherents, the Glamorganshire 'Peaceable Army' about 10,000. Again, independent observers accepted these figures. In Somerset, one estimate gave 6,000 men in arms, in Herefordshire

22. Ibid., p. 118.

3,000. Even if such figures were wildly exaggerated, the numbers must have been substantial at a time when only three armies in the kingdom consisted of 12,000 men or more. It is likely that the Clubmen outnumbered local forces in most Clubmen counties.[23]

Each Association began as an essentially popular peasant movement, growing out of a series of confrontations between village communities and soldiers demanding quarter or provisions (or general plunder).[24] In most cases, leadership then passed to the leading gentry who gave the associations greater administrative coherence and wider political programmes. Yet every Association remained distinct and retained characteristics reflecting local problems within a common concern for the traditional values of provincial society. At the heart of all the movements lay a yearning to halt the war, most Associations looking not just for a local pacification but for a national settlement along the same lines as those demanded by the bemused neutrals of 1642. Meanwhile they sought a local truce. Sometimes they envisaged themselves taking over full responsibility for raising and distributing contributions to remaining garrisons, sometimes they hoped to persuade both sides to withdraw all their forces, leaving the Clubmen as the sole military power. There were persistent demands for the full restoration of traditional methods of local government.

There is overwhelming evidence that most of the Clubmen were neutrals. In comparison with the rebels of Norfolk and Kent, they developed a convincing justification for their neutralism. This certainly did not preclude Associations from assisting either King or Parliament in particular circumstances, but this need not imply a betrayal of their neutralism. A tactical alliance with Fairfax, for example, helped the Devon and southern Somerset Clubmen to rid

23. There is no good published treatment of the Clubmen as a whole. O. Warner, 'The Clubmen and the English Civil Wars', *Army Quarterly*, Vol. 38 (1939), pp. 287–99, is superficial but offers a brief chronology. Underdown, *Somerset*, pp. 86–117 is excellent on Somerset and throws incidental light on other counties. For individual counties, see also Bayley, *Civil War in Dorset*, Vol. 2, pp. 150–63; C. Thomas-Stanford, *Sussex in the Great Civil War and Interregnum* (1910), pp. 160–73; G.N. Godwin, *The Civil War in Hampshire, 1642–1645* (1882), pp. 215–20. For the Clubmen and the New Model, see J. Sprigge, *Anglia Rediviva* (1854 edn), pp. 61–91. Harrison, 'Royalist . . . Wiltshire', ch. 6, is an important study of the Wiltshire Clubmen; Manning, 'Neutrals', ch. 5, is a useful synthesis of the printed sources. But see now G.J. Lynch, 'The Risings of the Clubmen in the English Civil War', University of Manchester MA thesis (1973), which I was unable to read until this chapter was completed. It is an excellent and judicious study.

24. It has been claimed that the Clubmen were responsible for introducing the word 'plunder' into the English language (Godwin, *Civil War in Hampshire*, p. 216; see also the *Shorter OED*).

themselves of Goring, who represented a threat to provincial liberties far greater than that posed, in the short term, by the New Model.

These Clubmen were not seeking to help Parliament win the war. They were using parliamentary troops to clear their own counties of the most potent immediate threat. Again, it is vital to point out that at the beginning of 1645, the war appeared evenly balanced; that the creation of the New Model did not immediately alert the country to a major shift in the balance of power; and that it took several months for the importance of the battle of Naseby to be appreciated. The Clubmen were assuming that a military stalemate still existed. Their primary task was to prevent their own shires from becoming major battlegrounds.

Furthermore, while many Clubmen assisted one side or the other, or at least had more sympathy for one side, their essential neutralism prevailed. To prefer King to Parliament did not preclude a preference for peace above both. Thus the Clubmen of the Marcher counties, above all Worcester and Hereford, necessarily directed their attention against the royalist forces occupying and plundering them. Their campaign was intended to 'tame' the royalists, force them to respect the wishes of the inhabitants and restore local civilian control. The Clubmen did not seek to destroy royalist power, only to control it. They pointedly rejected overtures from Edward Massey, parliamentarian governor of Gloucester, who marched forth hoping to make common cause with them. As the Somerset Clubmen wrote in reply to a similar approach from Colonels Blake and Pyne, this 'is quite contrary to the prime intentions of our Association, for instead of Mediators, we shall become Parties, instead of making Peace, we shall in all possibility lengthen the war . . .'.[25] So it was in the Welsh border countries. John Corbet, a man whose bigotry usually made him see things in terms of black and white, called them 'foolish neuters': they had given 'assurance that they were our friends, but could not declare for either side . . . these men were lost to us and to themselves also'.[26]

Edward Massey wrote to his colleague Sir Samuel Luke on 22 March 1645 in a way which reflected both his dilemma and his incomprehension:

> Sir, This Post can relate the Hereford busines the whole County being now in Armes in a confused manner and before the Citty of Hereford and some of the Worcestershire side haue ioyned with

25. BL, Thomason Tracts, E 300/13.
26. J. Corbet, *A True and Impartiall History of the Military Government of Gloucester* (1643), pp. 129–33.

them. I haue sent you a Coppie of their articles and demands from
the Gouernor of Hereford. Sir, upon this noyse I advanced upon
Wednesday last to Ledbury with 500 foote and 150 horse being as
many as I could spare or make at present and demaunded their
resolutions and desired them to ioyne with mee in observing the
Parliaments commands. They would faine have mee assist them (for
they dare trust mee) but they will not yett declare themselves for the
Parliament but they conceive themselves able to keepe of both the
Parliament's forces and the Kings alsoe from contribution and quarter in their County. That is their vaine hope and upon that ground I
understand they have taken up that resolution. Sir its an opportunity
offered to the Parliament if they lay hold on this occasion, and send
mee speedy force to gaine them all to the Parliament: if not the losse
will not bee small to us. Bee it how it will I have used all the best
arguments I can to moove them to declare themselves for the Parliament then they may haue proteccion and authority for what they
doe. Now their act is a perfect act of rebellion to bee justified by noe
Law or Statute and their confusion will be certaine.[27]

Here was the fundamental reason why neither side understood
the Clubmen. They both continually hoped to manipulate the Associations and assumed, once their overtures had been spurned, that
this implied a secret preference for the other side. They never
accepted the strength of the neutralist principle. The Clubmen
grounded their movement not on the authority of royal warrant or
parliamentary ordinance, but on the inherent rights of Englishmen
to defend their traditional and fundamental liberties. An assault on
local institutions and local rights gave each community a right of
resistance. The doctrine of popular sovereignty developed by the
Clubmen to justify a highly conservative political programme has
close affinities with the Leveller demand for radical extension of
local autonomy and liberty. Thus the Clubman vicar of Coombe in
Wiltshire, Henry Beech, denounced both King and Parliament for
abusing their power and their trust and called on his parishioners
to take the staff of state into their own hands to defend their inher-
itance.[28] Even more starkly, one Somerset Association denounced
taxation as arbitrary and defended the Clubmen's rights to resist
the violation of their liberties, 'for it is possible that a Parliament
may erre (and that foully) as well as a generall Councell'.[29]

27. See Webb, *Herefordshire*, pp. 150–62; HMC, *JP*, Vol. 4, The Letter Book of Sir
Samuel Luke, pp. 485, 490; HMC, *Portland MSS*, Vol. 3, p. 137; J. and T.W. Webb
(eds), 'A Military Memoir of Colonel John Birch', *Camden Society*, Vol. 7 (1873),
pp. 112, 216–17.
   28. BL Add. MS 22084 fo. 27.   29. BL, Thomason Tracts, E 300/13.

Fairfax illustrates the bemusement of parliamentarian observers well. To begin with, he hoped to win them over to the cause (and indeed in Devon and Somerset he succeeded), but later he tended to see them as crypto-royalist. He emphasised that the Dorset–Wiltshire leaders were 'such as are mainly *former* royalists', and gloomily reported that 'they are abundantly more affected to the enemy than to the parliament'. Yet in the same letters he also wrote that 'they take upon them to interpose between the garrisons of either side; and when any of the forces meet in places where they have sufficient power, they will not let them fight, but make them drink together', and that 'whatever party falls on them, they will join the other'. He also reported that the Wiltshire Clubmen were indifferently carrying through the agreement made with the parliamentarian garrison at Falstone and the royalist one at Langford whereby the Clubmen made themselves responsible for raising and paying over equal contributions to both.[30]

Fairfax's confusion can largely be explained by reference to the royalist backgrounds of many of the leaders of the movement. Of the fifteen directors of the Wiltshire Association, eleven had earlier acted as royalist officials, although four appear to have shown earlier preference for the parliament. But all the royalists had abandoned their offices in the summer of 1644 as a protest against royalist methods, and, even more significantly, several of them had been involved in the Wiltshire neutrality petition of October 1642.[31]

In view of this, and of the open royalist attempt to woo the leaders, Fairfax's scepticism of their ostensible neutrality is understandable. But he was too scrupulous not to report the contrary evidence, nor can he have been ignorant of the degree to which the Wiltshire Clubmen had hitherto directed their attention against the activities of the royalist garrisons like Devizes. The arrival of the New Model necessarily changed their priorities and energies. There is no reason to doubt that if Goring had burst out of the south-west, he would have been confronted by the same large Clubmen armies which were defeated by the New Model at Shaftesbury and Hambleton Hill in September. If, by then, the Wiltshire Clubmen were inclined to be more accommodating towards the royalists, this was a function of the hard line which the two Houses were now adopting and of the overriding threat posed by the New Model.

30. *LJ*, Vol. 7, p. 484; Rushworth, *Historical Collections*, Vol. 7, pp. 52–3.
31. Harrison, 'Royalist . . . Wiltshire', ch. 6, who believes, however, that the 'Club movement of 1645 was royalist in aim and neutral in character' (p. 435).

The supposed bias of particular Clubmen groups was often in the eye of the beholder. A parliamentarian newsletter might contemptuously dismiss them: 'they are Neutralls and such as like weathercockes they will turn this way and that with every blast; and will, I conceive, be ready to close in with the prevailing party, without respect to truth or justice'.[32] But the reality was rather different. It was the two High Commands who temporised. In the case of the Marcher counties, both sides sent representatives to negotiate with the Clubmen; in the southerly counties, both sides bought time, worried and alarmed by Clubmen strength. Fairfax gave passes for representatives to take petitions to Oxford and Westminster. The King sent a distinctly encouraging reply, Parliament blustered but issued no immediate command to Fairfax to suppress them by force. Indeed, it was only after the fall of Bristol, with the road open to the West Country and to Goring's final stronghold (this was six weeks after his initial confrontation with the Clubmen), that Fairfax decided to fight them. In the event, despite their numerical strength, the Clubmen collapsed at the first cavalry charge, but Fairfax had certainly anticipated much greater trouble.[33]

Few counties had experienced as much dislocation of normal procedures as the Clubmen counties. In others, such as Lancashire or Lincolnshire, divisions may have been deeper and fiercer, but there were few where civilian government had collapsed so completely, and where military requisition, uncontrolled plundering and free quarter were so widespread. Two related features also stand out. The first is the number of small garrisons in these counties, many of them almost completely independent of any central control; the other is the number of 'foreign' armies which tramped through these counties (particularly Somerset, Dorset and Wiltshire). Each one left additional garrisons or took over enemy ones. Weymouth, for example, had changed hands at least five times before the spring of 1645.[34]

Wiltshire can serve to exemplify the consequences of this. Throughout 1643 and 1644, law and order had been steadily eroded, as violence from both the armies and civilian population escalated. In February 1643, for example, the Earl of Pembroke's lands at Aldbourne were attacked 'by the tumultuous and riotous assembling together of multitudes of the commons'. A month later, a

32. BL, Thomason Tracts, E/288/11.
33. Sprigge, *Anglia Rediviva*; Warner, 'Clubmen'; Manning, 'Neutrals', *passim.*
34. See, for example, Webb, *Herefordshire*, Vol. 2, pp. 128–30; Birch, 'Memoir of Birch', pp. 110–12; *LJ*, Vol. 7, pp. 485–6 for protests against garrisons.

report from the county referred to 'a rough and ready club law' being practised by the countrymen of Wiltshire, and cited the recovery by a large band of peasants, of sheep, oxen and cloth plundered by Welsh royalist troops. In late August, a series of enclosure riots broke out on the Dorset–Wiltshire border (reminiscent of the massive unrest of 1627–31).[35] An observer noted: 'the said riots increaseth daily, and is growing towards an open rebellion, and resistance to all officers and government is there made'.

Throughout the summer, bands of countrymen plundered and attacked wayfarers and country houses. By the spring of 1644 both King and Parliament had ineffectually issued orders for their suppression. Things got worse later in the year. Almost half the royalist commissioners of array ceased to be active, seemingly in protest against the unchecked behaviour of royalist troops. In the Parliament-controlled part of the county, relations between the committee and garrison commanders similarly deteriorated, and the committee tried to prevent Sir William Waller from recruiting soldiers in the county. Meanwhile at Marlborough the commissioners of array sent out troops to attack recruiting sergeants from *royalist* headquarters. All attempts to raise the assessments were abandoned. Instead, each garrison commander laid claim to provisions from loosely delineated areas round about. This frequently led to skirmishing between foraging parties from different garrisons on the same side (for example Salisbury and Langford Castle). The climax of all this were the gatherings of those determined to halt the oppressions and to plead for a renewal of peace negotiations in July and August. The two were linked in a petition sent to the King, a copy of which was also read in the House of Lords. First the plea for further peace negotiations:

> Your Suppliants, having more deeply than many other parts of the Kingdom tasted the Miseries of this unnatural intestine War, which have been the more extremely embittered unto them by the Pressures of many Garrisons both here and in the neighbour Counties, and the opposite Armies continually drawn upon them by reason thereof, did lately hope, that, by means of the Treaty proposed by your Majesty to the Honourable Houses of Parliament, at Uxbridge,

35. D.G.C. Allan, 'The Rising in the West, 1628–1631', *Ec.HR*, Vol. 5 (1952–53); E. Kerridge, 'The Revolts in Wiltshire Against Charles I', *Wilts. Arch. and Natural Hist. Magazine* (1958–59). These revolts reveal the longstanding affinities of the Wiltshire–Dorset border population which may explain why, in this region alone, Clubmen organisation crossed county frontiers. The Dorset and Wiltshire Clubmen were the only ones seriously to co-ordinate their activities.

they might once again have reaped the blessed issue of their long-lost Peace, in the happy Accomodation of the present Differences. . . . [They] cast themselves at Your Majesty's Royal Feet, Humbly imploring, that . . . a farther Treaty of Peace . . . may prove for the Advancement of God's glory in the Maintenance of the true Reformed Protestant Religion, for the Safeguard of Your Majesty's Royal Person, Honour, and Estate, for the securing of the Privileges and Immunities of Parliaments, and for the Preservation of the Liberties and Properties of the Subject . . .

And second, for the running down of garrisons and local control of those that were to remain:

In case such a Treaty may be mutually and unfeignedly admitted, Your Majesty would once again be graciously pleased to press the Cessation of Arms during the said Treaty . . . [and that] you would be graciously pleased, that the Number of your Garrisons in this County may be lessened, in case the Two Houses of Parliament shall, upon Your Subjects Petition in that Behalf, do the like with the Garrisons in their Hands; and that all such Your Garrisons as shall seem necessary to be upheld within this County, for the Defence thereof, may be intrusted in the Hands of the said County, to be maintained at the Chardges of the Inhabitants thereof, and not to be delivered up by them unto any Persons, but such only as, by the joint consent of Your Majesty and the Two Houses of Parliament, shall be authorised to receive the same . . . and that all such Persons, that either are, or have been, in Arms, or otherwise assistant to either Party in this unhappy War, who for Fear have absented themselves from the Places of their usual Abode, or are Imprisoned only as Favourers of the Other Party, may be peaceably permitted to return to their wonted Habitations, and to the Obedience of the established Laws. . . . The like Petition to the Parliament, from the Clubmen, *mutatis mutandis.*[36]

A similar picture can be drawn for other Clubmen counties. In the south-west, in particular, Goring's army in the spring of 1645 was running amok, unpaid and vindictive. Small wonder that the Clubmen of the area were prepared to help Fairfax against him. In South Wales, Gerard's forces built up a secure reputation for trampling down all legal restraints. No wonder the most common complaint of all the Clubmen was the nation's 'bleeding under the devouring sword'.[37]

36. For the above, see Harrison, 'Royalist . . . Wiltshire', pp. 379–92, and the sources there cited. The Wiltshire petition is in *LJ* Vol. 7, pp. 485–6.
37. For example BL, Thomason Tracts, E/45/10.

But the winter of 1644–45 witnessed the crisis of the war in a wider sense. While fruitless negotiations for peace dragged on at Uxbridge, both sides completed radical military and administrative reforms. Parliament completed the overhaul of its Associations, implemented the Self-Denying Ordinance (which affected not only the Lord General and the Earl of Manchester but many important provincial commanders like Sir Thomas Myddleton and Sir William Brereton), and brought together the old armies of Essex, Waller and Manchester to form a New Model army under Sir Thomas Fairfax.[38] Charles, meanwhile, created his own new western high command at Bristol, administratively and militarily independent of Oxford, and also received a portfolio of projected reforms from his Oxford parliament.[39] Both sets of reforms reflected deep political divisions within the two leaderships, as well as administrative convenience. Historians have concentrated far too much on these changes and have looked at the Uxbridge negotiations only to write them off as party-political window-dressing.[40] If the negotiations *were* dragged out largely because both King and Parliament wanted to appear eager for a settlement, they succeeded only too well. For the negotiations had given false hopes and their breakdown became an important precipitant of the Club risings. Several Club Associations specifically lamented the collapse of the Uxbridge talks and called for them to be resumed.

The early months of 1645 were also a watershed in the negotiations between English and Scots divines for a presbyterian Church settlement. The formal abolition of the old Prayer Book and the agreement on a new Directory of Public Worship were the first fruits of these negotiations. It was this which precipitated the hitherto quiescent Wiltshire clergy into Clubman activity, and it was a theme taken up by several Clubmen Associations.[41]

Such things were essentially precipitants, but they may have had the effect of pushing the gentry into the movement. In every case, the initiative seems to have come from within peasant communities, particularly from amongst yeomen and other farmers. It was they who persuaded men from neighbouring villages to band together against plunderers or soldiers demanding quarter or contributions.

38. The best recent study is in Holmes, *Eastern Association*, pp. 181–220.
39. See Roy, 'Royalist Army', pp. 346–80.
40. For a convincing recent reinterpretation of the aims of the parliamentarian factions in the Uxbridge negotiations, see M.P. Mahony, 'The Presbyterian Party in the House of Commons, 2 June 1644 to 3 July 1647', University of Oxford D.Phil. thesis (1973), pp. 136–52.
41. See above, p. 127, and below, pp. 150–1.

As these *ad hoc* assemblies began to organise themselves (arrang-
ing for the ringing of church bells or some other signal for the
associates to gather), the gentry, clergy and other substantial men
(including a surprising number of lawyers)[42] appear to have been
drawn into joining the movement. They generally found themselves
able to institutionalise their social domination of the Association
(for example by having themselves proclaimed 'directors' at a mass
meeting), and they certainly broadened the political objectives and
diversified the activities of Club Associations. Above all they introduced the campaign for a national settlement.

One fact is immediately striking from a reading of Clubmen
programmes. That is, that while all Clubmen groups shared common values and aspirations, each retained its own personal characteristics and prejudices, reflecting local circumstances. In particular,
the degree to which the Clubmen emphasised grievances against
the armies, rather than grievances against the civil effects of the
war, varied greatly from county to county. The programmes of the
Hereford, Worcestershire and Wiltshire Clubmen, for example, were
almost entirely anti-military.[43] In Somerset, and even more in Sussex, however, the misdeeds of committees, even of royal proclama-
tions and parliamentarian ordinances, were given greater emphasis.[44]
In one case, Somerset, the differences in the experiences of men at
different ends of the county meant that each group issued its own
programme, and indeed went very much its own way.[45] Elsewhere
the county unit remained the essential organisational and inspira-
tional base.[46] Nonetheless, despite differences of emphasis, the
underlying unity of purpose in all the Associations is obvious, just as
the exact reproduction of a few phrases in several of the programmes
suggests an element of imitation.[47] Even more striking are the echoes

42. For lists of active Clubmen, see BL Add. MSS 22084, *passim* (BL, Thomason
Tracts, E 296/6 and /12; *LJ*, Vol. 7, pp. 484–5). The Wiltshire leaders, for example,
included several former commissioners of array, or JPs, some prominent citizens of
Salisbury (including former mayors) and lawyers. But see now, the much fuller
analysis of Clubmen leadership in Lynch, 'Risings of the Clubmen', pp. 207–29,
which could not be included here. He has identified 65 gentry, 36 clergymen and
only 7 lawyers amongst the 164 Clubmen who can be identified (ibid., p. 217).

43. HMC, *JP* Vol. 4, Letters of Sir Samuel Luke, p. 485. Willis-Bund (ed.),
'Townshend', Vol. 2, pp. 221–3; *LJ*, Vol. 7, pp. 484–5, *RP* doc. 22b.

44. BL, Thomason Tracts, E 300/13; BL Tanner MS 60 fos 252–4; see also BL
Add. MS 33058 fo. 71.

45. Underdown, *Somerset*, pp. 105–7.

46. Except for the close links which developed between the Clubmen of Dorset
and Wiltshire.

47. For example compare the Berkshire petition (HMC, *Portland MSS*, Vol. 1,
pp. 246–7) with the petitions from Wiltshire or Dorset.

of 1642, of the bemused neutrality of the 'Country' gentry on the eve of the war.

Above all, there was the same lack of perception of the gap between King and Parliament. The Clubmen petitions, like those of 1642, show a yearning for settlement, but had nothing new to offer. They asserted that the differences were small, negotiable; that there was agreement on essentials. The demand by the Wiltshire Clubmen for a settlement along the lines of the Protestation of 1641 ('the true reformed Protestant religion', the royal prerogatives, the privileges and immunities of Parliament, the liberties and properties of the subject) was typical, and it reflected the same vague and helpless hopes as those displayed by the men of 1642.[48] Indeed, some neutralist petitions then had called the Protestation the basis of a future settlement. The Clubmen were as profoundly ignorant of the reality of power politics as the 'pure' Country had always been. Something of the political rhetoric of the pamphleteers had rubbed off on them: a Wiltshire petition spoke of 'our ancient Lawes and Liberties, contrary to the Great Charter of England, and the Petition of Right, altogether swallowed up in the Arbitrary power of the Sword',[49] and the Sussex Clubmen refused to obey any warrant contrary to 'the knowne Lawes of Magna Carta or the Ordinances of Parliament except in cases of extraordinary apparent necessity',[50] but such loose, sonorous phrases were never tied down. As practical constitutional theorists, provincial leaders had learned little. But their localism and adherence to custom and to tradition had been strengthened. What does ring through the Clubmen petitions is the determination to return to known ways. Everything that had gone wrong was attributed to violations of traditional rights or of local autonomy: the restoration of the methods of the past and of local autonomy was the essential requirement for the return of order. Thus the Somerset Clubmen sought 'the benefit of those Lawes which are well knowne to us by the undoubted Seales, of King, Lords, and Commons . . . and that Judges and Officers may be authorised to, and secured in, their administration of Law and Right to all people'.[51] Elsewhere, the Somerset Clubmen characterised parliamentarian taxes as 'arbitrary' and enunciated the supremacy of custom over statute.[52]

This is the 'pure' Country constitutionalism of the 1630s which we encountered in Chapter 1, a constitutionalism not concerned

48. *LJ*, Vol. 7, pp. 484–5.   49. BL Tanner MS 60 fos 163–4.
50. Ibid., fos 252–4.   51. BL, Thomason Tracts, E 293/33.
52. Ibid., E 300/13.

with questions of sovereignty, power or political obligation, but with the simple supremacy of custom and of a localism guaranteed by effective self-determination. What the Clubmen resented more than anything else was outside interference in local affairs.

Thus the Clubmen were at pains to portray themselves as representing entire local communities joined together to repel 'invaders'. Much of their propaganda emphasises the 'neighbourliness', the 'mutual trust', the brotherly love on which the Association was built. The unity and integrity of the movement, and its reliance upon ancient forms of social organisation and activity, are other dominant motifs. This was reinforced by Clubmen institutions like the oath of association binding all members to assist one another if attacked or if seized, and the establishment of a common defence fund to provide pensions for maimed comrades or for widows.[53]

The deep embedding of local custom and local self-determination can only really be caught by a detailed example. The Articles of Association of the Wiltshire and Dorset Clubmen agreed at a meeting of 'neare 4,000 armed with clubs, swords, Bills, Pitchforks and other several weapons' presided over by 'Mr Thomas Young, a lawyer' were amongst the fullest but in no way untypical:

> (1) Every town, tything, parish, and great hamlet, make present choice of three or more of the ablest men for wisdom, valour, and estate, inhabitants of the same, unto whom at all times they may repair for assistance and direction.
> (2) That the Constable, Tythingman and other officers of the town etc. in pursuance of the Statute in that case provided, set a constant watch of two at the least, and they every night well-armed and if required by day also; the number of watchmen to be increased according to the direction of the chosen able men and officers.
> [(3) and (4) govern the behaviour of the watchmen.]
> (5) That all such as pretend themselves soldiers, and are taken plundering or doing any other unlawful violence, be presently disarmed and after examination (having confessed into which army he doth belong) to be safely guarded thither (together with sufficient witness to prove the offence) ...
> (6) That to avoid false alarms no man shall rise into arms but such as are summoned by the watchmen, unless they see apparent violence, or in case the watchmen be defective or surprised.
> (7) That all men furnish themselves sufficiently with as many and good arms and ammunition as they can procure: and the rich out of

53. See, for example, BL Tanner MS 60 fo. 545; BM, Thomason Tracts, E 274/24; Willis-Bund (ed.), 'Townshend', pp. 241–3; HMC, *Portland MSS*, Vol. 1, pp. 246–7.

a good conscience to relieve the poor herein, as also in their labours of watching, and other assistance in some proportionable measure.

(8) That the weekly contribution money and all other provision and necessary maintenance for armies, if it be demanded by a lawful warrant directed to an officer of the place, be not denied, but every man as he is able in some reasonable proportion forthwith to contribute: and for those truly unable, a certificate of inability to be made by the said officer with the advice of the said chosen able men of the place, unto their Commander in Chief from whom the warrant issued, with petition for respite and mitigation of the proportion of the warrant required, until they shall be better enabled.

(9) That if quarter be demanded according to Order Martial, the soldier is to be friendly entertained behaving himself fairly in his quarters, but if he plunder or offer any other violence then he is to be restrained and delivered up unto the Commander in Chief to be by him corrected.

(10) That whatsoever person, though seemingly associated himself, shall be found to occasion any outcry or by any means to assemble any in favour or opposition to either party, King or Parliament, or on behalf of any person not associated, or in any way contrary to the articles of our Association: he shall be accounted unworthy of our protection as dissembling his inclination to our party in frustrating according to his power our real intentions for the Counties good.

(11) That no person or persons upon any pretext whatsoever presume to search a house or seize the person or goods of any of the Associated in inhabitants of the County but only Constables, Tythingmen and other sworn officers of the County for that place and upon lawful warrant.

(12) Not to admit any man to subscribe to the Articles of Association with you who is in arms for either party, or is known to be no Protestant neither are you to protect any man who doth not associate.[54]

The conviction that only a rigid application of traditional methods could restore order is to be found time and again. They insisted that taxation could be raised only by the direction of formal warrants via the head constables to the petty constables to be executed 'according to the rule'. Several Associations specified that all searches, distraints and assessments were to be made only by 'constables, Tythingmen, and other sworn officers of the county'. If ancient parochial officials were to be restored to their traditional powers, the Associations were even more adamant about the speedy return of civil administration by the JPs at quarter sessions. Dorset Clubmen appealed to all justices to return home so that the laws could be

54. A.R. Bayley, *The Civil War in Dorset, 1642–1660* (1910), pp. 472–5.

duly administered. The Somerset Association, in other respects very suspicious of the gentry, pointedly invited all justices – whatever their political persuasion – to return home and undertook to protect them in the execution of their duties.[55]

But the Sussex Clubmen were exceptional. They specifically called for the return of the 'ancient ways', roundly condemned wartime expedients such as the Excise tax and assessments, implicitly denounced many of the powers granted to the sequestrators, and launched an uncompromising assault on the record of the county committee:

> The insufferable, insolent, arbitrary power that hath bin used amongst us contrary to all our auncient, knowne lawes or ordinances of Parliament, upon our persons and estates by imprisoning our persons, imposeing of somes of money, lighthorse and dragoones, and exacting of loanes by some particular persons stept into authority whoe have delegated their power to men of sordid condicon whose wills have bin lawes and commands over our persons and estates by which they have overthrowne all our English liberties and have endeavoured to make us desperate.

This was not simply an attack on individuals, or on a single committee. It was an attack on a new ethos of government, created and fostered by the war, an ethos in which alien values, priorities and commitments were allowed to override custom and the 'knowne lawes'.[56]

None of the Associations found it necessary to maintain a standing army. It was enough to organise an alarm system which could bring the members together in the event of a threat. An early Dorset resolution specifically required 'able men to maintain husbandry and useful trades'. Some Associations arranged that all should foregather whenever a potential enemy was sighted. Others laid down that the alarm was only to be raised once members had been directly threatened.[57]

Similarly, some Associations instructed all their members to turn out as soon as the alarm was sounded, but in Dorset 'to avoid false alarums no man shall rise into arms but such as are so summoned by the watchmen, unless they see apparent violence, or in case the watchmen be defective or surprised'. Later, however, Dorset, in

---

55. Ibid., p. 479.   56. BL Tanner MS 60 fos 252–4. See also *RP* doc. 22c.
57. Bayley, *Civil War in Dorset*, pp. 473–5; BM, Thomason Tracts, E 287/7, E 293/33; Willis-Bund (ed.), 'Townshend', pp. 221–3.

conjunction with Wiltshire, amended this rule. Elected representatives in every village ('three or more sufficient men') were to list all fit men and appoint those who were to appear when the bells were rung.[58] Other Associations expected that local elected officials would take responsibility for ensuring the acquisition and maintenance of arms and ammunition.[59] In Somerset, even the officers in the Club army were elected (elsewhere this ceased with the coming of gentry leadership), and Somerset alone discouraged gentlemen (*sic*) who had ever been active for either side from joining the Association (although such men were invited to return home and carry out their duties as JPs).[60] The organisation certainly bears out David Underdown's assertion that it possessed a 'sophistication that reminds us that however humble, these were men of independence long familiar with the processes of self-government'.[61] Certainly, adherence to traditional forms coupled with elements of village democracy are the hallmarks of Clubmen thinking.

Beyond this, the Clubmen were broadly in agreement about how to reduce the burdens of military rule. The similarity of the programmes from Wiltshire, Dorset, Somerset and Berkshire is particularly striking. Pending a negotiated settlement at national level, local pacifications were to remain in force. All field armies were to depart, and all 'unnecessary garrisons' were to be abandoned. Both sides were to retain their major strongholds (or, by agreement, hand them over to be held by Club forces), and the Associations pledged themselves to raise money indifferently for the upkeep of all such garrisons as were retained. These proposals for local affairs were far more sensible and apt than their plans for a national settlement. But again, within this general framework, each county made its own adjustments. In Somerset, it was proposed to allow each side an equal number of garrisons and half the contributions. In Wiltshire, the commanders of garrisons for both sides attended a conference at Salisbury and accepted a package deal over supplies and quarter. Each county adopted a different attitude to quartering. In Wiltshire, regulations for assessments were carefully laid down. Warrants for specific sums were to be directed by the head constables to the petty constables who were to require all members of the community to contribute. However, those in straitened circumstances could have their assessments reduced by the village

58. Bayley, *Civil War in Dorset*, p. 477.
59. For example Willis-Bund (ed.), 'Townshend', pp. 221–3.
60. BL, Thomason Tracts, E 293/33; Underdown, *Somerset*, p. 98.
61. Ibid., p. 107.

committees who then sent certificates to the garrison commander with the expectation that he would deduct the relevant sum from the assessment.[62]

There was much of the bemusement and half-articulated provincialism and traditionalism of 1642 about the Clubmen. But it was not a simple resurrection of the pre-war movement for peace. In 1642, most neutrals were men who were committed to both sides, men who believed that a war between King and Parliament would open the way to anarchy, to the rule of the 'many-headed monster'. By 1645 this had changed. The danger now came from the royalist and parliamentarian movements themselves. Both were getting out of control, and in their determination to defeat one another both were trampling on the very values they were pledged to defend. The resultant neutralism was more self-confident and more independent than that of 1642.

Nonetheless the Clubmen had to fight to defend their independence. For both King and Parliament sought to infiltrate the Associations, and many Clubmen inevitably brought residual sympathies or antipathies with them when they joined the movement after active careers as royalists or parliamentarians. But time and again we find the Associations rejecting tempting offers of help which would have required a denial of principles.[63] Even when an Association did ally itself to King or Parliament it was unusual for the Clubmen openly to acknowledge the general superiority of that cause (but see the New Forest Clubmen in September 1645).[64]

The pressures exerted by the two sides were, however, of very different types and serve to explain the different reactions of different Clubmen groups.

Parliament's public pronouncements were always antagonistic towards the Clubmen. The Houses consistently refused to consider reconvening the Uxbridge negotiations, denounced the Clubmen as rebels whose actions were without any authority or grounding, and threatened retribution if they persisted (local committees and commanders were often much more conciliatory).[65] Yet on the ground, and in practice, Parliament took a much softer line and did not provoke confrontations. The New Model was in fact rapidly becoming the only reasonably well-disciplined (because well-paid?)

---

62. Bayley, *Civil War in Dorset*, pp. 473–7, BL, Thomason Tracts, E 287/7, E 292/5; Manning, 'Neutrals and Neutralism'; Harrison, 'Royalists in Wiltshire'.

63. See above, pp. 134–6.

64. Underdown, *Somerset*, pp. 113–17; BL, Thomason Tracts, E 297/4.

65. See, for example, *CJ*, Vol. 4, p. 187.

army in the kingdom. Fairfax dealt swiftly and fiercely with those of his men handed over by the Clubmen as plunderers.[66] He and his army earned the respect of the countrymen of the areas through which he passed, and this was crucial to his success in winning over the south-west Clubmen in his campaign against Goring. The New Model indeed fulfilled the main requirements of the Clubmen: they paid for their quarter, kept out of civil matters, and refrained from plunder. In comparison with Goring's thugs, the New Model were friends indeed.

Fairfax himself had seen that this was the key. He wrote: 'nothing carries our business with more advantage than keeping our soldiers from doing violences.'[67] Meanwhile in Wiltshire, the Clubmen had pointedly compared the excesses of the Devizes' cavaliers with the behaviour of the New Model.[68] An observer in Hampshire, even more subtle than Fairfax, observed that the way to win over the Clubmen was 'to ease the Countrey and given them such a breathinge time from oppression as to permitt their quiett gatheringe in their harvest'.[69]

Parliament's solution was simple: give no concessions on principle and discourage further outbreaks by advocating repression. Meanwhile, do everything possible at a local level to reform abuses and implicitly acknowledge past failings, hoping thereby to earn respect and subsequently support. The King's strategy was precisely the reverse. He was completely unable to restrain his troops, who rampaged through the countryside. Instead he reacted moderately and soberly to all Clubmen proposals, expostulating that he too wanted peace and carefully taking up their slogans as his own, hoping thereby to assimilate them into the royalist cause. If this policy failed wherever royalist practice was all too evident, it did have some successes in those areas mainly under Parliament's control (such as Sussex and Hampshire, whose main experience of royalist armies had been of the comparatively gentle Hopton).

The King's problem was complicated by the fact that he had tried a rather similar tactic the year before. In the summer of 1644 he had given a series of addresses in the West Country (notably at Chard in Somerset) calling for the election of 'a full and free convention' to settle the nation's ills and meanwhile for 'one-and-all'

66. For example Sprigge, *Anglia Rediviva*, pp. 17, 22; BL, Thomason Tracts, E 262/21.
67. R. Bell (ed.), *Memorials of the Civil War: Comprising the Correspondence of the Fairfax Family* (2 vols, 1849), Vol. 1, p. 245.
68. BL, Thomason Tracts, E 262/20.   69. BL Add. MS 24860 fo. 133.

to join in a popular uprising to defeat the rebels and to impose peace. The idea had been taken up with varying degrees of enthusiasm in neighbouring counties but had essentially fizzled out by early 1645. Ironically, some of the carefully chosen slogans (like the idea of 'the pure religion of Queen Elizabeth and King James') had struck reverberant chords and became Clubmen slogans in the course of 1645.[70]

Fair words had failed in 1644, and they failed again in 1645. Any residual enthusiasm for the royal response was dampened by awareness of his duplicity in the border counties, in which local commanders had negotiated settlements with the Clubmen, who had then disbanded and returned to the plough. In each case Prince Rupert or Prince Maurice had then arrived, disowned the agreements, and imposed financial burdens and rigorous oaths on all those concerned (oaths specifically denouncing parliamentarian and neutralist principles).[71] Most futile of all were the efforts made by Goring to woo the Clubmen. His extravagant promises were immediately placed in perspective by fresh outrages.

Under such circumstances, the royalist strategy had little chance of winning over the Clubmen. But the efforts to infiltrate agents from Oxford, the desperate and blinding desire for peace, and residual respect for the monarchy led to a few local successes. And furthermore, the King did have one clear advantage over Parliament. On questions of religion, he could play on Clubmen sympathies with considerable hopes of success.

The Wiltshire Clubmen, as we saw, were dismayed at the ban on the use of the Prayer Book, and calls for its restitution appear in three other Clubmen programmes. More generally, both the Dorset and the Wiltshire Clubmen called for a return to 'the pure religion of Queen Elizabeth and King James'; while in Berkshire, Sussex and elsewhere the plea was for the continuity of the reformed protestant tradition. In Sussex, for example, the Clubmen complained about 'imprimis the want of Church government whereby our churches are decayed, God's ordinances neglected, orthodox ministers cast out without cause and never heard, Mechanickes and unknowne persons thrust in, whoe were never called as Aaron but by a Committeeman, whereby God and the Parliament are dishonored and the people grieved'; and they petitioned for the

---

70. Rushworth, *Historical Collections*, Vol. 5, pp. 688–90, 717–18; C.E. Long (ed.), 'The Diary . . . kept by Richard Symonds', *Camden Society*, Vol. 74 (1859), *passim*; Willis-Bund (ed.), 'Townshend', pp. 182–98.
71. Webb, *Herefordshire*, Vol. 2, pp. 157–63.

maintenance of patronage rights, a ministry reserved to men 'whoe have received orders', and a general moratorium on innovation. In general, all the Clubmen appear to have favoured an Erastian settlement, with a restricted episcopacy, a Prayer Book shorn of offensive rubrics, and a good deal of latitude for individual ministers and congregations to go their own way within the framework of a royal supremacy. The Dorset petition, which called for the retention of the Prayer Book, but for 'freedom of our consciences in matter of ceremonies', supports the view that the Clubmen wished to endorse the mild Church puritanism of 1590–1640. What they decisively rejected was all clericalist presumption, all thought of the attainment of Zion, the godly reformation through ecclesiastical upheaval.[72]

The King made the most of the advantage this gave him. He could plausibly claim such a view as his own, despite its 'pure' Country pedigree. But it is not a sign of the Clubmen's conversion to royalism. It was a sign of the integrity of county ideals through the war years. If the Clubmen felt sympathetic to the King or Parliament, it was only because both these movements made great efforts, in their own ways, to conform to those ideals.

The Movement for One-and-All

The Clubmen, like the earlier rebels in Norfolk and Kent, were confronting the war and the agents of war. They stood against all invasions and innovations. But there were many more who fought similar battles while remaining within the system, as committee-men or army officers using their position and influence to protect older values. To treat the rows within county committees or between central and local bodies in such terms is to risk oversimplification, but it does add a perspective to such disputes which has not been adequately treated in the past.

For example, the commissioners of array for Caernarvonshire issued a passionate protest in April 1644 of which the central theme

72. For example BL, Thomason Tracts, E 287/7, E 300/13; BL Tanner MS 60 fos 252–4; Bayley, *Civil War in Dorset*, pp. 473–7; BL. Add. MS 22084, *passim*. On the other hand, the Clubmen were completely anti-catholic, and this certainly prejudiced some of them against a royalist cause reputedly saturated with papists. See also the views of the 'Peaceable Army' in South Wales, who complained bitterly that 'the book of common prayer hath been traduced, and several Sundays omitted in Cardiff, which we apprehend as a forerunner of its final rejection, had some their desires, and were we not resolved by the help of God to continue it' (*RP* doc. 23a).

was that the county's interests had been overridden and that local men and methods had been ignored.[73] Similarly, an important dimension of the conflicts within the royalist leadership in Devon and Cornwall in 1645 was a widespread determination to put local interests first and to restrict the authority of 'foreign' crown nominees. A meeting at Crediton early in the year agreed to raise a fresh army in Devon, in the King's name but responsive solely to local commanders and local needs.[74] The accountability of all agents to 'such persons as shall be nominated and appointed for that purpose by us the inhabitants' was also an important element in a Cornish petition to the King in June 1645. Furthermore, the petitioners expressed concern at the expediency of royalist taxes: 'you cannot find that wee once murmured at the payment of the rates or taxes imposed on us. But at the manner of payment and the partyes to whom.' Localism and traditionalism were once again conjoined.[75]

It was precisely these values that Charles had appealed to when he launched his campaign for a national popular uprising in the late summer of 1644. In a series of speeches (beginning with one at King's Moor in Somerset in July) he proclaimed that he wanted to relieve his people 'from the violence of a rebellious army'. He promised that all national problems should be settled by a new, freely elected 'convention of Parliament'. Meanwhile the counties should rise *en masse*, under their own chosen officers and march on London (though they would be free to return home to bring in the harvest). He undertook to restrain his standing army from all disorders if the county agreed to supply it. His scheme spluttered only fitfully in Somerset but caught fire elsewhere.[76] In Worcestershire, for example, it seems to have inspired the general meeting of 'all the Nobility, Justices of the Peace, Gentry and Clergy; together with all the freeholders and copyholders for lives or years of any lands or tenements of the yearly value of 40s[hillings] and upwards' which met in December to agree on proposals to remove the 'extreme pressures and intolerable grievances' of the county. The careful prescription of those invited to participate clearly suggests a strong feeling that the consequent decisions could be legitimated by issuing them in the name of 'the body of the community'. At the

73. Howells (ed.), *Letters Relating to North Wales*, p. 62.

74. T. Carte (ed.), *A Collection of Original Letters and Papers Concerning the Affairs of England From the Year 1641 to 1660* (2 vols, 1739), Vol. 1, pp. 99–101; Coate, *Cornwall*, pp. 169–79, 191–7; Andriette, *Devon and Exeter*, pp. 137–48. See *RP* doc. 19f.

75. BL Clarendon MS 23 fos 10–11.

76. Rushworth, *Historical Collections*, Vol. 5, pp. 688–90, 715–16; Underdown, *Somerset*, pp. 75–80.

meeting, a declaration was drawn up calling for a national settlement. But if Parliament did not respond positively, the country would rise on the King's behalf. The meeting also decided to invite the counties of Shropshire, Hereford, Stafford and Monmouth to join with them. The initiative was a local one, and the aims too were more genuinely localist than the King had sought, but he welcomed the movement nonetheless. Significantly, the terms which the Worcestershire 'One-and-All' leaders invited Parliament to accept were those of the Protestation of 1641.[77]

But the movement rapidly turned sour on its initiators. The continued indiscipline of royalist troops and the indecisiveness of the commissioners of array led the grand jury to return a very severe presentment against both on 17 January 1645. Within weeks there was to emerge a popular Clubmen movement which accepted the premises of the 'One-and-All' leaders (that the war must be brought to a speedy end by a mass rising) but denied the predicate, that this should be done in the King's name. Nonetheless, a moderate royalist party continued to exist, opposed both to Clubmen neutrality and to the subjugation of the county to the priorities laid down at Oxford.[78]

A similar movement developed in Staffordshire.[79] Neutralism had been particularly strong there in 1642, and following what were termed 'invasions' by both royalist and parliamentarian forces (notably from Derbyshire), a special sessions of the peace was convened at which it was agreed to raise a 'neutral' peacekeeping force of 1,000 men. But the continuing intervention of 'foreigners' (royalists from Shropshire, parliamentarians from Cheshire) eroded confidence, and an attempt to strengthen the peacekeeping force at the Epiphany sessions failed. What appears to have driven many gentlemen finally into the royalist camp was a rising by the Moorlanders, inhabitants of the bleak forest and upland region in the north-west of the county. Attempts by 'foreign' royalists to recruit men there at the end of 1642 led to the renewal of the violence which had simmered ever since a particularly vicious battle between troops and civilians at Uttoxeter during the marches north in the second Bishops' War (1640).[80] The Moorlanders were initially

77. See above, p. 144.
78. For the above, see Willis-Bund (ed.), 'Townshend', Vol. 2, pp. 182–200.
79. J.T. Pickles, 'Studies in Royalism in the English Civil War, 1642–1646, with special reference to Staffordshire', University of Manchester MA thesis (1968), chs 2 and 3.
80. PRO, SP 16, Vol. 460/8.

uncommitted to either side, but they later made a rather uneasy deal (one he later regretted) with Sir William Brereton. The prospect of this alliance between a 'foreign' commander and a rabble 'of all sorts convened together, being neither disciplined nor armed; some with birding guns, others only with clubs, others with pieces of scythes, very few with muskets',[81] finally induced the moderates to declare for the King. But even then they simply undertook to defend the county against all invaders. They would hold Staffordshire in the King's name, but nothing more.

The civilian council established by the local gentry proved unable to contain the parliamentarians, however, and by mid-1643 the initiative on the royalist side had passed to military commanders nominated by the Oxford High Command and to the garrisons at Lichfield and Dudley. For almost two years, royalist control over Staffordshire was maintained by force and through military requisition.

It is unsurprising, therefore, to find the erstwhile civilian commissioners embracing the 'One-and-All' movement and using it to demand the reform of royalist methods and the removal and punishment of official military leaders.[82] With the parliamentarians steadily strengthening their control of the region, and the collapse of popular support in those areas still in royalist hands, the King acceded to their demands. He created a new Association out of the Marcher counties with Rupert as the nominal head, empowered to raise 2,000 more foot (200 of them from Staffordshire). Thereafter all forces were to be under local control, with locally elected officers; the contributions necessary for these forces should be raised with the assent of the grand jury of each county; all the profits of sequestration and half the (non-existent) receipts from the Excise were also to be retained for local defence. Additional clauses safeguarded civilians from arbitrary imprisonment and plunder. Garrisons were made strictly accountable to treasurers nominated by each county. Local forces were to be raised 'in the nature of a *posse comitatus*' (the ancient shrieval force) and would be subject only to the common law. They were to remain in their own county, or at least in the Association.[83] As John Pickles says of the commissioners negotiating these terms: 'in seeking to establish their authority over

81. HMC, *Hastings MSS*, Vol. 2, p. 91; for the Moorlanders, see also Pennington, 'County and Country'; Pickles, 'Studies in Royalism', pp. 85–95.

82. See, for example, the letter of Sir Jacob Astley to Charles I in W.A. Day (ed.), *The Pythouse Papers* (1879), pp. 20–1.

83. Pickles, 'Studies in Royalism', pp. 112–15; compare the King's Declaration to Worcestershire, Willis–Bund (ed.), 'Townshend', Vol. 2, pp. 195–8.

the local military commanders and in emphasising the rights of civilians and the preservation of the county, the commissioners showed, in effect, as much sympathy with the aims of the Clubmen as with those of the King.'[84]

Two important consequences stem from this surrender by Charles. On the one hand, he probably averted the emergence of a Clubmen movement in Staffordshire. He had surrendered to the elements of localism and conservatism which were the hallmarks of the Clubmen. On the other hand, such surrenders hastened the collapse of his central organisation. Where, as here and in other key counties, he effectively cut himself off from all the financial resources necessary to maintain his field armies, Charles abandoned all hope of facing the New Model on equal terms. Parliament experienced a milder crisis in the demands of the Eastern Association counties at a conference at Bury St Edmunds that the integrity of their Association and their overriding local responsibilities be acknowledged. In surviving this crisis and breaking the Eastern Association, Parliament ensured that its streamlined army would be adequately paid and supplied for most of 1645.[85] Financial thrombosis killed the royalist cause; Parliament recovered from a threatened blockage in its arteries of war and became certain of victory.

The Attack on the Committees

Similar tensions and preoccupations formed one strand within the infinitely varied and tangled skein of conflicts within parliamentarian county committees throughout the 1640s. Once more, we must remember that every county was unique, subject to different pressures working through different power structures, and that the interaction of national and local events was inevitably complex.[86]

One of the few easy generalisations to make about this problem is that public confrontation and mutual denunciation characterised the history of most parliamentarian county establishments at some

84. Pickles, 'Studies in Royalism', p. 117.
85. For the Bury conference, see *LJ*, Vol. 7, pp. 177–8, and Everitt, 'Suffolk', pp. 32–4, 83–9. For the Committee's petition to the Houses, see *RP* doc. 16a.
86. In general, see Underdown, *Pride's Purge*, pp. 25–40 and *passim*; also Holmes, 'Edward King'. Holmes emphasises 'the interplay of national issues and local ties', and his book on the Eastern Association has taken up this theme in much greater detail. There is certainly a difference of emphasis between him and me on these matters, and the following section would have been adjusted had I read *The Eastern Associations* before writing this.

point during the years 1643–47. This is in itself a sign of the instability of the parliamentarian ideals. Again and again the charges and counter-charges resulting from these disputes return to a few principal themes. One was the question of overlapping jurisdictions.[87] Another – already alluded to – was the series of problems resulting from the creation of sub-committees of accounts. Another was the lack of definition in the relationship of military and civilian authorities.[88] Questions of corruption and favouritism often joined with clashes of personality or even the continuation of ancient feuds and rivalries to intensify disputes in particular counties.[89] However, while it was unusual for these problems not to be present, it was also unusual for these to be the only factors at work in dividing the local leadership of a parliamentarian county.

In most counties, deeper political and religious divisions cut across or coincided with these more immediate problems. But, as in the 1630s, these 'national' problems were crucial not just as abstract issues but precisely because they affected local communities in distinctive ways. This is perhaps most clearly seen in the religious divisions of the period. Obviously the essentially national conflict over the basic nature of the religious settlement was in itself reflected in each county. But while at Westminster politicians and divines struggled to work out a blueprint for the future, a coherent overall plan, in the provinces committees were daily required to cope with an ecclesiastical vacuum, the immediate problem of supplying men to empty pulpits, expelling or retaining men whose political or religious views were of borderline acceptability, exercising jurisdiction over important matters hitherto the work of the now defunct Church courts. A host of *ad hoc* decisions had to be made long before a strategy for the future could be worked out. In general, historians have oversimplified religious issues and once again presumed the very real polarities of the artificial world of Westminster to exist in much the same form elsewhere. The terms 'presbyterian' and 'independent', like the terms 'royalist' and 'parliamentarian', 'puritan', or 'Country', must be used with utmost care. It seems to me that at a local level, in explaining the religious

87. For example Shropshire: see *CSPD, 1645–1647*, pp. 358–9, 459, 470; *RP* doc. 16b. BL Tanner MS 60 fos 444, 461, 463; Auden, 'Colonel Mytton'.

88. See above, pp. 80–90; for perceptive comments on the tensions necessarily produced by accounts committee even in a stable county, see Everitt, *Kent*, p. 184.

89. For example Montgomeryshire: see Dodd, *Studies in Stuart Wales* (2nd edn, 1971), p. 116 and *passim*; PRO, SP 28, Vol. 256, unfoliated, *passim*; *CSPD, 1645–1647*, pp. 441, 458–9, 491. Also G.M. Thomas, 'Sir Thomas Myddleton, 1588–1666', University of Wales MA thesis (1967), Appendix 5.

tensions of the 1640s in the counties, the terms are positively mis-leading. In their exercise of patronage and discharge of their temporary ecclesiastical jurisdiction, committees were often more fundamentally divided in two overlapping ways.

On the one hand, committees were divided about the religious nature of the revolution. Rigid presbyterians and congregationalists might agree that the revolution was a prelude to the creation of a godly nation, fired by enthusiasm and sound doctrine and forced into obedience to their vision of the moral commonwealth by godly magistrates. Men like Oliver Cromwell looked for men represent-ing 'the different forms of godliness in this nation', who shared this essential faith in an imminent Zion. In Cheshire, strict presbyterians and visionary congregationalists made common political cause against the 'worldly' party. Only at the end of the 1640s and early 1650s did this union disintegrate. Other men, including 'presbyterians', congregationalists and episcopalians, sought only to purge rem-nants of popery from the existing Church, discharge unfit men from the ministry, cleanse and restore the Church to an exalted but not dominant role in a flawed and fallen world.

On the other hand, committees were deeply divided over the integrity of the parochial system. The parish represented the con-junction of spiritual and temporal jurisdictions (it was a crucial fiscal and administrative unit) and was defended as providing every one with a church where they had a right and a duty to worship. On the other hand, it was claimed that the essential unit should be the gathered congregation to which only those with a 'call' should be admitted. For many committee-men, the possibility of the co-existence of the two forms became increasingly attractive, but there were many 'independents' (who believed in the autonomy of each parish) who opposed the toleration of a separatist congregation *within* a parish. 'Independency', indeed, comprehended extreme separatists and those who believed in a loosely federated parochial structure (with many gradations between), while 'presbyterianism' comprehended a strict, regulated theocracy (on the Scottish or the Genevan model) and men who sought a federal parochial structure linked by largely advisory (and probably lay-gentry) *classes* and synods. Many crucial problems, including those of tithes, augmentations and the nature of toleration, were subsumed within this conflict. On many issues, the basic polarity lay between an 'Erastian' alliance of moderate episcopalians, presbyterians and independents, and a 'Godly' alliance of strict presbyterians and congregationalists (but excluding the sects). While, at Westminster, the establishment of a national liturgy and doctrine, and the theological problem of toleration created different polarities (the role of the Scots very much complicating the issue), in the localities the realities of coping with the ecclesiastical anarchy on a day-to-day basis did create alliances unthinkable at a higher level.[90]

Men who wanted to purge the nation of its evil ways and inaugurate a new age were likely to adopt punitive attitudes towards those responsible for the civil war.[91] On the other hand, moderates were acutely aware of the accidental ways by which many of their opponents had found themselves unhappily active for the royalists. Many common civilities and contacts continued despite the war, and many county committees found themselves expected to sequester and harass old friends, relatives and neighbours.[92] Quite apart from such bonds, however, many moderates temperamentally favoured conciliation of the defeated as a better way to restore security and peace than repression. To the Godly, however, condign punishment of all who had opposed a just cause was necessary and proper. The position of neutrals was one which excited particularly fierce controversy within county committees. Certainly the campaign by radical groups to enforce rigorously the terms of the sequestration ordinances became a major source of conflict. In many counties, moderates retained control of sequestrations and reacted sympathetically and generously to individual tales of misfortune and mischance. As Nathaniel Bedle, the solicitor for sequestrations in Norfolk, told the central committee on 8 July 1644:

> I have truly sett forth the causes, & causers of the disservice to the Commonwealthe. In the Causers, it is partly, as you saye, their connivance & Principally their partiallyty, but not as you sayd their Timourousnes, but rather as I may saye, their bouldnes to adventure to proceede contrary to the letter & intent of the ordinances. Presuming that through their greatnes & friends, & their plausable speeches & carriages and specious pretences & other meanes that

90. For a general discussion, see Underdown, *Pride's Purge*, ch. 1. For good county studies, see Underdown, *Somerset, passim*; Bayley, *Civil War in Dorset*, ch. 14; Coate, *Cornwall*, ch. 15; Wood, *Nottinghamshire*, ch. 15. But for the particular points made here, see Morrill, *Cheshire*, pp. 264–72 and *passim*.

91. See, for example, the remark of Richard Fitzgerald, agent for the collection of the assessments for Ireland, in discussing committee divisions in Monmouthshire in 1646. He spoke of those 'more godly than others in their own and their brethren's conceits' (HMC, *Egmont*, Vol. 1, p. 343). See his other letters from Wales, ibid., pp. 350–2, 360–1, 362–3, 410–11, 450–1.

92. See, for example, the comment of a Dorchester parliamentarian on the inactivity of his local sequestration committee: 'affinitie and consanguinitie marse al . . .' (BL Clarendon MS 22 fo. 33). *RP* doc. 17c.

they can use, through the Corruption of the times, they may doe any-
thinge and never be questioned, or not soe as shall harme them. . . .
Indeed a maine cause of their partiall proceedings is their relation
of kindred & friendshipp &c. A maine hinderance to proceedings in
generall is because the Parliament & Committees of Parliament have
not time to receive informacon. If they had, things had bin better in
this county, then they are, if my writings could have bin read &
considered, & my speeches heard. Twoe or 3 lines from the Parliament
or the Comitte would have sett things Right presently. The course
that I caused to be taken had brought Mr Sotherton & others to be
yeilding to our faire proceedings for the benifitt of the publique till
Sir John Hobart and the Rest procured that last order from the
Lords and Commons which incouradged them in their unfaire proceedings againe . . .[93]

Elsewhere, the 'Godly' maintained a rigorous and austere husbandry
over the estates and persons of the delinquents.[94]

In Parliament itself, the one issue which unquestionably created
and sustained organised parties was the minimum terms for a settlement with the King. On the very possibility of a negotiated settlement rather than a military one, and on the constitutional safeguards
to be required, a minority of MPs took up clearly defined positions
and worked on the indecisive majority of members, each with
his own preferences and prejudices which might incline him one
way or the other as a host of considerations influenced him at any
given time.

This issue, so dominant at Westminster, was never so clear-cut in
the provinces. There is little evidence, for example, that county
committees divided over, or took particular positions in relation to,
the negotiating terms at Uxbridge in 1645, or indeed during any of
the other peace initiatives (whereas many counties did express their
views about the developing ecclesiastical settlement). There is little
evidence of heightened local tension or conflict during the parliamentary crises over the peace question.

Clearly, all committee-men were keenly interested in the outcome
of all negotiations, but the question of local pacification or victory
was of greater significance. And in this respect both moderates and

93. Bl Harl. MS 5508, fo. 16. See above, p. 111 and references, for examples
from Lancashire and Dorset. See also Essex (Quintrell, 'Committee of S. Essex',
pp. 88–98) and Wiltshire, BL Add. MS 22084 fo. 15 (letter to the county committee,
22 December 1646), etc. See also *RP* doc. 17d.
94. For example Kent (Everitt, *Kent*, chs 5–6, *passim*); Somerset (Underdown,
Somerset, ch. 6); Cambridgeshire (PRO, SP 20, Vol. 1, *passim*; BL Harl. MS 5494,
passim).

radicals were agreed on and committed to clearing royalists from their own county or Association. The views of men like Sir John Gell, a pugnacious and aggressive leader in Derbyshire, determined to drive the royalists out of the north midlands with never a thought of a local compromise, but a peace party man at Westminster, were quite consistent.[95] There were crucial differences within many counties (as we have seen) about what price could be paid to ensure local victory but not about the desirability of outright *local* victory.[96] After the end of the war, local committees were again more preoccupied with questions of local settlement: the disbandment of local forces (and the control of residual garrisons), security against future trouble from within their own communities. Clearly very few committee-men envisaged the failure to reach a settlement: republicanism grew more slowly in the counties than in Parliament. In a sense, this was a latent issue. The *lack* of settlement did not create tensions; the achievement of any particular agreement (over the Heads of Proposals in 1647, for example) might well have brought out hidden divisions within the counties. But until any such settlement was reached, the constitutional issues lay dormant.[97]

The civil war transformed the bureaucracy of local government. Before 1642 local officials could be fairly easily divided into three groups whose responsibilities matched their social status: a senior group (justices, Deputy Lieutenants, sheriffs, drawn from the upper gentry and nobility), a middling group (grand jurymen, high constables, escheators, bailiffs, drawn from the yeomanry and minor gentry) and the drudges (petty constables, overseers, surveyors, drawn from the small householders and labourers). The civil war introduced a much less rigid hierarchy of duties, above all greatly expanding the number and importance of middling executive posts (sequestration collectors, agents, commissioners; treasurers,

95. For this seeming paradox, see Morrill, *Cheshire*, pp. 139–51, 158–63.

96. Ibid.; Everitt, *Kent*, pp. 143–55, 200–18; Holmes, *Eastern Association, passim.* See also Cromwell's clearly voiced denunciation of the narrowly focused aims of the Essex committee – to force the royalists from the county and its environs, but then to feel that enough had been done: 'is this the way to save a kingdom where is the doctrine of some of your Countye, concerning the trained bands and other forces not goeinge out of the association? Lord Newcastle will advance into your bowells, better ioyne when others will ioyne, and can ioyne with you, then stay till all be lost' (August 1643; BL Egerton MS 2643 fo. 17).

97. It is, of course, clear that a national 'Peace' party leader like the Earl of Denbigh would carry his local supporters in counties like Warwickshire and Staffordshire with him in the event of a national or local ceasefire. But this potentially divisive fact did not in practice contribute to the open conflicts within those county committees. The problem remained latent.

assessors, collectors for numerous funds; clerks, messengers, secretaries). As the need for senior county commissioners also grew, at a time when the divisions and casualties of war reduced the pool, social mobility within the structure also increased. Supernumerary army officers (often experienced in organising and collecting tax assessments) were also available for promotion. This had little to do with ideology. It happened within *provincial* royalist administrations as much as within parliamentarian ones, but after 1646 it certainly continued to take place. In many areas, county committees came to recruit senior men from backgrounds which would have barred them from membership of the pre-war élites. Furthermore, in some counties, this development in itself added to the political struggles already discussed. The new men (minor gentry with a sprinkling of townsmen) proved to be political and religious radicals who further alienated and sometimes displaced those members of the old traditional élite who had earlier constituted the parliamentarian leadership.

David Underdown has shown that the crucial turning point was often the same period in late 1644 and early 1645 which marked the crisis of the war in so many other ways, and he has argued that this period witnessed a vital radicalisation of the county committee structure. Underdown himself carefully puts the argument in perspective but there is a danger that others might distort its significance. In a majority of English counties, that group of traditional governors who adhered to Parliament in 1642–43 remained in control until 1649. This included most of East Anglia, the south (Dorset and Wiltshire) and the midlands (Northamptonshire, Derbyshire, Lancashire). In counties where the royalists had held overall control for any length of time, Parliament found it difficult to find former governors who had not compromised themselves, and necessarily looked to less prominent men who had avoided committing themselves or who could more readily disguise past indiscretions. This was the pattern in much of northern England and Wales: also in counties like Worcestershire.

Nonetheless, the social background of many of the new committeemen did form an important element in the struggle for power in a number of counties of which Kent, Sussex, Somerset, Staffordshire, Cheshire and Nottinghamshire are prominent examples. In all these cases the 'new men' tended to be more radical in religion, more determined in the harassment of delinquents, tougher in their preparedness to sacrifice the independence of the county to win local or regional military control. However, those men of 'middling rank' (yeomen, townsmen) who did achieve high office did so because they were determined and capable and because they were sponsored by prominent radicals already in key posts (as MPs, committee chairmen, etc.). Similarly minor gentry, yeomen and townsmen formed a high proportion of the accounts sub-committees which Donald Pennington has shown to be the local agencies of the 'presbyterian' party at Westminster. These sub-commissioners systematically attacked the methods of the more radical committees. Often they were specifically the allies of the local moderates.[98]

The above factors interacted differently in each county. In Staffordshire, social and military disputes predominated;[99] in Dorset religious and sequestration policies were most important;[100] in Montgomeryshire, long-standing local feuds going back to the 1590s combined with jurisdictional disputes between the main committee and the accounts committee to create a situation where each group attempted to arrest and sequestrate the other.[101] Cheshire affords probably the clearest example of a self-contained local struggle over local military priorities, the intrusion of 'new men' and the pursuit of a hard line against royalists and neutrals.[102] Somerset, Kent and Lincolnshire, in very different ways, reveal the interaction of national and local events. In Somerset, John Pyne involved himself directly in the campaign to weaken the power of the Earl of Essex and with the development of a radical programme to impose limitations on the royal prerogative and to usher in a Godly reformation.[103] In Kent, Anthony Weldon reluctantly subordinated Kentish interests to those of the South Eastern Association and later the New Model Ordinance, but only in order to strengthen his own control over the county and to force continued support for Parliament from a

98. The above is based on the large number of county studies used above. There is an excellent summary (with references) in Underdown, *Pride's Purge*, pp. 29–39. For a case study, see Everitt, *Kent*, particularly pp. 146–55, or Pennington and Roots, *Committee at Stafford*, pp. xxii–xxiii, lxxiv–lxxxii. For the changing social composition of committees, see the tables in various theses (for example B.G. Blackwood, 'The Lancashire Gentry, 1625–1660', University of Oxford D.Phil. thesis (1973), ch. 6; A.M. Morton-Thorpe, 'The Gentry of Derbyshire, 1640–1660', University of Leicester MA thesis (1970), ch. 5). For the social structure of royalist organisations, see Pickles, 'Studies in Royalism', ch. 6; Blackwood, 'Lancashire Gentry', ch. 5. For accounts committee, see Pennington, 'Accounts of the Kingdom', and above, pp. 97–9.

99. Pennington and Roots, *Committee at Stafford*, PRO, SP 28, Vol. 256, unfoliated accounts committee correspondence.

100. Bayley, *Civil War in Dorset*, ch. 15; Mayo (ed.), *Standing Committee of Dorset*, *passim*.

101. See pp. 99–100.   102. Morrill, *Cheshire*, chs 4 and 5.

103. Underdown, *Somerset*, pp. 121–2 and *passim*.

majority apathetic to Parliament's national objectives.[104] Lincolnshire is the most involved county of all; Clive Holmes has brilliantly un-ravelled the way local groups pursued their feuds at Westminster, and has shown how the great parties in the two Houses used local incidents to promote much wider political strategies.[105]

Amidst so many problems, the characteristic conservatism and localism of the 'Country' tradition is difficult to isolate and was clearly not a crucial element of conflict within parliamentarian com-mittees. But it did exist. Since all the commissioners had accepted office under the terms of specific ordinances it was hard for them to challenge such powers without courting disaster. Neutrals could and did claim that Parliament was acting *ultra vires*; royalist com-missioners could play the King at his own game, taking advantage of his professed institutional conservatism by calling for a full restora-tion of traditional methods. Parliamentarians had to tread more carefully, had to denounce their radical colleagues for *abusing* their powers only, and to outflank them by calling for the restoration of older institutions (such as quarter sessions, jury trials, the shrievalty) alongside the county committees. But they could not directly chal-lenge the propriety of the ordinances. Their criticisms had to be veiled, indirect.

I have offered elsewhere a detailed case study of how the mod-erates in Cheshire sought to protect traditional values against the fiercely puritan, hard-line anti-royalist party headed by Sir William Brereton.[106] In a series of petitions, the established gentry leaders called for restraints on Brereton's nominees. They sought to bring all local forces under their personal control as Deputy Lieutenants; they sought local autonomy in the handling of delinquents' estates (again asking that the Lieutenancy be empowered to take composi-tions), and made it clear that their policies would be lenient ones. In strategic terms they were content that Cheshire should particip-ate in a regional movement of liberation, but they sought to em-phasise the independence and integrity of each county in a federated Association. Each county should control and pay its own men, and they rejected the pooling of men and resources sought by Brereton and exemplified by East Anglia. Above all, the Cheshire moderates sought to return authority to old county institutions (shrievalty, Palatine courts, quarter sessions) and to men 'who have respons-ible estates', the 'cheefe Gentlemen of the County whose interests

---

104. Everitt, *Kent*, pp. 186–7, 200–4 and *passim.*   105. Holmes, 'Colonel King'.
106. Morrill, *Cheshire*, chs 4–5, particularly pp. 155–63.

will make them more vigilant and industrious then others and their counsells more secret'. On another occasion they described themselves as the 'discreet gentlemen'. By contrast, a leading preacher hailed Brereton's faction as 'the Godly'. This sums up the basic division within the parliamentarian movement in many counties: between those who had only joined the cause to preserve existing values and structures, to conserve their own power and influence, and those who saw the war as preparing for a transformed world. The group attacking Brereton in 1644–46 had almost all been leading neutrals in 1642 before reluctantly declaring for Parliament. Their fundamental attitudes had not changed at all.

Brereton was also involved in a power struggle in Staffordshire. Here the issue for a long time concerned the policies and abilities of the Earl of Denbigh, commander-in-chief of the West Midlands Association. But the dispute ran deeper. At Michaelmas 1645 a sessions of the peace was held at Stafford, and the grand jury (at the instigation of moderates within the county committee) delivered a stinging rebuke to the radicals. Much of their presentment aimed to restrict the expense and modify the behaviour of county forces. But other clauses indicated the need to distinguish civilian and military offices (a self-denying ordinance for committee-men was proposed), to strengthen the commission of the peace by the swearing in of 'some Gentlemen of quallity', to restore petty constables in name and function, and to regulate the judicial powers of the committee. Their powers to arrest, imprison or sequester were not challenged directly, but the grand jury demanded that the committee should regulate their judicial proceedings by issuing sufficient warrants showing cause for their actions.[107]

This last point bears out evidence from counties like Essex and Suffolk where the established gentry for so long controlled the activities of the committees. There, they modelled their work as nearly as possible on traditional lines, at times eschewing the powers granted by ordinance in order to follow local precedent. Brian Quintrell, for example, says of the Romford committee that 'procedure bore striking resemblances to that of the Court of Quarter Sessions and its divisional subordinates'.[108] Similarly, Alan Everitt has written that the Suffolk committee 'was in fact a kind of exclusive country club comprising most of the brains and much of the wealth of the shire . . . the county gentry put at the service

107. Pennington and Roots, *Committee at Stafford*, pp. 343–7.
108. Quintrell, 'Committee of S. Essex', p. 35.

of the [Eastern] Association an administrative machine built up over the past three generations and a wealth of local precedent and experience.'[109]

The pre-war élites, left to themselves, ran committees in accordance with custom and local traditions. Elsewhere, men (often with no experience of governing) took their cues from the ordinances and from Westminster and invariably provoked hostile reactions to their rule.

Above all, moderate opinion was alarmed by committees' powers of arbitrary arrest and punishment. Typical was the complaint of John Musgrave, a committee-man in Cumberland, against his fellows there who imprisoned without trial, ignoring customary legal safeguards. He had himself been locked up for months without trial 'for refusing to answer Interrogatories otherwise than according to law by writing, or to stoop unto the arbitrary and illegal proceedings of a committee, who admitteth the parties accused to sit with their hattes on, and committeth the accusers to prison'.[110] This was a theme taken up by the parliamentary critics of the committee system. Thus Sir John Holland, in calling for their discontinuation and replacement by the old institutional framework, claimed that

I ame one of those that shall humbly desire you to disolve your Committees that you employ at present in the several Countyes for though they were at first of absolute necessity in the beginning of your troubles, yett I think them not now for there are other Hands to bee found will better doe your worke. I shall bee bold to say that the people of this kingdome never groaned under soe heavy a burthen in the worst times as these Committees are in most places become through ther usurpations & misgovernment. For it may be sayd of them truly what was falsly & scandalously printed of a worthy Member of this House, that they take cognizance of all Causes & hold jurisdiction over all persons as well Ecclesiasticall as Temporall within ther several Dominions & truly Sir they are in some places grown to that height that they will give noe manner of observation either to your orders or ordinances for they will Judg, by noe other Rule then that of ther owne wills & those Judgments shall be sure to bee putt in execution with all manner of rigour & they are lookt upon as your Instruments, which will in a short time render your government more oppressive & hatefull to the people then the former have been, which will endanger the affections of the kingdom which what

109. Everitt, *Suffolk*, pp. 16–17.
110. BL, Thomason Tracts, E 323/6. See particularly Musgrave's letter to Sir Arthur Heselrig.

opinion soever we may have of the strength of our armyes may bee of Infinite perill to us.[111]

Holles (but with the wisdom of hindsight) attacked committees for putting their victims 'to an oath as ill as ex officio' and wrote of other (central) committees created by Parliament: 'that of Sequestration . . . came to be worse than any spanish Inquisition, few escaping that were ever questioned . . . the Committee of Examinations . . . what a continual horsefair it was.'[112]

Parliamentary Reactions

From at least the middle of 1645 a chorus of voices demanded the abolition of county committees. The presbyterian party leaders, particularly in the Lords, led the way.[113] A committee to examine the powers exercised by county committees was established in December 1645. A full-scale debate on their future was held in June 1646. A specific ordinance to abolish them was passed by the Lords in August. In February 1647 the Journal recorded that 'the Lords have many Months since sent an Ordinance to the House of Commons for the taking away County Committees, which is expected from both Houses, according to the several Declarations of Parliament, *to bring things to the old course and way of Government . . .*'[114] (author's italics). Meanwhile the presbyterian newspaper, the *Scottish Dove*, led a prolonged campaign for their dissolution.[115] David Underdown, indeed, has argued that 'the issue had now become one of the principal bones of contention between Presbyterians and Independents'.[116] Certainly the various attacks were initiated at times when the presbyterian party generally was making the running in the Houses. But they certainly failed to carry backbench opinion with them in the Commons, and nothing was in practice achieved until 1649 when the purged Rump drastically curtailed the powers and independence of county committees.[117] Furthermore, in 1647

111. BL Tanner MS 321 fo. 7. See *RP* doc. 24b.
112. Holles's Memoirs in F. Maseres (ed.), *Select Tracts Relating to the Civil Wars* (1815), Vol. 1, p. 191.
113. See Underdown, *Pride's Purge*, pp. 38–9; Holmes, 'Colonel King', pp. 481–3.
114. *LJ*, Vol. 8, p. 719.
115. Numerous articles between November 1646 attacked committees. For example BL, Thomason Tracts, E 341/17, E 345/11, E 346/10, E 351/10, E 353/19. See also *Perfect Occurrences* (9–16 April 1647) (BL, Thomason Tracts, E 354/8, printed in *RP* as doc. 24a).
116. Underdown, *Somerset*.   117. Ibid., ch. 10.

the campaign against them was loudest in the Army where they were denounced both by the Levellers and by the Grandees, allies of the 'independent' leaders in the Commons. Thus in June the Grandees accused committees of exercising 'vast and arbitrary powers to vex, delay, fine and imprison at their own pleasure or judgement any that they can bring within the compass of Accomptants, and to proceed upon their own judgement . . .'.[118] Furthermore, the grievances of individual regiments handed in by their officers at the Saffron Walden Army debates in May show a consistent antipathy to county committees, specifically to their quasi-judicial powers.[119]

The attempt to abolish them may have been thwarted less by the 'independents' than by backbench defiance both of a hostile 'presbyterian' leadership and of the indifference of an 'independent' party unwilling to cross the Army. Parliament contained a minority of 'party' politicians, men actively concerned with the broad terms of the future settlement of the kingdom. It also contained a much larger number of county bosses and their clients. Men like Sir Anthony Weldon, Sir William Brereton, Sir Nathaniel Barnardiston, Sir Thomas Myddleton, Sir John Gell held totally different views on the sort of national settlement with the King which they would accept. But they shared in common the fact that they had built up powerful local machines in their counties which they were reluctant to dismantle. Such men followed 'party' lines on general issues, but not necessarily when their 'party' threatened their local power base. It is possible that such men would join together against any move to abolish committees altogether. Clive Holmes has certainly shown how cross-voting took place when the committee of Lincolnshire was under attack.[120]

If the county bosses wanted to oppose both parties, they would carry many votes with them. From the autumn of 1645, by-elections were held to fill the seats made vacant since 1642 by death or by the deprivation of royalist MPs. David Underdown has shown how a parliamentary struggle ensued to control the issue of writs. He has also argued that the parties at Westminster sponsored candidates in the counties. Michael Mahony, while accepting and developing the former point, sees a different significance in the elections themselves. Rather than directing the elections from Westminster, the

118. BL, Thomason Tracts, E 392/9.
119. Worcester College, Oxford, Clarke MSS 41, *passim*, for example fos 108, 119. See also the seventh article of *The Humble Representation of the Army* (4 June 1647), Rushworth, *Historical Collections*, Vol. 7, pp. 505–10.
120. Holmes, 'Colonel King'.

main parties were awaiting instructions from local caucuses broadly
sympathetic to their aims and were making parliamentary procedure
fit local requirements. He has shown that the recruiter elections
were a triumph for localist interests. Carpetbaggers had never had
such a thin time (only one army-sponsored candidate succeeded
outside his home base in the West Country, for example). 'The control of the seals was important not so much in the form of central
management, but in that of responding to local circumstances.' Sir
William Brereton sponsored his own friends and relations in the
elections in the north midlands, for example, and looked to his
allies at Westminster to control the timing of the writs. Some of those
he supported were likely to be moderates at Westminster despite
their loyalty to him in local affairs. Conversely, Brereton reported
that the election of a local enemy of his, Edward Leigh, at Stafford,
need not mean that the radicals might not gain his support on
national issues.[121]

Most commentators now agree that only a minority of MPs were
'party' men. There existed a number of small groups of members,
related by marriage, by patronage or by regional ties. These groups
made working alliances with one another on major issues and sought
to gain the support of the majority of the uncommitted members.
At most periods of the war, there were three such alliances, but the
configuration was regularly disturbed, notably in early 1644, the
winter of 1646–47 and the autumn of 1648. At times (as in early
1645 and the summer of 1647) national issues led to the effective
polarisation of the Houses into two or three clear groups. But at
other times, the caucuses of thirty or so members had to work on
an amorphous body of placemen and backbenchers, all of whom
would have their own ideas on national questions from which they
could be deflected. Thus, in late 1643, many MPs 'cross-voted',
supporting a 'party' they generally opposed. For the members most
enthusiastic for the Scots alliance included many from the northern counties which would be liberated in consequence, while support for Waller's independent army included West-Country MPs
normally sympathetic to the 'peace' party aims championed by the
Earl of Essex, the bitter opponent of Waller.

On many other issues there were no clear-cut party lines and for
much of the time, while the caucuses struggled to control the executive and to mobilise backbench opinion, the most divisive issues

---

121. D.E. Underdown, 'Party Management in the Recruiter Elections, 1645–1648',
EHR, Vol. 83 (1968); Mahony, 'Presbyterian Party', pp. 486–506; Morrill, *Cheshire*,
pp. 173–9.

saw no clear party pattern. It was perfectly possible for most members to remain generally uncommitted, subject not to a party whip but to their own consciences and to their calculation of the best interest of their own county communities.[122]

The Revolt of the Provinces

In the summer and autumn of 1647, England was more clearly on the verge of anarchy than at any other time in the century. Parliament had polarised almost completely and fundamentally over a related series of problems: how to proceed against an intransigent King; how to disband a recalcitrant army; how to reach a religious settlement and then how to impose it; how to halt the Levellers, a genuinely popular, revolutionary movement which skilfully linked together the grievances of the rank and file of the army with those of the articulate sub-political groups in the metropolis and other towns (and with related proposals calculated to appeal to the mass of the peasantry). Each group in Parliament, the Grandees in the Army, the Levellers, the Scots and the King all looked inflexibly for the achievement of incompatible aims in their proposals for settlement. No wonder the political group in power, the 'Presbyterians', made such a mess of things.[123]

Provincial communities were certainly aware of the gravity of the crisis. But they were just as aware of the collapse of order at a local level, the rising popular violence, the clashes of soldiers and civilians, the continuing dourness and increasing isolation of committees. Never was the yearning for settlement, meaning a restoration of the old ways, more clearly expressed.

The problems were universal. There were serious mutinies amongst garrisons and local forces in most counties in 1646–47. In

---

122. The above is based on Mahony, 'Presbyterian Party', *passim*; Underdown, *Pride's Purge*, particularly ch. 3; and the articles of Valerie Pearl cited above. Despite differences over detailed points of interpretation, there is a basic and persuasive unity of approach amongst these historians. The alternative approach by MacCormack, *Revolutionary Politics*, is totally unconvincing. Insofar as the above differs from these writers, it is by applying some of the insights in A.B. Worden, *The Rump Parliament* (1974) back into the 1640s. Shortage of space has forced this section to be drastically curtailed.

123. J.S. Morrill, 'Mutiny and Discontent in English Provincial Armies, 1645–1647', *P. and P.*, Vol. 56 (1972), particularly pp. 72–4; V. Pearl, 'London's Counter-Revolution' in G.E. Aylmer (ed.), *The Interregnum* (1972); Mahony, 'Presbyterian Party', chs 8 and 9.

several cases the mutineers captured and imprisoned committee-men, holding them to ransom for their arrears.[124] In several counties there was a renewal of Clubmen activity, usually directed against troops sent to take free quarter. There was sporadic Clubmen activity in Somerset throughout 1646, for example.[125] In 1647 the grand jury there asserted that unless action was taken urgently to remove troops quartered in the county ('either by the *Posse Comitatus* or some other lawful way') they feared 'the tumultuous Meetings and the Risings of the Country in Arms'.[126]

There were bloody skirmishes between troops and civilians in Wiltshire and Hampshire, a fight between rival religious groups in Leicestershire, Excise riots in a number of towns, some of them involving crowds of women.[127] The Moorlanders rioted against the county committee in Staffordshire, and a similar movement developed among the loosely structured communities of north Yorkshire and Northumberland (the Dalesmen and the Mosstroopers). The latter seized the High Sheriff and were powerful enough to induce Major General Lambert to negotiate with them rather than to attack.[128] As David Underdown has remarked, 'in a country wracked by plague, food shortages, and high prices . . . something like a complete breakdown of law and order' took place.[129]

124. Morrill, 'Mutiny and Discontent', Underdown, *Pride's Purge*, pp. 40–1, 77–9.

125. Underdown, *Somerset*, pp. 135–7. See also the re-emergence of the old Clubmen leader, Humphrey Willis, and his savage renewed attack on the county committee in *Time's Whirligig*, BL, Thomason Tracts, E 355/3.

126. *LJ*, Vol. 9, p. 172.

127. Underdown, *Pride's Purge*, pp. 79–83, 90–1; BL, Thomason Tracts, E350/21; E402/2; E 511/24; BL Tanner MS 59 fo. 442; HMC, Portland MSS, Vol. III, pp. 157–8. In Haverfordwest in September 1644, it was reported that: 'On Monday last the commissioners for the excise came to this town and having shown us their commission we yielded obedience unto it, and thereupon they sent out their warrants for the summoning of the inhabitants before them. And having sat yesterday in the afternoon on it there came to the town hall a company of the poorest sort of women of this town and there made a mutiny and forced the commissioners thence to their lodgings. And having complained unto us, we thought by the authority of the civil power to suppress them and for that purpose entreated the commissioners to sit again this day and that we would assist them therein. And we and the said commissioners being in the town hall thinking to proceed on the service, the said women came again and would have forced into the hall, whereupon we committed some of them to the sheriff thinking they would have yielded obedience thereunto, but they fell again into such a mutiny that for safeguard of the commissioners' we were forced to leave the hall, and having repaired with them to their lodging with an intent to see them safe out of the town, the said women followed us thither and would have forced on them in their chamber in such manner as for the space of six hours we could not pacify them . . .' (Haverfordwest, Corporation MS No. 244, printed in B.E. and K.A. Howells (eds), *Pembrokeshire Life, 1572–1843* (1972), p. 15).

128. Rushworth, *Historical Collections*, Vol. 7, pp. 809–70, *passim*.

129. Underdown, *Somerset*.

The reaction of moderate gentry and freeholders was entirely characteristic. They renewed their call for an end to the committee system and for the restoration of local autonomy and ancient institutions. There were other echoes of the consistent Country programme unchanged since 1640, 1642, 1645. In May 1647, for example, the Devon grand jury presented a long list of grievances. Prominent articles spoke of the want of able ministers and neglect of the Lord's Supper, criticised the Excise (which should be regulated by 'Justices and Gentry') and attacked the continued resort to free quarter. They also denounced the maladministration and corruption of the sequestrators, who should render account, 'not only to the Committee, but to such other just and honest Men of this County' as should be thought fit.[130]

Even more dramatic was the Dorset petition of 1648. The ten thousand signatories claimed that they had 'engaged [their] lives, liberties and estates on the same grounds under the slighted and unprosperous notion of Clubmen. Notwithstanding our sufferings then, our ends are still the same and we doubt not our endeavours will be more successful.' Specifically they called for the release of the King, a religious settlement worked out by clergy elected from each 'county or *diocese'* (sic), the return of authority to 'men of visible estates and of unquestioned repute', an end to committees, sequestrations, and for fresh elections. Above all, they asked 'That the common birthright of us all, the Laws, may be restored to their former purity, and that we may enjoy them without corrupt glosses and Comments of their Arbitrary Power, or unequal Ordinances and practises between them and their Committees.'[131]

This petition provides the key to the second civil war. Like the 'royalist' movements in Kent and Norfolk in 1643, the great majority of those who rose for Charles I were reacting against Parliament and centralisation, not *for* the King.[132] More than ever 'social and political grievances combined to foreshadow a counter-revolutionary

130. *LJ* Vol. 9, pp. 171–2. See also the Cheshire grand jury presentment at the Easter Great Session [assize] of 1648, printed in *RP* doc. 24c: 'First we present unto your Lordship that wee have for diverse yeares last past and yet doe lye under an Arbitrary and unlimited power exercised by most of the Deputy Lieutenants of this county in their taxeing and Imposeing many great burthens and payments upon us in the name of Mizes . . . and in leavying the same upon our estates by distress without any act of or Ordinance of Parliament enabling or directing them thereunto . . . which tends to the losse of our propertye as freeborne Englishmen and is directly against the Liberty of the Subject and the Law of the Land for which we have lately and ever will ingage our Lives and estates' (PRO, Chester 24/127 no. 1, unfoliated).
131. Bayley, *Civil War in Dorset.* For the full text, see *RP* doc. 25b.
132. Underdown, *Pride's Purge*, pp. 146–9. See *RP* doc. 21b.

explosion'.[133] Food prices reached their peak for the century, and food riots were widespread, particularly in the West Country. Elsewhere, as at Canterbury, Exeter or Norwich, there were riots to mark the prohibitions on Christmas festivities or the King's birthday.

The following months saw an unprecedented wave of petitions, both from the Levellers and other 'Country' groups: they represent an 'overwhelming demonstration of opposition to military government and centralisation'. Many of them came from a 'region hitherto mainly parliamentarian in its loyalties'.[134]

All the main revolts which made up the second civil war grew out of popular demonstrations which

> were compounded of many different elements: excise and assessments, petty tyranny by county committee, violation of the traditional rights of the county through government from Westminster. Once again can be felt a widespread yearning for the good old days, for a return to the old government of J.P.s and locally controlled militias, even at the cost of some crucial elements in the programme for which Parliament had gone to war.[135]

Most of the petitions called for an accommodation. But as ever, the call was unspecific and rather unenthusiastic. There were no references even to such empty formulae as the Protestation of 1641. The nature of the accommodation seemed almost irrelevant. What mattered was an end to much more frightening dangers nearer home.

There is no evidence that anyone saw a settlement between Parliament and the King as solving any of the basic problems. It would remove some of the paralysis which prevented effective action from being taken to halt the advance of anarchy. In any case, few ex-royalists were involved in the risings. Most royalists felt that Charles's Engagement with the Scots was a betrayal much worse than his accommodation with the Irish in 1643. A typical royalist reaction was that of John Aston in Cheshire: 'the Scots have eternally lost their honour with us, therefore we heed not their invasion'.[136] Too many royalists had just paid composition fines, were crippled by debt and desperate to avoid further costs or risks.[137] It was the old provincial moderates, men disillusioned with Parliament for its failure to adhere to their view of the conservative objectives of the war,

133. Underdown, *Pride's Purge*, p. 89.   134. Ibid., pp. 90–2.
135. Ibid., p. 98.   136. BL Add. MS 36914 fo. 237.
137. Wood, *Nottinghamshire*, pp. 146–50; Ketton-Cremer, *Norfolk*, p. 357; Underdown, *Somerset*, pp. 147–9.

who hesitated longest. Even then, most of them finally threw in
their lot with the New Model.[138]

In the event, several small groups of royalists rose (incoherently, at
different times) in many counties. But the only areas where a serious threat to the army occurred were those where the royalist coup
coincided with a popular rising against the army and county committees. Even then, it was more a question of coincidence than union.

The clearest example is afforded by Kent, where a full-scale revolt
broke out in May. Alan Everitt has brilliantly unravelled the background to this revolt in the growing isolation of the committee from
moderate opinion of all shades. By 1648, it was so vindictive and
obsessed with its own power that 'rebellion was not impossible, as
contemporaries thought: it was inevitable'.[139]

On Christmas Day 1647, a riot against the prohibition on festivities took place in Canterbury and was whipped up by royalist agit-
ators. Arrests were made, but when the cases came up at the assizes
in May, the jury refused to indict. The judges, backed by the Committee, refused to accept the jury's findings and recommitted the
accused to prison. This example of committee arrogance and disregard for the law immediately provoked meetings throughout the
county in which the whole community articulated its pent-up rage
against the Committee. It was, says Alan Everitt, 'a revolt of the
whole countryside, like that of Cornwall in 1497 and like the Northern Rebellion of 1536 . . . it was the last of the great local insurrections of English history.' Almost six hundred gentry were involved,
'the entire county establishment backed by their tenants'.[140]

The Engagement drawn up by the leaders and the succeeding
remonstrance reveal a total preoccupation with ridding the community of the consequences of parliamentary rule: the army, committees, over-taxation.[141] The attempt of a royalist minority to exploit
this mass movement was wholly unsuccessful. Originally, only a small
number of the Kentish rebels declared for the King, but as royalists
from other counties moved into Kent (plundering as they came) all
hope of lasting co-operation dissolved. Parliament skilfully exploited
the divisions within the movement, sowing self-doubt in the hearts
of many moderates. The movement was disintegrating by the time
the New Model arrived. The royalist minority cut their losses and

138. For example, Broxap, *Lancashire*, pp. 159–62.
139. Everitt, *Kent*, p. 185. For what follows, see ibid., pp. 231–70.
140. Ibid., p. 241.
141. See also H.F. Abell, *Kent in the Great Civil War* (1901), pp. 174–5, 185–7, and
RP doc. 25a.

headed north to join another group of local dissidents gathered at Chelmsford.[142] To quote Everitt again:

> The rebellion had begun with a petition against the County Commit-
> tee and few of the rebels ever thought of themselves as more than
> petitioners. Only the Cavaliers saw the need of co-ordinating county
> grievances with the political requirements of the state.[143]

They were, of course, branded as traitors and malignants: they were, in fact, as they always had been, the 'Country'.

The other main area of revolt was South Wales, where the defiance of former parliamentarian leaders encapsulates the essential continuity and integrity of the provincial communities throughout the 1640s. The adjacent counties of Glamorganshire and Pembrokeshire had been brought under royal control at the outset of the conflict through the decisive action of the Marquises of Worcester and Hertford (the Earl of Pembroke had not attempted to mobilise his important faction). But the history of the two counties took rather different courses.[144] In Glamorgan, mounting royalist demands for cash and recruits, coupled with the intrusion of 'foreign', English commanders, led to a crisis in the summer of 1645. The commissioners of array, reacting to popular demonstrations, renounced their financial and military agreement with the King and formed a 'Peaceable Army' in the county whose aims were entirely consistent with those of the contemporary Clubmen in neighbouring English counties.[145] The King initially capitulated to their demands but later appeared to be planning to invade the county to reassert his authority. The leaders of the revolt made a tactical alliance with the parliamentarians now ascendant in Pembrokeshire, by which the effective autonomy and self-sufficiency of Glamorganshire under nominal parliamentarian sovereignty was acknowledged. But the leaders of the Peaceable Army soon found the counties' institutions were being

142. For the second civil war in East Anglia, see A. Kingston, *East Anglia and the Civil War* (1910), pp. 252–71; Ketton-Cremer, *Norfolk*, pp. 231–53.

143. Everitt, *Kent*, p. 170.

144. The following is based on four main secondary sources: J.R. Philipps, *The Civil War in Wales and the Marches* (2 vols, 1874); A.L. Leach, *The History of the Civil War in Pembrokeshire and on its Borders* (1937); J.F. Rees, *Studies in Welsh History* (n.d.); and C.M. Thomas, 'The First Civil War in Glamorganshire, 1642–1646', University of Wales MA thesis (1963), *passim*. Many biographical details come from Dodd, *Studies in Stuart Wales* and Lloyd, *Gentry of South West Wales*. All material not otherwise attributed comes from these sources.

145. BL Harl. MS 6804 (Papers of Sir Edward Walker) fos 210–11. Walker's papers are full of details of the Peace movement, and have never been fully used. But see now Lynch, 'Clubmen', pp. 182–94.

undermined by parliamentarian ordinances, new men obtruded into county government, and the traditional rites and observances of the Church of England suppressed. Twice in February 1646 and June 1647 they rebelled, charging parliamentary committees with tyranny, innovation and breach of the agreement of September 1645.[146] Each time the revolt was crushed by force.

In neighbouring Pembrokeshire, where the Tudors had failed to impose English customs and values outside the towns and the area known as the 'Englishry', the pattern was rather different. Almost uniquely, the Welsh areas were purely neutral, genuinely *apathetic*, in a sense we have not encountered elsewhere. In the towns, too, the majority were neutral, ready to follow the line of least resistance.[147] For most men this entailed acquiescence in royalist control. Only eight gentlemen made early declarations for Parliament and had they not been able to seize Pembroke Castle and be supplied for the next three years by the fleet, they would soon have given in. The most prominent of them were John Poyer, who, as Mayor of Pembroke in 1642, first raised troops to meet a fabricated papist plot,[148] and Rowland Laugharne (the key figures throughout this story). Gradually, as these determined men, sallying forth periodically from Pembroke, gained effective control over a wide area (the royalists had few troops in the area precisely because they were so remote from any other parliamentarian forces), they induced many others to assist them passively. It was the usual pattern of men acquiescing in all recognisable authority. But Poyer was not a man who stuck to niceties (to declare for Parliament where and when he did signifies bullheadedness) and his tendency to cut corners in his financial dealings antagonised the more careful converts, men like the Lort brothers of Stackpool. In April 1645 the Committee (created in mid-1644 to mark the achievements of Poyer and Laugharne), all but the two of them ex-royalists, denounced Poyer for 'insatiable and insolent oppressions'.[149]

In the following years this bitter feud simmered nastily. In December 1647, the situation reached crisis point. Poyer's power rested entirely on his governorship of Pembroke Castle. Once out of his command, he would be extremely vulnerable to his enemies

---

146. *LJ*, Vol. 9, pp. 682–3; HMC, *Portland MS*, Vol. 1, pp. 270, 345–6, 351–2 (*RP* doc. 23a); Rushworth, *Historical Collections*, Vol. 7, pp. 578–9; BL Tanner MS 58 fos 173, 230.

147. The best example is Haverfordwest, which met the demands of both sides throughout the war.

148. HMC, *Portland MS*, Vol. 1, p. 31.   149. BL, Tanner MS 60 fo. 115.

who controlled the county committee. In December 1647, as part
of the rationalisation of commands following the New Model's victory over the 'presbyterians', Poyer was required to hand over the
castle to a detachment of the New Model. He refused, asserting
that he and his men would not disband without their arrears and a
special indemnity. Mutiny had long been accepted as a legitimate
political manoeuvre and he could expect to be bought out. But
with the beginning of the second civil war, his plan misfired. Made
desperate by the delays, Poyer met and talked with royalist agents,
although he never accepted a commission from the King and all his
warrants were issued in his own name. The gentry of Glamorgan
rose for the third time against parliamentary misrule, but the tone
and details of the petition of both groups of South Wales rebels
were entirely in the traditions of the old neutralist programmes of
1642 and 1645. They demanded that:

> the Just prerogative of the king, Privileges of Parliament, Lawes of
> the Land, Liberties of the People, may be maintained, and preserved
> in their proper bounds, and the Protestant religion, as it now stands
> established by the Law of the land, restored throughout the king-
> dom with such regard to tender consciences as shall be allowed by
> Act of Parliament.[150]

The bluff had failed. Cromwell was despatched with a substantial
proportion of the New Model. Laugharne's 'ill-assorted body of royalists, presbyterians, Episcopalians, ex-supernumeraries, sympathisers
from various parts of England and Wales, local Clubmen armed only
with staves', about 8,000 in all, crumbled in a brief encounter with
Cromwell at St Fagans. After a dour eight-week siege of Pembroke
Castle, Poyer and his followers surrendered. The war was over.

Poyer had overreached himself. He had tried to negotiate and to
bluster his way out of a local feud, and failed; he had tried to
outflank his local enemies, and had become enmeshed in a much
wider network of conspiracy; he had put out a programme in which
the authentic voice of protest against the violation of traditional
rights and civil liberties can be heard. He sums up the complexities
of the English revolution. Here was a man praying that the 'lawes
of the land and liberties of the people may be all established in
their proper bounds'.[151] The great majority of Englishmen had never
asked for any more and had yet to learn that a civil war can only
protect such liberties by abrogating them.

150. BL, Thomason Tracts, E 435/9; see *RP* doc. 23b.   151. Ibid.

Conclusion:
The Revolt of the Provinces *Revisited*

Introduction

This final essay explores my personal sense of the enduring value of a book written to meet the historiographical needs of twenty years ago. It is an exercise in scholarly auditing. It will be principally concerned with noting those aspects of the book that have been so absorbed into the general historical understanding that the accounts given here have lost their freshness if not their value; with those aspects of the book that have been shown by subsequent historical research to be inaccurate or unhelpful characterisations – or explanations – of the past; and with those aspects of the book which may be still uniquely valuable as we continue to seek to make sense of the period. To put it a different way, this essay will be a historiographical review of work published in the past twenty years and an attempt to show how that work has *absorbed* the arguments of this book, *rejected* the arguments of this book, and *overlooked* the arguments of the book. It is an exercise in sifting of wheat from chaff.

It is emphatically not an attempt to say how I would write the book if I was writing it today. The field has moved on and I have moved on. Could anyone nowadays write a book that is so anglocentric, so uninterested in the interpenetration of events in England, Scotland and Ireland (or at least in the ways that consciousness of events elsewhere in Ireland and Scotland affected the behaviour of English men and women)?[1] Or even, for that matter, could anyone write an

1. For the recent explosion of work on 'the War of the Three Kingdoms' or 'the British Problem' and how it might impinge on the subject matter of this book, see C. Russell, *The Causes of the English Civil War* (Oxford, 1991) and *The Fall of the British Monarchies, 1637–42* (Oxford, 1992); John Morrill, 'The Britishness of the English Revolution' in R. Asch (ed.), *Three Nations – A Common History?* (Bochum, 1993),

account that made so little reference to events on the continent of
Europe or about how the *experience* of war for the English compared
with the experience of people in contemporary Europe?[2] These are
simply two of the most obvious ways in which new approaches to
the period would have transformed how this work would have been
conceived. If I was writing this book in 1998 I would not be starting
from here.

The Coming of War: (a) The 1630s

The first half of the opening chapter of *The Revolt of the Provinces*
was thinly researched. It was intended simply to provide a context for the better-researched second half, which in turn set out to
demonstrate two things above all. The first is the absolute necessity
of understanding that there was no simple connection between the
issues which alienated the vast majority of the people of England
and Wales[3] from the Crown and its policies in 1640, and those that
led so many of them to support or to oppose the King with a
radically different group of ministers and raft of policies in 1642.
And the second is that most Englishmen – or at any rate most of
the gentry and urban governors of England and Wales – were reluctant to go to war and sought to avoid having to take sides, and that
many of them petitioned for peace and for further negotiation
and/or actively organised to prevent the war from spreading into
their area.

---

pp. 84–112, and 'Three Kingdoms and One Commonwealth: The Enigma of Mid
Seventeenth Century Britain and Ireland' in A. Grant and K.J. Stringer (eds), *Unit-
ing the Kingdom? The Enigma of British History* (London, 1995), pp. 167–92. For the
way new textbooks deal with it, see David L. Smith, *The British Isles in the Seventeenth
Century, 1603–1707: The Double Crown* (Oxford, 1998) or Martyn Bennett, *The Civil
Wars in Britain and Ireland 1638–1651* (1997). For a discussion of how and why study
of the English civil war after 1900 came ever more to be disconnected from these
wider contexts and then reconnected to them from 1980 onwards, see J.S. Morrill,
'The War(s) of the Three Kingdoms' in Glenn Burgess (ed.), *The New British History*
(forthcoming, 1999).

2. For an example, see Ian Roy, 'England turned Germany? The Aftermath of the
Civil War in its European Context', *TRHS*, 5th ser., Vol. 28 (1978), pp. 127–44.

3. I am damned if I use this formula and damned if I don't. The book assumes
that the Welsh theatres of the English civil war can be treated as part of a single war,
and that while each Welsh theatre will be distinctive from the others and from each
English theatre, that will be for the same reasons and within the same parameters as
the variations between English theatres. Welsh examples were under-represented in
the text and in the documentary appendices, but they are present and I will use this
formula rather one that subsumes Wales into England.

That first half of 'The coming of war' has received more attention than any other part of the book, and can ill afford to take close scrutiny. It is based more on a series of intuitions and assertions than demonstrations. Many of the intuitions have proved valuable, but few of the assertions stand up to close scrutiny. The intuitions need to be expressed in very different terms.

The first of the intuitions was that the civil war was not a war of the 'ins' versus the 'outs', the beneficiaries of the 'Renaissance state' with its 'ever-expanding bureaucracy' against those who 'mutinied . . . against the vast, oppressive, over-extending apparatus of parasitic bureaucracy that had grown up around the Crown and above the economy' – i.e. it was a struggle of Court versus Country.[4] To this I countered that both those terms were being used in unhelpful ways; and that 'Country' in particular[5] was better seen as a number of discrete groupings and attitudes, clustered around two poles which I termed the 'official country', groups of would-be courtiers and office-seekers alienated from the personnel, policies and practices of Charles I and his ministers, but aiming to remedy misgovernment by what Hanoverian politicians were to call 'storming the closet'; and the 'pure country', men with a reflex suspicion of the operations of central government. I went on to suggest that in 1640 there was a very clear Court versus 'official Country' divide and a deeply alienated rather than suspicious 'pure Country'; but that that configuration did little to explain the loyalties of 1642. Rather, the courtiers of 1640 were divided in 1642, most (those not driven into exile) on the King's side but others (including the Earls of Pembroke and Northumberland) on the parliamentarian side, while the official 'Country' was split down the middle; meanwhile the 'pure Country' provided a mass of anti-war neutralist or localist sentiment. I was later to suggest that a more helpful way of examining patterns of protest to the Crown was in terms of three 'modes of opposition' – localist, constitutionalist, and religious, the first leading into neutralism in 1642 and the second, unless reinforced by the third, into royalism.

4. Above, pp. 26–7.
5. It is perhaps as well that I said so little about the Caroline court given the transformation of our understanding of the nature and significance of the Court and of the 'politics of intimacy' in the early modern period. For the 1630s, we are fortunate to have Kevin Sharpe as an informed and able guide in such essays as 'The Image of Virtue: The Court and Household of Charles I 1625–42' in D. Starkey *et al.* (eds), *The English Court: From the Wars of the Roses to the Civil War* (1987), pp. 226–60; *Criticism and Compliment: The Politics of Literature in the England of Charles I* (Cambridge, 1987).

All this was a helpful oversimplification. It failed to allow for the ways in which many local gentry were linked to those who had court connections or to aspiring courtiers: it created a false dichotomy between men who operated on a national and a purely local or provincial stage. What I had overlooked was that many were temperamentally committed to 'Country' values, but realistic enough to know that they needed to be able to dirty their hands by contact with the men and institutions of central government. 'Pure country' Members of Parliament were, after all, strutting unconfidently on a national stage. My eyes were opened when I read Derek Hirst's essay on the 'Court, Country and Politics before 1629' in which he wrote of the struggle of Court and Country within the heads of individuals, and the mutual need of the one for the other: the epithet 'Janus-like' was applied earlier to some of the 'Country' politicians, but it is applicable also to some who were paid servants of the Crown.[6]

A similar point was made by Clive Holmes in a penetrating article (published in 1980) which argued against the self-containedness and introspection of county communities and for greater institutional and intellectual congruity of centre and provinces than works like *The Revolt of the Provinces* allowed for.[7] Although I think I may have misstated the question, I think I gave the correct answer.

The second of the intuitive points made at the opening of the book was that while 'by the 1630s there were more sources of information than ever available to the gentry [who were] better educated than any previous generation . . . what united them in their opposition to the Crown in 1640 was their *lack* of understanding of royal policies'.[8] I supported this by referring to the preoccupation with the *effects* of royal policies 'rather than their origin or purpose which remained concealed'; and I cited a number of gentry letter collections which appeared to trivialise or at any rate anecdotalise major public events. All this was too sweeping. The work of Johann Sommerville, Glenn Burgess and others has demonstrated the nature and extent of public discussion of political theory

6. D.L. Hirst, 'Court, Country and Politics before 1629' in K.M. Sharpe (ed.), *Faction and Parliament* (Oxford, 1978), pp. 105–38 at 120–2.

7. Clive Holmes, 'The County Community in Stuart Historiography', *JBS* 19/2 (1980), pp. 54–73. This was followed up by his study of *Seventeenth-Century Lincolnshire* (Lincoln, 1980) in which he provides a case study of the proliferation of local and national identities in this period. For a commentary on Holmes's work that both welcomes it and seeks to combine it with my own work, see John Morrill, *The Nature of the English Revolution* (1993), pp. 179–93.

8. Above, pp. 27–30.

and its application to political practice in the early Stuart period as a whole,[9] and Tom Cogswell, Peter Lake and Richard Cust have been in the forefront of demonstrating the sophistication of local leaders in responding to central initiatives.[10] We also know far more than we did twenty years ago about the dissemination of news, not only in the form of printed separates but also manuscript newsletters.[11] Here I think I would want to give more ground. I now regret that I wrote so exclusively about the gentry; that I omitted any discussion of religion, given that I was going to put such weight on the significance of the emergence of religious militancy in 1640–42; and that I misrepresented the sophistication of regional awareness of, and response to, events at the political centre and in other regions. Neutralism and localism in 1642 were not the product of ignorance and incomprehension, but of an analysis more sophisticated than I realised of who was who, what was what, of what was right by God, by the Ancients and by the rule of law. It was also based on a chronic inability to see how civil war would solve anything. Whatever the drift towards tyranny that many could see in the actions of Charles I and his ministers, the anarchy that would result from civil war would be worse. The paragraph on pp. 37–8 of this edition is probably the most inaccurate and insupportable in the whole book and should be treated with special caution.

The book then moves into a more informed discussion of the collection of ship money in 1634–40. It is based on a fairly thorough analysis of the correspondence between sheriffs and other local officers and the Privy Council in those years, and it concludes by noting that despite all the vocal protest, it is the success not the failure of ship money which needs to be stressed. Collection collapsed after it became clear that Charles would be constrained to call a Parliament which was likely to put an end to ship money.

9. See especially Johann Sommerville, *Politics and Ideology in England 1603–1640* (1986), and Glenn Burgess, *The Politics of the Ancient Constitution: An Introduction to English Political Thought 1603–42* (1992) and their other influential writings.

10. T. Cogswell, *The Blessed Revolution: The English People and the Coming of War 1621–1624* (Cambridge, 1987); the essays by Cust, Hughes, Cogswell, Sommerville and Lake in R. Cust and Ann Hughes (eds), *Conflict in Early Stuart England: Studies in Politics and Religion 1603–42* (1989); and – striking at the heart of my exegesis – R. Cust and P. Lake, 'Sir Richard Grosvenor and the Rhetoric of Magistracy', *BIHR* 54 (1981), pp. 40–53. See also A. Fletcher, 'National and Local Awareness in the County Communities' in H. Tomlinson (ed.), *Before the English Civil War: Essays in Early Stuart Politics and Government* (1983), pp. 151–74.

11. See especially the following theses: Michael Frearson, 'The English Corantos of the 1620', University of Cambridge Ph.D. thesis (1994) and David Cockburn, 'A Critical Edition of the Letters of the Revd Joseph Mead 1626–7', University of Cambridge Ph.D. thesis (1994).

I maintained that it was the administrative incoherence and the perceived inequities of its geographical and social distribution that made it so resented, not its doubtful legality: 'the constitutional propriety of ship money was not the main reason for opposition to it. What had changed between 1634 and 1640 was not the gentry's opinion of Charles's constitutional arguments but the breakdown of peace, quiet and order in the local communities.'[12]

This has proved a contentious interpretation. It became a revisionist rallying point and my interpretation – and especially the claim that ship money should be seen as fundamentally a government *success* – was supported by Conrad Russell and by Kevin Sharpe (who provided massive additional evidence to support it).[13] But a number of scholars have pointed out that the reports of sheriffs were not a reliable source for my purpose: they were likely to exaggerate for their own purposes the sheer administrative difficulty facing them; and it has been shown that they needed to broker deals by which they could get more co-operation from their friends and colleagues only if they could get for them special concessions from the Council.[14] Others have suggested that there was considerably more ideologically-driven *anger* if not ideologically-driven effective obstruction than my account allowed.[15]

My own reading of the conflicting evidence is that the account in *The Revolt of the Provinces* oversimplifies more than it misrepresents. By far the most careful and thorough review of all the evidence concludes that while all the administrative problems that I identified (disputes over the quotas as between counties, as between counties and corporate towns, as between cathedral towns and cathedral chapters) were significant in and of themselves, they were frequently if not commonly used as a device to disguise more fundamental objections.[16] My view that the King's victory over Hampden

---

12. Above, p. 44.

13. See Conrad Russell, *The Causes of the English Civil War* (Oxford, 1990); K.M. Sharpe, *The Personal Rule of Charles I* (1992), pp. 545–98.

14. Peter Lake, 'The Collection of Ship Money in Cheshire during the Sixteen Thirties: A Case Study of Relations between Central and Local Government', *Northern History* 17 (1981), pp. 44–71. Cf. Pamela Colman, 'The Wiltshire Sheriffs of Charles I: To Whom the Loyalty', *Wilts. Archaeological and Natural History Magazine*, 84 (1991), pp. 117–30.

15. e.g. Kenneth Fincham, 'The Judges' Decision on Ship Money in February 1637: The Reaction of Kent', *BIHR* 57/136 (1984), pp. 230–7; C.A. Clifford, 'Ship Money in Hampshire: Collection and Collapse', *Southern History* 4 (1982), pp. 91–106; and John Fielding, 'Opposition to the Personal Rule of Charles I: The Diary of Robert Woodford 1637–41', *HJ* 31 (1988), pp. 769–88.

16. Alison Gill, 'Ship Money in the Reign of Charles I', University of Sheffield Ph.D. thesis (1991).

was widely accepted cannot be sustained; but my view that ship money was sulkily but generally paid until the prospect of a Parliament made people suspend their payments is still arguable, although it is clearer that new procedural spanners were becoming available to jam the works. In particular, it is clear that many lawyers were advising their clients that writs from the Court of *Exchequer* for the distraint of goods for non-payment of sums owing to the *Admiralty* were illegal; and that they could sue the sheriffs for theft. The intuition that ship money was more successful than any of the textbooks allowed and that opposition to ship money contributed to the scale of protest against misgovernment in 1640 but not directly to the formation of a parliamentarian movement in 1642 (and that many more of its most vociferous opponents were royalist rather than parliamentarian), was sound enough.

The Coming of War: (b) Reactions to Crisis 1640–42

When *The Revolt of the Provinces* was published, there had been no thorough source-based study of the internal dynamics of the Short Parliament and of the Long Parliament in its first two years since S.R. Gardiner's *History of England from the Accession of James I to the Outbreak of the Civil War* (10 vols, 1883–84), with the partial exceptions of the first part of Brian Wormald's *Clarendon: Politics, History and Religion* (1951) and of several chapters in Perez Zagorin's *The Court and the Country: The Beginnings of the English Revolution* (1969). My account of the factional regroupings and polarisation (pp. 47–9) looks very dated in the wake of the publication of so many of the parliamentary diaries for the period since 1976 and the appearance of the strictly complementary accounts of those internal dynamics in magisterial books by Anthony Fletcher and Conrad Russell[17] and a range of detailed articles.

Fletcher was concerned with chronicling and understanding the waves of petitions from shires and cities which poured in to King and Parliament and which were subsequently published. These waves of petitions were in part procured by groups within Parliament, were a spontaneous reaction to events in Whitehall, Westminster or elsewhere (e.g. the Irish Rebellion) and in their own time helped

---

17. Anthony Fletcher, *The Outbreak of the English Civil War* (1981); Conrad Russell, *The Fall of the British Monarchies 1637–1643* (1991).

to shape factional reactions at court and in Parliament. It was a much more dialectical process than I had allowed. Russell's book is a highly sophisticated and powerful analysis of high politics, which takes Fletcher's perspective as read, and it gives a gripping account of how MPs struggled to restructure the institutions through which they hoped and believed (with decreasing confidence) the King would feel himself bound to govern responsibly, while also having to deal with grimly-determined Scots seeking to procure the reformation of the English Church and the creation of confederal institutions to new model the Anglo-Scottish Union, and to come to terms with rebellions and massacres in Ireland. The three-kingdom dimension is completely lacking from my account, as is its dark shadow, the strength and significance of anti-popery whether as a conspiracy at the heart of government or as the threat of an invasion of savage Irishmen hell-bent on pillage, rape, torture and the extinction of protestant liberty.[18]

The discussion on pp. 47–51 suffers from a lack of these perspectives. But the fundamental point – that 'men at Westminster were acutely aware of the interplay of personality and politics, had lived through and corporately experienced the great debates and traumas of 1640–41, above all were subject to forces which tended to polarise and divide. In the counties, on the other hand, the pressures tended to unite the ruling groups and make them increasingly confused about the nature and unsure of the importance of events at Westminster and Whitehall. The central reality for them was the increasing evidence of the collapse of order' – has only been reinforced and nuanced by subsequent scholarship, not invalidated by it.

The account of that collapse of order and the gentry panic has been confirmed by much subsequent work. The assumption behind other work of the 1960s and 1970s, that popular violence was anti-monarchical and helped to build a popular parliamentarianism,[19] has been blown away by subsequent research, which reveals that many of those engaged in riots in 1641/42 were apolitical as far as the growing polarisation into 'royalist' or 'parliamentarian' movements are concerned and many looked to King against Parliament. Some did appeal to Parliament against the Crown and its agents,

18. As fully revealed by Caroline Hibbard, *Charles I and the Popish Plot* (Chapel Hill, NC, 1983). See also W.M. Lamont, *Richard Baxter and the Millennium* (1979) for a gripping account of one man's obsession with the reality of the Popish Plot in 1641–42.

19. See the work of Brian Manning, especially 'The Peasantry and the English Revolution', *Journal of Peasant Studies* 2 (1975), pp. 133–58 and *The English People and the English Revolution 1640–1649* (1976, 1993).

but many did not do so.[20] So I see no reason to modify my conclusion that 'fear drove some men into royalism; it drove far more into neutralism'.[21] There may have been some understatement of the degree of collusion between royal courtiers or parliamentary leaders and local gentry groups in the framing of petitions, especially those relating to religion and to the military build up of 1642 (the Militia Ordinance, the commissions of array),[22] but the gatherings of gentry at the spring and autumn assizes and at Midsummer quarter sessions and the co-ordinated campaigns for local peace and petitioning against the national drift to war *were* a challenge to the hopes and fears of the men of the centre and that section of the book seems in little need of modification.

The Choice of Sides

In 1976 it was still possible in writing a book on the 1640s to dwell on the allegiance of the gentry. Most of the impetuses behind the rethinking of the civil wars were so many exotic funguses growing out of the decaying trunk of the felled 'Gentry Controversy' after all; and the 'county community' school of history was at its zenith – and the 'county community' was construed as a gentry community. The many-headed monster was seen as a source of anarchy and its activities were seen not as significant in themselves but as something that conditioned the behaviour of the gentry. Its role was contingent. The middling sort wandered in and out of the story in rather fuzzy and unclear ways.

20. K.J. Lindley, *Fenland Riots and the English Revolution* (1982), chs 3–4; Buchanan Sharp, *In Contempt of All Authority: Rural Artisans and Riot in the West of England 1586–1660* (Berkeley, 1980), chs 7–8, and his essay 'Rural Discontents and the English Revolution' in R.C. Richardson (ed.), *Town and Countryside in the English Revolution* (1992), pp. 251–69; Andy Wood, 'Beyond Posy-Revisionism? The Civil-War Allegiances of the Miners of the Derbyshire "Peak Country" ', *HJ* 40/1 (1997), pp. 23–40. See in general on this subject, J.S. Morrill and J. Walter, 'Order and Disorder in the English Revolution' in A. Fletcher and J. Stevenson (eds), *Order and Disorder in Early Modern England* (Cambridge, 1985). John Walter's forthcoming study of the riots around Colchester and in the Stour Valley (in press) will be a fundamental breakthrough in our understanding of these matters.

21. Above, p. 54.

22. Judith Maltby's Cambridge Ph.D. thesis on Prayer-Book loyalism, to be published while this book is in press under the title *Prayer Book and People in Elizabethan and Early Stuart England*, contains a detailed and persuasive account of the development of a petitioning campaign to safeguard the Prayer Book in 1641; T.P.S. Woods, *Prelude to Civil War: Mr Justice Malet and the Kentish Petitions* (Salisbury, 1980) is an especially valuable contribution to our understanding of the dialectic between centre and county in 1642.

The Revolt of the Provinces was published almost simultaneously with Brian Manning's *The English People and the English Revolution*, which sought to change all that, and, had my book not yet gone to press, I would have had to recast it in order to take Manning's claims into account. In essence, Manning argued that with the gentry fatally divided, it was politicised and militant sections of the middling sort who grabbed the initiative and forced the country into bloody civil war; and their participation was to ensure Parliament victory over the King. Their class-driven demands were to transform our understanding of the nature of parliamentarianism from a struggle between rival groups within the élite towards a revolutionary outcome. I never accepted Manning's thesis and reviewed it very harshly[23] but it compelled me (more than for several years I cared to admit to myself) to take the question of popular allegiance seriously.

In the aftermath of writing *The Revolt of the Provinces* I was working on a study of Cheshire electoral politics 1543–1974 and on a study of the Cheshire grand jury 1625–59, both of which compelled me to look at popular participation in government in wider contexts, and I concluded that while Manning had correctly identified strands of militant puritan-parliamentarianism amongst the middling sort, and that those strands made a distinctive contribution to 'Roundhead' political culture – and to the outcome of the civil war – he had wilfully failed to look for and had therefore overlooked the strength of Crown and Prayer-Book loyalism that produced equally strong middling-sort royalism (and, I should add, strong middling-sort neutralism too). Much of my work in the late 1970s and early 1980s – resulting for example in the essay on anglican survivalism in the later 1640s – arose from this concern.[24] My own work was then overtaken by that of David Underdown, first in a lecture to the Royal Historical Society[25] and then in his book *Revel, Riot and Rebellion: Popular Politics and Culture in England 1603–1660* (Oxford, 1985). Although I engaged in vigorous and good-natured debate with him on the thesis of his book that popular allegiance could be related to the conditions prevailing in particular and distinctive agricultural and urban regions (*pays* perhaps), with distinctive social, religious, and political popular cultures,[26] I was quite

---

23. Reprinted in J.S. Morrill, *The Nature of the English Revolution* (1993), pp. 214–23.
24. Ibid., ch. 7.
25. David Underdown, 'The Problem of Popular Allegiance in the English Civil War', *TRHS*, 5th ser., Vol. 31 (1981), pp. 69–94.
26. 'The Ecology of Allegiance in the English Civil War' (with a reply by David Underdown) in *JBS* 26/4 (1987), pp. 451–79.

clear (and still am) that Underdown had established that in the 1640s England had a civil war different from all previous civil wars. It was different in that men (and to a minor extent women) deep into society were sufficiently independent economically, socially, culturally (in terms of their access to news and information) to be able to make free political choices.[27] I was also convinced that the proportion of each social group who were active royalists and active parliamentarians was similar. There is a consequence of this in which *The Revolt* anticipates more recent work. I suggested as an aside that the scale of the war and the squeamish, pacifistic sides of so many of the nobility and gentry – 'the divisions and casualties of war' – led to social mobility within *both* parliamentarian and royalist structures, with men from outside the traditional governing élites securing positions of prominence. If anything, there were more plebeian colonels and majors in the royalist armies by 1645 than there were in the New Model.[28] There would have been as many problems in accommodating the personal and political aspirations of these men in the wake of a royalist victory as there were in the wake of the parliamentarian victory. This general point, about the free political choices of the many and not the few and the social consequences of that freedom, has thus left me unpersuaded by the claims of John Adamson (which were deeply influential on the thinking of Conrad Russell, for example) that the civil war was most helpfully seen as a baronial revolt.[29]

The final section of the first chapter therefore needs to be read in that light. It offers an account of the choice of sides that I still believe in *so far as it goes*. The most important thing it does is to

27. Mark Stoyle's *Loyalty and Locality: Popular Allegiance in Devon during the English Civil War* (Exeter, 1994) reaches the same conclusion. A magnificent study of popular as well as élite allegiance inspired by Underdown's work, it too reaches very different conclusions about the prevalence of royalism and parliamentarianism in particular types of *pays*.

28. Above, pp. 73–4. For the social structure of the royalist armies, see Peter Newman, 'The Royalist Officer Corps 1642–1646: Army Command as a Reflection of Social Structure', *HJ* 26 (1983), pp. 226–43; Ronald Hutton, 'The Royalist War Effort' in John Morrill (ed.), *Reactions to the English Civil War* (1982), pp. 51–67; Martyn Bennett, 'Leicestershire's Royalist Officers and the War Effort in the County', *Trans. of the Leics. Archaeological and Historical Soc.* 59 (1985), pp. 44–51; and cf. Ian Gentles, *The New Model* 'Officer Corps in 1647: a collective portrait', *Social History* 22.2 (1997), pp. 129–44.

29. J.S.A. Adamson, 'The Baronial Context of the English Civil War', *TRHS*, 5th ser., Vol. 40 (1990), pp. 93–120. There was a baronial *dimension* to the war and the King may have seen it as a war; but the peers and their allies at Westminster could not launch the war under the slogan 'support your local baron': they had to deploy religious language and a language of popular liberties to get men into the armies they were creating.

show the sheer difficulty and contingency of so many people's choice of sides. If I was reacting in 1976 against a tradition that saw allegiance in positivist or determinist terms, the attempt to explain political behaviour by reference to external social and cultural circumstance,[30] the same discussion protects us against the equally dangerous tendency of seeing the chattering classes of the seventeenth century as deciding what to do on the basis of careful intellectual reflection on literary debates such as those generated by the Militia Ordinance or Charles I's Answer to the Nineteen Propositions. My account also allows for *armchair* politics; for men (and their wives and widows) making their choices on the basis of rational discussion. It allows for *zealous* politics, as religious passion and fear that created millenarian and hellish visions of politics. But it also allows for *deferential* politics – an inability to make a decision and therefore a willingness to accept the lead of a local magnate; it allows for *prudential* politics and a choice of sides that removed or reduced the prospect of immediate plunder; and it allows for *vindictive* politics, a choice of sides to spite a local rival or enemy.[31] It allows for a few men to determine the behaviour of much larger groups of men, as pre-existent local factions hung together against the threat of outside force. Above all it allows for the fact that only a small number of people felt a war was necessary or desirable. Throughout the 1980s I was to argue that that minority were driven by religious militancy (on both sides) and that there were few if any constitutional militants (religious fanaticism created in some of them a constitutional militancy – but never vice versa). Militancy was a

30. I am perfectly happy to accept that I may have over-reacted to the positivism of a previous generation who treated the words of men in the early 1640s as rationalised actings out of culturally conditioned behaviour. Being a member of a rising or a declining family, possessing ancient or recently-acquired wealth and so on, might well have been (almost certainly was) a background factor, creating what in the computer age we might see as the default setting for allegiance. I am currently working on a paper that appears to show a very strong correlation between ownership of former monastic property and active parliamentarianism; and there is much of interest in Conrad Russell, 'Issues in the House of Commons, 1621–1629: Predictors of Civil-War Allegiance', *Albion* 23 (1991), pp. 23–39; and in Wilfrid Prest, 'Predicting Civil War Allegiances: The Lawyers' Case Considered', *Albion* 24 (1992), pp. 225–36.

31. A case in point is my discovery, subsequent to writing the book, that the origins of the feud in Cheshire which divided the county élite at the time both of the 1640 elections and the 1642 choice of sides lay in a struggle for precedence between those who had paid good money to become baronets and those who had paid better (or at any rate more) money to become barons in the Irish peerage. Which group was to take the higher seats at quarter sessions or more prominent places in funeral processions?

psychological condition not an intellectual proposition and it was religion that induced (or at any rate represented the articulated manifestation of) that condition.[32]

All this was a reaction against a way of studying allegiance that began with two boxes, one marked 'royalist' and the other 'parliamentarian' (often with a third marked 'side-changers, neuters and others'). Individuals were then placed in one or other of the boxes, and once this process was complete each box was tipped out and the contents analysed for distinctive characteristics.[33] My argument was and is that such a technique was fundamentally flawed because it forced together men who in 1642 pushed themselves forward, raised troops, garrisoned towns, bullied others in assisting them with money or supplies and those who yearned for peace, worked for peace, tried desperately to prevent the collapse of order in their own localities, but who eventually – with heavy hearts and lack of conviction – gave hesitant and qualified help to one side or the other, perhaps because of a marginally greater fear of sectarianism than of popery, perhaps because they *trusted* the collective wisdom of the men of Westminster more than that of the coterie around the King. It makes no sense to mulch down the many who wanted no part in the war with the few who did. One phrase of mine and one of Brigadier Peter Young's dominate my thinking now as in 1976. Mine was to recognise that it is often less of a political act to obey an order than to disobey it, especially when the person making the order has the power of arrest or the ability to plunder your property. But the sending of a servant to join a regiment, or of a cart of provisions to supply it would be seen by the other side as an act of war, and someone who simply obeyed an order under duress could then find himself on the other side's proscribed list and thus prudently drawn into more and more close links to the side that had originally constrained him.

Brigadier Peter Young's wraith will not, I suspect, mind me saying that two bottles of wine at lunchtime sharpened his wit and gift

32. Morrill, *Nature of the English Revolution*, chs 2–7, which also examines (ch. 2) the objections to my trying to separate out politics and religion. The best and shrewdest analysis that exposes the clumsiness of my earlier attempts to isolate religious motivation by false dichotomies is in Ann Hughes, *The Causes of the English Civil War* (1991).

33. The fullest attempt of this kind is B.G. Blackwood's *The Lancashire Gentry and the Great Rebellion* (Manchester, 1978), an exemplary piece of research but with all the hermeneutic problems here discussed. A full account of my difficulties with this approach can be found in a review article focusing on Blackwood's book and republished in *Nature of the English Revolution*, ch. 9.

for the apt aphorism. Lecturing thus to a roomful of sixth-formers
in the Education Centre in the Tower of London, he explained that
there was much latent royalism in Kent, but that cut off from the
rest of the country by the sea on three sides and parliamentarian
London on the fourth, almost all the gentry felt it prudent to go
along with the prevailing power. His summary had the clarity that
only claret can bring: 'if London had been where Birmingham is,
Kent would have been royalist.' Now that *is* an effective round of
historiographical grapeshot.

The Progress of War

The title of the second chapter was deliberately ambiguous and
ironic. It was about how war was fought, it was about the development of the bureaucracies of war, and it was about the similarities
and differences between the organisations created by the two sides.
There was an inexorable development of sophisticated means of
waging war and supporting the effort of war. But it was also about
the costs of war, the loss of civil liberties, the sufferings of a people
caught up in a war beyond anything that had hitherto been known.
My own subsequent work suggested that one in nine of all Englishmen between the ages of 16 and 50 were in arms at any one point
in the campaigning seasons of 1643–45, and perhaps one in three
or one in four bore arms at some point. One recent estimate is that
more than 80,000 men were killed in the 635 battles, skirmishes
and sieges of the English wars from wounds received in battle and
many more from the contingencies of war,[34] and while many reviewers think this figure may be too high, it is indicative of a death-
rate that was almost certainly higher than that experienced by Britons
in either of the World Wars of the twentieth century.

The burdens of taxation, of free quarter and of plunder varied
enormously from area to area, but everywhere caused immense short-
term hardship to the mass of the population.[35] Parliament alone
was raising more money every six weeks from direct taxation than
ship money had ever raised in a year (or, to put it another way,
Parliament was raising a parliamentary subsidy every fortnight); while

34. Charles Carlton, *Going to the Wars: The Experience of Civil War in the British Isles,
1638–1660* (1994), summarised in Charles Carlton, 'The Impact of the Fighting' in
J. Morrill (ed.), *The Impact of the English Civil War* (1991), pp. 17–31.
35. For one particular aspect graphically described, see Stephen Porter, *Destruction
in the English Civil Wars* (Stroud, 1994), well summarised in 'Property Destruction in
the English Civil Wars', *History Today* 36/8 (1986), pp. 336–41.

the introduction of excise duty (for which there was no precedent) on absolutely basic commodities like salt (the only preservative of meat before the age of the refrigerator) and beer (the staple drink of all the population, given the shortage of safe drinking water, before the arrival of infusion drinks like tea and coffee) hit at the poor even more than the rich. Both sides had to find ways of ensuring that their armies were large enough to hold the area already under control and to liberate other areas; and they had to pay, provision and equip those armies. To do all this required the creation of central, regional and local administrative structures with the ability to run the war.

All this had been explored in depth in a series of important county and urban studies published in the years (indeed in the decades) before 1976, but *The Revolt of the Provinces* was the first attempt to collate this work and to offer an overview that did three things. First, it set out to present coherently the ways in which the experience of war differed from one region to another. But everywhere there was inefficiency, internal disputes and feuds, and tension between local men trying to minimise the disruption of local life and concentrate resources on the defence of their own area, and men at, and of, the centre trying to syphon off resources from the regions to fuel the central war effort, the national armies and the armed struggle in Ireland and Scotland. Secondly, *The Revolt* set out to explain how, in order to win the war, Parliament had to set aside those institutions of local government which depended on local consent and to institute committees that acted by *droit administratif*, policing their own activity (with arbitrary and unlimited powers of arrest, imprisonment and distraint, powers they were widely believed to have abused and misused). It also set out to explain how the King was less willing to suspend existing local institutions and procedures (e.g. quarter sessions) and preferred to try to seek the consent of grand juries to his taxes and sequestrations. Thirdly the chapter seeks to show that Parliament's greater administrative ruthlessness was a major reason for its victory over the King. Unpopular and resisted as many of their military and administrative policies were, they kept their armies in the field and limited the violence of the soldiery against the civilian population. As the King's armies disintegrated from lack of resources, it was the parliamentarians who stayed the course. But they defeated the King only to lose the goodwill of the people at large.

I think this account has stood the test of time. Rereading it after many years, I realised that the cuts required to shoehorn the work into the prescribed maximum length had caused a loss of structural clarity which the changes in this version are intended to ameliorate; but the three-pronged argument seems to me to have been in essence sustained by the mass of scholarship to have appeared since. If in the rest of this section I notice those works that modify aspects of the thesis of the chapter, they seem to me to be refinements rather than challenges. All the major surveys of the decade rooted in primary research, such as those of Robert Ashton, Derek Hirst, John Kenyon and Martyn Bennett,[36] confirm the points I am making, I think. A wealth of specific scholarship has confirmed crucial links in the argument. Ross Lee's edition of the grand jury charges given to the Bedfordshire quarter sessions in the mid-1640s[37] contains graphic accounts of the anger of 'moderates' at the arbitrary powers of county committees; William Epstein's article on Judge David Jenkins is a study of one of the great scourges of county-committee rule, who was tried for treason on account of it;[38] while a series of articles by Jean Mather follow up on the themes of the book.[39]

The Revolt of the Provinces grew out of my own doctoral thesis on Cheshire, a Palatine county with a particularly tightly-knit gentry community and a characteristic set of county institutions that made it one of the most self-contained and inward-looking of all the shires. At the time that I was writing, the leading study was Alan Everitt's *The Community of Kent and the Great Rebellion*. Kent too was an unusual county – as we just reminded ourselves, with sea on three sides and London on the fourth, and with a social system that was unique and made for a high rate in intermarriage within the county. Although I had read and taken note of more than a dozen other counties, I now recognise that I allowed two counties at one end of the spectrum for self-containedness to be my stereotypical counties. Coming from a background in the study of Cheshire had

36. Robert Ashton, *The English Civil War: Conservatism and Revolution 1603–49* (1978, 1989); and his essay 'From Cavalier to Roundhead Tyranny, 1642–9' in Morrill (ed.), *Reactions to the English Civil War*, pp. 185–206; Derek Hirst, *Authority and Conflict: England 1603–58* (1986); J.P. Kenyon, *The Civil Wars in England: A Military History of the Three Civil Wars 1642–1651* (1988); Martyn Bennett, *The Civil Wars in Britain and Ireland 1638–1651* (1997).

37. Ross Lee (ed.), *Law and Local Society in the Time of Charles I: Bedfordshire and the English Civil War*, Bedfordshire Historical Record Society 65 (1986).

38. W. Epstein, 'Judge David Jenkins and the Great Civil War', *Jnl. of Legal History* 9 (1982), pp. 187–221.

39. See especially Jean Mather, 'The Parliamentary Committees and the Justices of the Peace', *Am. Jnl. Legal History* 23/2 (1979), pp. 120–43; and 'The Moral Code of the English Civil War and Interregnum', *The Historian* 44 (1982), pp. 207–28.

a second distorting effect: the absence of corporate towns and parliamentary boroughs other than the county town of Chester. Town–country tensions were largely missing from the book. Since then the major county studies have all had a corrective effect: Ann Hughes's study of Warwickshire most obviously, but also Clive Holmes's study of Lincolnshire and Stephen Roberts's study of Devon; and there has been an explosion of urban studies for cities and towns of all sizes: Bristol, Exeter, Gloucester, Coventry, Windsor, Devizes, Pontefract, Bridgnorth and many more.[40]

The cumulative effect is to show an even greater range of responses by particular communities to the onset of civil war and a greater sense that loyalties to areas *smaller* than that of a county and *larger* than that of a county were more significant than this book recognised. In this respect perhaps the most important study of all was Philip Tennant's study of a *war zone*, the south midlands corridor spreading out from the strategic crossroads and frontier zone formed by the area in south and north Warwickshire bounded by Coventry, Oxford and Evesham.[41] The fluidity of county borders, the fact that military zones were defined by physical geography and not by administrative districts could have been more fully brought out in this book. It is now clear that the fact that the bulk of the records were generated by county committees created an archivally-driven emphasis on county-mindedness that overstated an important case. It is also clear that in exploring the heavy-handedness of county committees I may have understated the violence and intimidation perpetrated by soldiers. The English civil war saw little of the wilful destruction of civilian life and property, little of the scorched-earth policy of some theatres of the Thirty Years War or the Irish theatre of the War of the Three Kingdoms, but that was small comfort to those who lived in the suburbs pulled down by defenders so that houses close to thick medieval walls could not be used by besieging armies; it did not console the churchgoers of Scarborough who found cannon mounted in the church so that it could be protected from hostile fire as it lobbed cannon balls through the great East window into the castle; it did not console the inhabitants of Bolton and Leicester after they had been sacked

40. I traced fifteen through a search on *The Royal Historical Society Bibliography on CD-ROM: The History of Britain, Ireland and the British Overseas.* A particularly interesting cluster of articles can be found in R.C. Richardson (ed.), *Town and Countryside in the English Revolution* (1992) – i.e. Keith Lindley on London, David Scott on York, Ann Hughes on Coventry, David Harris Sacks on Bristol and Ian Roy on Oxford.

41. Philip Tennant, *Edgehill and Beyond: The People's War in the South Midlands 1642–1645* (Gloucester, 1992).

by Rupert. The book could have done with a paragraph or two on these matters.[42]

On the other hand subsequent work has only reinforced the evidence for the way that administrative confusion – the untidy creation of overlapping jurisdictions for example – and internecine strife on both sides weakened the war effort, but left all too many civilians caught in the crossfire. Forthcoming work by Sue Sadler, on the imprisonment, violence and torture practised by one group of Cambridgeshire commissioners on another will add spectacularly to this account.[43] Her work also explains how a constant dread of marauding armies and the reality of taxation, the more ruthlessly raised because of the lack of plunder and free quarter, could create an atmosphere of fear and despair almost as great as that in warzones more torn by fighting. In that sense her work bears out the thesis of this book especially well.

Only on one major point has the argument of this chapter been strongly challenged. Ann Hughes has suggested that my account of the 'tyrannical' practices of the county committees is exaggerated, perhaps to the point of distortion. Certainly jury trial, access to habeas corpus, local assent to rates, were suspended; but the committees followed forms of due process recognisably based on earlier patterns of behaviour by those commissioned by Exchequer or Chancery. More importantly, she has argued that my view of localism as intrinsically antipathetic to the functional radicalism of war, a natural obstructiveness that had to be overcome and coerced, is too simplistic:

> Overcoming localism was not the key to victory in the civil war.
> Rather in a political system characterised above all by an inextricable
> intertwining of local and national concerns, the political basis for
> victory involved the harnessing of local interests, cooperation with,

42. Porter, *Destruction, passim*; Mark Stoyle, 'Whole Streets Converted to Ashes: Property Destruction in Exeter during the English Civil War', *Southern History* 16 (1994), pp. 62–81; Ian Roy, 'England Turned Germany? The Aftermath of the Civil War in its European Context', *TRHS*, 5th ser., Vol. 28 (1978), pp. 127–44; Ian Roy, 'The English Civil War and English Society', *War and Society*, Vol. 1 (1975), pp. 24–43; B. Donagan, 'Atrocity, War Crime and Treason in the English Civil War', *Am. Hist. Review* 99 (1994), pp. 1137–66; B. Donagan, 'Codes and Conduct in the English Civil War', *P. and P.* 118 (1988), pp. 85–115; B. Donagan, 'Prisoners in the English Civil War', *History Today* 41/3 (1991), pp. 28–35; Jack Binns, '*A Place of Great Importance': Scarborough in the Civil Wars* (Stroud, 1994), pp. 142–3.
43. To be presented in a Ph.D. from Anglia Polytechnic University, and hopefully then published. See also D.F. Mosler, 'The "Other Civil War": Internecine Politics in the Warwickshire County Committees, 1642–1659', *Midland History* 6 (1980), pp. 58–75.

not a challenge to, localism, and the maintenance of the maximum of harmony between the local and the national. Parliament, for a variety of structural, institutional and ideological reasons, was better able to work with localism than was the King.[44]

Her case study of the operation of the Indemnity Committee, which protected soldiers and civilian officers for things done *tempore et loci belli* by setting aside judgements against them in the restored common law courts, is especially telling.[45]

I think that what she has exposed is a rhetorical confusion in my work. I was (still am) on the side of the victims of the war. I was seeing it through their eyes and reporting what they saw. There was a failure of objectivity in such statement as 'this chapter is largely concerned with the development and nature of parliamentarian tyranny' (above, p. 76). It should at the very least have contained a 'what many who experienced it took to be' before the last two words. I can see now that the committee-men and the generals were basically upright men fighting a desperate war and scrambling with endless new contingencies, scrapping for scarce resources not only with the enemy but with other groups on their own side, caught between the demands of generals and captains for men, money and supplies and a civilian population desperate for peace. They were caught between instructions to send money off to Westminster for a national war and to their local garrison commander to spare him the necessity of relying on military requisition. For the most part they tried to follow rules of natural justice and to adapt customary procedures to the special circumstances of total war. My respect for their attempted integrity was much enhanced by detailed study of one of the most unattractive of them – William Dowsing, the commissioner for the counties of the Eastern Associ-

---

44. Ann Hughes, 'The King, the Parliament and the Localities during the English Civil War', *JBS* 24 (1985), pp. 236–63 (quotation is from p. 241); 'Militancy and Localism: Warwickshire Politics and Westminster Politics 1643–1647', *TRHS*, 5th ser., Vol. 31 (1981), pp. 51–68. Ann Hughes's admirably fair and firm characterisation and criticism of the 'county community' school is as much directed against the work of Ronald Hutton and Anthony Fletcher as against *The Revolt of the Provinces* (and especially against Ronald Hutton, *The Royalist War Effort 1642–1646* (London, 1982) and the essays of Hutton and Fletcher in Morrill (ed.), *Reactions to the English Civil War*).

45. Ann Hughes, 'Parliamentary Tyranny? Indemnity Proceedings and the Impact of the Civil War: A Case Study from Warwickshire', *Midland History* 11 (1986), pp. 49–78. Cf. Robert Ashton, 'The Problem of Indemnity' in C. Jones, M. Newitt, S. Roberts (eds), *Politics and People in Revolutionary England* (Oxford, 1986), pp. 117–40 and William Epstein, 'The Committee for Examinations and Parliamentary Justice 1642–1647', *Jnl. Legal Hist.* 7/1 (1986), pp. 3–22.

ation appointed to remove the monuments of idolatry and superstition from all the churches. He was, as I termed him, the bureaucratic puritan, the grim reaper of saintly effigies and images in glass, the clipper of angels' wings on roof-beams and of haloes on fonts. But he stuck to the letter of the ordinances under which he served, and since the ordinances required him to remove images of the host of heaven and of sanctified human beings but did not refer to images of Satan, he removed the former, but left the Devil intact.[46] So I would accept that I overstated the case for parliamentary tyranny and the degree of coercion involved.

But I have remained puzzled by some aspects of Hughes's argument. I never denied that many county committee-men, especially those committed to an outright victory and to godly reformation, were willing to co-operate with the centre; simply that those who had been reluctant to get involved in war were reluctant to see traditional forms and structures set aside in a war which they saw as intended to preserve a rule of law menaced by the King and now wrecked by the managers of the war, and I cannot see that interpretation challenged by her work. And while it may be true that 'on the evidence of surviving correspondence it seems that Royalist military commanders were *generally* more contemptuous of civilian participation than their Parliamentarian counterparts',[47] it is unclear to me why this was not the *consequence* of the process I described, the King's insistence that consent be sought for all royalist contributions, grand jury indictment necessary for the sequestration of parliamentarian property etc. An over-reliance on co-operation created shortages in supplies that created the frustration and abuses that she chronicles. It is true that *some* royalist commanders would have been more impatient and haughty in any case (Prince Rupert most obviously),[48] but I would dispute her 'generally'. The fullest study of one of the royalist generals with a bad reputation – Henry Hastings, Earl of Loughborough – tends to confirm my interpretation: he worked with and through a civilian administrative system as patiently and as long as he could, and his attitudes to

46. John Morrill, 'William Dowsing, the Bureaucratic Puritan' in John Morrill, Paul Slack, Daniel Woolf (eds), *Public Men and Private Conscience in Seventeenth-Century England* (Oxford, 1993), pp. 173–204. This has now been reworked and developed in 'William Dowsing and the Administration of Iconoclasm in the English Revolution' in Trevor Cooper (ed.), *The Journals of William Dowsing*, Ecclesiological Society, (forthcoming, 1999).
47. Hughes, 'King, the Parliament and the Localities', p. 253.
48. Above, pp. 115–18.

plunder were no different from that of his parliamentarian opponents in the east midlands.[49] I would thus stick by my view that 'generally' the King's party seemed the more restrained and committed to co-operation with the localities until his cause began to collapse, at which point his commanders were forced back, with varying degrees of willingness, on extortion and terror.

Nonetheless, I believe that Chapter 2 is still the best and most important chapter in the book. Its motto was the words of Lord Wharton: 'they were not tied to a law, for these were times of necessity and imminent danger', and they still seem to me the motto of the decade. Honourable men struggled to act justly within that framework. In the end, the dialectic between a rhetoric of fighting to protect liberties and the reality of the times of necessity produced an administrative system that won the war. But the effect of that kind of war on local communities the majority of whose members had never believed in that necessity, had sought to avoid involvement, and who fervently believed that it could have been avoided and could still be settled by negotiation was precisely the pattern of resistance that is chronicled in Chapter 3.

Reactions to War, 1643–49

This third chapter looks at the way the war effort of both sides was impeded by the inertia and passive resistance of individuals and groups at two major waves of violent resistance: the Clubman risings of 1644–46 and the 'Revolt of the Provinces' itself – the English aspects of the second civil war of 1648. The motto of this chapter can be found in its second paragraph, and I *almost* stand by it now:

> Instead of a nation full of fearful neutrals, undecided which way to turn, there developed a nation full of embittered, desperate neutrals, seeking first to hide from the war and then, driven from their hiding places, determined to stand and fight the implications of war, the betrayal of fundamental rights and liberties. In 1642, the political nation feared the spectre of mob rule. By 1645 it confronted those in power who had shown themselves to be mindless of shared values and traditional rights. (See above, p. 123.)

49. Bennett, 'Leicestershire's Royalist Officers', pp. 44–51; and he reinforces the point in his comparative article on the funding of war by the two sides in the north midlands: 'Contribution and Assessment: Financial Exactions in the English Civil War, 1642–1646', *War and Society* 4/1 (1986), pp. 1–11.

It is now clear that I tried to impose too much coherence and unity on the mindset of those in the various 'Clubman' movements and 'Peaceable Armies'; and I think I mistook an aspect of the second civil war for its core. I would no longer defend the final pages of the book. I should also admit that I think there is a serious gap or eloquent silence in the book which is only partially explained by the extreme pressure of space. In retrospect it was a mistake and a distortion to ignore the Levellers.

They matter because the Leveller movement (and I do believe there is one) was as much a manifestation of popular revulsion at the effects of war as the other movements which I did describe. I did not discuss them for a variety of reasons. One was that they were essentially a London-based movement and I was not considering London as a province of England (that itself is now something I would challenge). Another was that they appeared to have been studied too much and too repetitively.[50] Ironically my work on provincial armies and work-in-progress on the internal history of the New Model Army in 1647[51] persuaded me that the Levellers made even less impact outside London than I had thought. That did not, however, absolve me from explaining the nature of their thought as a manifestation of the despair at a war won at unacceptable cost; nor from explaining just why 'the radical conservatism of the Clubmen was more characteristic of the later 1640s than the iconoclasm of the Levellers' (above, p. 122). In fact, we still do not have a thorough answer to that question. The Levellers have the great advantage that their thought is so readily accessible in hundreds of pamphlets, many of them containing narratives of the movement and its sufferings, and this has absolved historians from the need to undertake fundamental archival work to establish the lineaments of the movement. Murray Tolmie's discussion of the way so much Leveller activity in 1646–49 was parasitic upon the structures of the London General Baptist churches is the most important contribution to the structures of the movement to have appeared so far;[52]

50. *The Royal Historical Society Bibliography on CD-ROM: The History of Britain, Ireland and the British Overseas* indexes fourteen books and nineteen articles published between 1900 and 1975 which deal extensively with the Levellers (half of them in the 1960s and early 1970s). It lists one article on the Clubmen – untranslated from the Russian!

51. The resultant essays are reprinted in Morrill, *Nature of the English Revolution* as chs 17 and 16.

52. M. Tolmie, *The Triumph of the Saints: The Gathered Churches of London 1616–49* (1977), chs 7 and 8. Cf. Norah Carlin, 'Leveller Organisation in London', *HJ* 27 (1984), pp. 955–60.

but Phil Baker's forthcoming Cambridge Ph.D. exploring the history of more than 100 men associated with the dissemination of their ideas will transform our understanding. Meanwhile, Brian Manning's account of the attempt by the Levellers to create a programme of social and economic reform to answer the clamours of the countryside deepens the mystery of their lack of success outside London.[53] If, as Mark Kishlansky and I have argued,[54] there was in Leveller rhetoric a fundamental suspicion of standing armies and if there was far less Leveller support in the Army than was thought in 1976, and if the Levellers – a few major petitions apart – organised through General Baptist churches which were simply too thinly scattered and autonomous to act as a national distribution network, the general failure of the movement to evangelise seems likely to have been organisational rather than ideological.

That perspective apart, much of this chapter remains uncontentious and undisturbed by more recent work. The case studies of individuals caught up in the war, of village communities trying to hold it at bay, refusing to allow vendettas and feuds to add to their miseries, stand up to most subsequent work.[55] Similarly, the anti-war stirs of 1643, and the ability of King and Parliament to make common cause with those resentful of the wartime impositions of their opponents – as in the 'Movement for One-and-All' in 1644 – have been largely uncontentious. Indeed, I suspect that the radical implications of the sections on the parliamentary reactions to the collapse of support for them in 1646–47 (pp. 169–72) as they failed to turn military victory into constitutional settlement have still to be fully worked out.

We are still some way from understanding the dynamics of the Long Parliament. The older mechanical accounts of 'two or three parties' (or even more) have long been unsatisfactory, although David Underdown's account of the later 1640s in his *Pride's Purge* (1970) combines a traditional taxonomy with a sensitive account of the mood-swings amongst the majority of MPs, whose loyalties were

53. Manning, *English People*, chs 10–11.
54. M.A. Kishlansky, *The Rise of the New Model Army* (Cambridge, 1979) and a string of articles, perhaps most notably 'Consensus Politics and the Structure of Debate at Putney', *JBS* 20/1 (1981), pp. 50–69. See also J.S. Morrill and P. Baker, 'The Case of the Army Truly Re-Stated', forthcoming.
55. Bill Cliftlands in 'The Godly and the Well-Affected in Essex 1642–9', University of Essex Ph.D. thesis (1984) has shown while what I say on pp. 125–32 above is broadly true for Essex, there was more co-operation from within some communities over the identification and punishment of 'delinquents' and over the cleansing of churches of monuments of idolatry and superstition than my account allowed for.

less to power-groups at the centre than to their local communities. Since then, the most convincing analysis of the way bicameral groups operated and shifted in relation to one another is that of John Adamson in his unpublished Ph.D. thesis,[56] some parts of which have been published in article form.[57] Mark Kishlansky[58] and others have convincingly demonstrated the way that evidence has been abused to strengthen the thesis, and that the particular claims about the relations of the parliamentary caucuses to the Army Grandees are clearly wrong. But the analysis of fluid groupings and their kaleidoscopic relations one to another has a conceptual force that previous accounts lacked. The task now is to show how these groups had to work to secure the support of blocs of provincial MPs – ex county bosses and their allies – for many of whom the reduction of the military presence, fiscal burdens and the end to county committees was crucial. Two studies offer a very clear lead in this respect. Lotte Mulligan has shown how MPs whose estates were under parliamentarian control had a very different attitude to peace negotiations from that of MPs whose estates were occupied by the royalists.[59] David Scott has shown how the occupation of the northern counties created a political reaction in Westminster amongst MPs from that region.[60] These are two straightforward demonstrations of how a better understanding of the reactions to war in the provinces could affect the ability of caucus leaders to command majority support in the two Houses. And the perspectives of this book could help with the elucidation of that set of problems.

The Clubmen and the Peaceable Armies

The Clubmen were perfectly well known before I wrote about them in *The Revolt of the Provinces*. Two theses had been written about

56. J.S.A. Adamson, 'The Peerage in Politics 1645–1649, University of Cambridge Ph.D. thesis (1986).

57. Especially J.S.A. Adamson, 'Parliamentary Management, Men of Business and the House of Lords, 1643–9' in Clyve Jones (ed.), *A Pillar of the Constitution: The House of Lords in British Politics 1640–1784* (1989), pp. 21–50; J.S.A. Adamson, 'The English Peerage and the Projected Settlement of 1647', *HJ* 30 (1987), pp. 567–602.

58. M.A. Kishlansky, 'Saye What?', *HJ* 33 (1990), pp. 917–37; J.S.A. Adamson, 'Politics and the Nobility in Civil War England', *HJ* 34 (1991), pp. 231–55; M.A. Kishlansky, 'Saye No More', *JBS* 30 (1991), pp. 399–448. This seems to have settled the issue.

59. L. Mulligan, 'Property and Parliamentary Politics in the English Civil War, 1642–1646', *Historical Studies: Australia and New Zealand* 16 (1975), pp. 341–61.

60. David Scott, 'The Northern Gentlemen, the Parliamentary Independents, and Anglo-Scottish Relations in the Long Parliament' *HJ* (forthcoming).

them[61] and they had been discussed in a number of regional mono-graphs, most notably David Underdown's study of Somerset in the civil war and interregnum (1973). But little or no notice was taken of them in any of the standard textbooks and that at least has changed. The existence of groups determined to put local people back in charge of their own area and to limit the demands that could be and were made by marching armies and settled garrisons on the civilian population, and who were in many cases willing to put pressure on Parliament and on the King for an early negotiated settlement, is now a commonplace of all the new generation of civil-war textbooks. But much more detailed work has been under-taken on particular Clubman risings and several aspects of my dis-cussion have been challenged.

I argued that the Clubmen and the Peaceable Armies originated within local communities (usually along war corridors) which formed natural farming and marketing regions within particular counties or occasionally straddling the boundary of adjacent counties (most obviously the Dorset–Wiltshire border). Leadership lay with articu-late, literate middling sorts and country lawyers, sometimes with active support, even leadership, from clergymen. Each Clubman group was reacting against one or both of the regional armies of King or Parliament and local experience often prejudiced them more against the one than against the other. Their aims were either to threaten force as a way of keeping armed troops from both sides out of their area, or to confine them to garrisons while the Clubmen themselves assessed, levied and handed over whatever taxes or contributions they thought fair and just to the garrisons. They were willing to talk to local, regional and national commanders and to enter into deals with them, thus sometimes appearing to favour one side more than the other. And they were willing to put forward proposals to encourage a national peace settlement. I cer-tainly recognised that there were differences as between the move-ments in different counties, but I sought to assimilate them to a shared commitment to limiting the effects of war. The differences were over tactics rather than underlying philosophy. The motto of my interpretation was that while some groups preferred King to Parliament or Parliament to King, they preferred peace above both. Peace was the aim, deals with one side or the other a means to that end. It led me to a clear overstatement: 'there is overwhelming

---

61. Those by Manning and Lynch itemised in the list of acknowledgements to the 1976 edition and reprinted above, p. vii.

evidence that most of the Clubmen were neutrals' (above, p. 134). It is a view that has been influential and entered into most of the textbooks of the period and into some more specialist articles and books. Gerald Aylmer, in his Presidential Address to the Royal Historical Society on 'Collective Mentalities in Mid Seventeenth-Century England', preferred my interpretation to those which had sought to modify it, 'remaining inclined to the more old-fashioned view [*sic!*] that the Clubmen were against whichever army was on their backs at a particular time and place'.[62] The broadest and most detailed analysis of groups of Clubmen has been provided by David Underdown. His study of the Clubmen of Dorset, Wiltshire and Somerset was an important part of his more general study of what I termed 'the ecology of allegiance', the ways in which the economic and social structures of the uplands and the downlands (the wood/pasture and sheep/corn regions), together with their power structures, and (in the broadest sense) their religious and political cultures helped to shape the response of the middling and lower sort of people to the collapse of royal government. For him there were regions with 'royalist' (as against pro-royalist) Clubmen and 'parliamentarian' (as against pro-parliamentarian) Clubmen: 'support for King or Parliament was influenced by the type of community in which they lived.' For me the bias in any Clubmen group depended on the state of the war in a region; for Underdown it was a predisposition based on the life-experience of the inhabitants. My doubts about the Underdown thesis on the Clubmen can be found as part of my general scepticism about his general thesis.[63] But I have to say that may be a mistake; for Mark Stoyle, whose superb study of popular allegiance in Devon seems to me *the* outstanding contribution to the debate, while generally critical of Underdown's 'ecological' pattern, finds for him very clearly on that point:

> pre-existent allegiance patterns,[64] rather than an automatic response to military depredations, were what chiefly determined the stance of the Devon Clubmen . . . We must conclude with Underdown that the

62. G.E. Aylmer, 'Collective Mentalities in Mid Seventeenth-Century England: IV. Cross Currents – Neutrals, Trimmers and Others', *TRHS*, 5th ser., Vol. 39 (1989), p. 8.

63. David Underdown, *Revel, Riot and Rebellion: Popular Politics and Culture in England 1603–1660* (Oxford, 1985), chs 6, 8, 9; David Underdown, 'The Chalk and the Cheese: Contrasts Amongst the English Clubmen', *P. and P.* 85 (1979), pp. 25–48. And see the debate between us, initiated by my article 'The Ecology of Allegiance in the English Revolution', *JBS* 26/4 (1987), pp. 451–79.

64. These patterns are not, for Stoyle, determined by the sheep/corn, woodland/pasture dichotomy (Stoyle, *Loyalty and Locality*, Part III).

Clubmen were not true neutrals and indeed, to regard the Clubmen as belonging to a distinct movement of any sort, let alone a truly neutralist one, may well be a mistake.

In a most telling passage he shows how those who, armed with clubs and agricultural implements, resisted royalist incursions in 1643–44, when there was no parliamentarian army around, came from precisely the same parts of the county as the anti-royalist Clubmen of 1645–46: 'it is surely misleading to divorce the second group of risings from the first and treat them as a phenomenon which was altogether new'.[65] Other historians have challenged the freedom of the Clubmen movements from gentry infiltration and subversion by agents of the two sides. Ronald Hutton found the Worcestershire Clubmen being infiltrated and ultimately destroyed by royalist agents.[66]

I am prepared to haul up a white flag in the presence of Stoyle's argument. I think I did not sufficiently relate the movements of 1645–46 to the movements of 1642–44 which I had described earlier in the book. But while showing that there was a touch of naiveté in my portrait of the true neutralism of the Clubmen (a willingness to take rhetoric at face value which was a general hazard of my writing in the 1970s and 1980s, I think), nothing in Stoyle's account damages the significance I wanted to attribute to the Clubmen: the problem they represented to both sides in trying to win the war and the problems for the parliamentarians in being able to control the country after the war was over. Something that Ronald Hutton wrote, with the Worcestershire Clubmen in mind, strikes me as just as significant and as being deeply supportive of my argument:

> If one adopts a purely local viewpoint, then they represent an eminently sensible reaction to the war, to set up workable local mechanisms for the preservation of the countryside from plunder . . . On the other hand, if one adopts any wider view they represented all the short-sightedness and ignorance of truly backward people. They wilfully destroyed the one chance of the one body potentially powerful enough to exert any proper control over an undisciplined regular soldiery and preserve local order [i.e. the royalist Gentry Association].[67]

65. Ibid., ch 6; quotations from pp. 131 and 132.
66. Ronald Hutton, *The Royalist War Effort 1642–6* (1980), chs 15–16; Ronald Hutton, 'The Worcestershire Clubmen in the English Civil War', *Midland History* 5 (1979), pp. 39–49; cf., however, Paul Gladwish, 'The Herefordshire Clubmen: A Reassessment', *Midland History* 10 (1985), pp. 62–71.
67. Hutton, 'The Worcestershire Clubmen', p. 43.

This is compatible with my view and Stoyle's. The Clubmen were a square-peg movement, radical in their challenge to national bodies and values, radical in their defiance of gentry leadership and power, conservative in their adherence to the forms, processes, values of rural life. No wonder Frances Dow, in her survey of *Radicalism in the English Revolution 1640–1660* (Oxford, 1985), mentions them several times, but in the end offers a lengthy discussion only in an appendix to her fifth and final chapter.

The Second Civil War: A Very British Crisis

In the first draft of this book, back in 1975, I wrote more than 10,000 words on the second civil war, and I dubbed it *The Revolt of the Provinces*, a revolt against the failure of the victorious Parliament to achieve a settlement with the King, its failure to scale down the Army and the taxation to finance the Army, and its failure to stand down the hated county committees. I cut that chapter back to a five-page coda of Chapter 3 of the book because of pressure of space and am now very glad that I did so. For a wealth of subsequent scholarship has shown that I had mistaken the part for the whole. There was a link between the seething discontent of provincial communities across England in the first half of 1648 and the armed uprisings and insurrections in Kent, East Anglia, the Welsh Borders, North and South Wales and the northern counties and more spottily in the midlands; but it was simplistic to conclude that the events of the second civil war were essentially 'a revolt of the provinces' and that disillusionment and defeatism, paralysis brought on by the effects of sequestration and composition – and anger at the Scots treaty which appeared to commit the King to presbyterianism – made the old cavaliers stay at home while disaffected parliamentarians and those hitherto non-aligned rose in uncoordinated spasms of despair and yearning for a settlement. In essence, I gave the case study which most nearly fits the thesis I wanted to advance – the revolt in South Wales – and a confused account of another – the Kentish revolt – and it is just as well I did not overstate my case at inflated length.

In essence there were two separate sets of events in 1648 and they were much more loosely connected than the truncated account in this book (and in the suppressed full version) would allow. There were all the manifestations of frustration, anger and disaffection of which I wrote; but they did not turn generally or normally to armed insurrection.

It is now clear that there was more *organised* backlash against the Long Parliament and its committees, and against the standing army in 1647, than I chronicled in 1975. There were more petitions to the Parliament, more protests by grand juries, more direct action at local level against committee-men and their agents. Perhaps the most startling aspect of this is what in 1983 I christened 'the Prayer Book rebellion' as all over England bands of men and women acted to remove from their pulpits and parsonages ministers intruded by parliamentary committees and to reintrude ministers removed for ceremonialism or Prayer-Book loyalism years before. Ministers who refused to use the proscribed Book of Common Prayer, especially in the administration of the sacraments or at funerals, were confronted and assaulted. This happened in hitherto solidly parliamentarian areas as much as in hitherto royalist areas.[68]

There were riots in at least six counties in late December 1647 against the ban on the celebration of Christmas and its accompanying secular festivities. As winter turned to spring, there were demands for a number of incompatible things from different counties or from different groups in the same county: for the overturning of Parliament's Vote of No Addresses and an immediate personal treaty with the King; for Parliament to restore the use of the Prayer Book or to revoke the tolerationist ordinances of 1647 and legislate for the full implementation of presbyterianism; for an end of the standing army, the removal of garrisons, for the payment of arrears to local standing militias; for the end of county committees; for the return of moneys from the sequestration of royalist estates and from composition fines paid by delinquents to discharge local debts (e.g. to discharge debentures for quartering). Some of these activities drifted into demonstrations and some of the demonstrations into spontaneous violence, such as the Clubmen risings in defence of Prayer-Book loyalists in Dorset in March, or the riots in Bury St Edmunds following scuffles around a maypole in early May, and above all the widespread riots in Kent after the re-arrest of men by the county committee acquitted at the assizes for an illegal game of football at Christmas. In the south-west, in the Welsh Marches, and most notably in Pembrokeshire, local military forces mutinied over arrears and mistreatment by local committees, and called for a

---

68. For this paragraph see Robert Ashton, *Counter-Revolution: The Second Civil War and its Origins 1646–8* (London and New Haven, 1994), esp. chs VI–VIII; and for the 'Prayer Book Rebellion' see Morrill, *Nature of the English Revolution,* pp. 170–5. Ashton's book should have been titled *The Origins of the Second Civil War,* for it runs out of steam and conviction on 1648. But its discussion of 1647 is indeed magisterial.

national settlement as a context for the just settlement of their own
particular grievances. In many of these incidents there were calls
for a personal treaty and a national settlement; but not in every one
of them; and in those that did call for a personal treaty, it was a call
for a *negotiated settlement.*[69]

At the same time, often in the same areas but also in the far
north, former royalist army officers and prominent *known* royalist
gentry and nobles were trying to raise fresh troops to serve in the
King's name and to restore him unconditionally. They were preoccupied with a *non-negotiated settlement.*[70]

And there is the rub. These are the two dimensions to the English unrest of 1648 and they were not readily miscible. As the most
perceptive of all those to write on the events of 1648, Brian Lyndon,
put it:

> It was the Royalists' business to co-ordinate [m]uch [of the] sporadic
> and purely particularist outbreaks, just as it was the Parliament's
> terror to think of such a concerted, concentric onslaught. That such
> Royalist co-ordination was intended and attempted is beyond ques-
> tion. Provincial disturbances, at the least, would serve as distractions
> for Parliamentary forces until Scots troops entered England in the
> King's interest.[71]

He has also offered a detailed case study of the way a series of
separate protests in Essex – over military matters, taxation and religion – were all infiltrated by ex-royalists, and of how the leaders of
each of those protests fell away and a minority of those who had
joined their localist movements got sucked into a much nastier
insurrection to their ultimate misfortune.[72] And in his last and most
compelling article he demonstrated that point for county after
county across the south and west of England.[73]

69. Brian Lyndon, 'The South and the Start of the Second Civil War', *History*, 71/
233 (1986), pp. 393–407. Shortly after the publication of this article, Brian Lyndon
died in a car crash, leaving the major study he was completing tragically unfin-
ished. For this paragraph see also Ashton, *Counter-Revolution*, ch. XII, Bennett, *Civil
Wars in Britain and Ireland*, pp. 284–310 and D. Hirst, *Authority and Conflict* (1986),
pp. 276–85.

70. The most robust up-to-date narratives of these and other aspects of the second civil war are in John Kenyon, *The Civil Wars of England* (1988), pp. 176–99 and
Bennett, *Civil Wars in Britain and Ireland*, pp. 284–310.

71. B.P. Lyndon, 'The Parliament's Army in Essex, 1648', *Jnl. of Army Historical
Research* 58 (1980), pp. 140–60, 59 (1981), pp. 230–42 (quotation from Vol. 58,
p. 142).

72. Brian Lyndon, 'Essex and the King's Cause in 1648', *HJ* 29 (1986), pp. 17–40.

73. Lyndon, 'The South and the Start of the Second Civil War'.

This is where I had elided things. I had assumed that the major risings of the second civil war were a subset of the murmurings and protests that could be found everywhere in those months. I had filtered out the separate royalist risings that blazed out in East Anglia and the south-east. I had treated the Scottish dimension as wholly separate, whereas the *fact* of the King's Engagement with the Scots was something that deterred the 'personal treaty men' from joining the 'imposed settlement men'. And I had left out of account entirely the King's willingness to make deals with Irish nobles – albeit protestant ones – for the delivery of troops from Ireland to assist the war effort. By now, no Englishman with pro-vincialist attitudes would look complacently at *any* troops sent over from Ireland. The clause in the Engagement which allowed the King to bring Irish catholic troops into Britain so long as they served under British officers only made that matter worse.

The second civil war was *not* a series of uncoordinated localist risings. There was consistent royalist striving to stimulate and to link up all kinds of protest everywhere. In South Wales there was slightly more royalist involvement with the disaffected parliament-arian officers than I allowed for (but the story is in essence as I described it in pp. 174–6), but in Essex, the motley combination of forces from at least six counties who became holed up in Colches-ter were hard-core royalists leading a motley assortment of ex-cava-liers and of men who had risen up as part of the various protest movements and who then became syphoned off – as their original leaders slipped back into the woodwork – into a royalist army. Per-haps the best way of looking at the complexities and swirling cross-currents of 1648 is the way Ian Gentles looked at London's élite. He speaks of the city fathers – the equivalent of the malcontent wartime élite of remoter shires – pressing for a personal treaty but finding themselves

> in an excruciating dilemma . . . Would they yield to the weight of pub-lic opinion . . . to bring the King back at almost any price? Or would they toe the line laid down by the Commons [and Army]? . . . The dilemma explains the political paralysis at the height of the crisis. Detesting [the Army] and all [it] represented, they could still not bring themselves to risk everything with the insurgents.[74]

In 1976 I suggested that in 1648 the men of provincial England seized the initiative in a way they had failed to do in 1642. They

74. Ian Gentles, 'The Struggle for London in the Second Civil War', *HJ* 26/2 (1983), p. 304.

were principles in the struggle for power and their values were the ones over which that second civil war was fought. I was wrong. In 1648, just as in 1642, they aspired and gave up without a real fight. Provincialism in 1648, like provincialism in 1642, went off not with a bang but with a whimper. That is why this book has rightly been renamed *Revolt in the Provinces,* a less sympathetic and less challenging title than the original. This version for the Millennium leaves us with the victims, but cannot sustain the view that they were also heroes, of the English Civil Wars.

Maps

Map 1   England and Wales in the Civil Wars, 1642–8

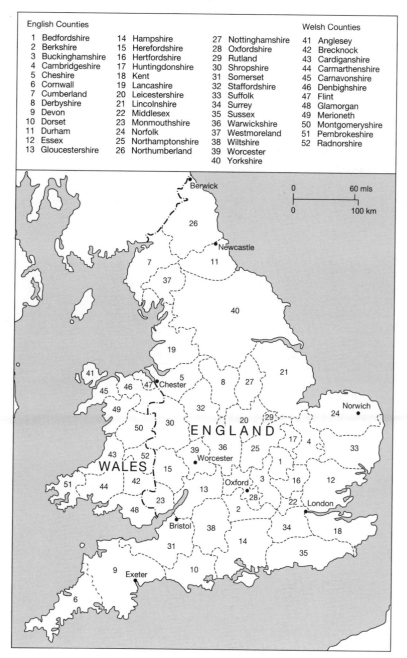

Map 2 English and Welsh counties at the time of the Civil War

Index

Abbot, George, Archbishop of Canterbury, 69

Accounts Committee at Cornhill, *see* Committee for Taking the Accounts of the Kingdom

Accounts, County Committees of, 97–9

Admiralty Court, 183

Advancement of Money, 95, 119

Aldbourne (Wilts.), 138

alehouses, 35, 126

'Ambidexters', 98, 124

Amounderness Hundred (Lancs), 40

Anabaptists, 72

Anglo-Scottish Covenant, 184

Answer to the Nineteen Propositions, 50, 188

Antiquarianism, 38

Arminianism, *see* Laudianism

Army Plots (1641), 49

Ashmole, Elias, 55

Ashton, Robert, his work discussed, 2, 3

Assessments, Monthly, 29, 80–1, 84–5, 85n, 93–4, 96, 100, 109, 110, 116, 118, 121–2, 146 190

Assizes, 35, 56, 93, 116–17, 205

Associations, 82, 100–2, 109–11, 120–1, *see also* Eastern, Midlands, North Wales, Northern, Southern, South Eastern, East Midlands, West Midlands Assocations

Astley, Sir Francis, and ship money, 40

Aston, John, 172

Aston, Sir Thomas, 40, 70–1

Attempt on the Five Members, 49

Aylesbury, Thomas, 127

Aylmer, Gerald, his work discussed, 3–4

Bacon, Francis, 1st Viscount St Albans, 33

Banbury, 115

Baptists, 198–9

Barnardiston, Sir Nathaniel, 56, 167

Baronetcies, sold and disputed, 38, 112

Baxter, Richard, 73

Baynton, Sir Edward, 88–9

Beauty of Holiness, 70

Bedford, Earls of, *see* Russell

Bedfordshire, 102, 192

Bedle, Nathaniel, 158

Beech, Henry, 136

Berkshire, 30, 46, 95, 133, 147, 150

Birmingham, 190

Bishops' Wars, *see* Scotland, wars with

Blake, Robert, 135

Bolton, massacre at, 193–4

Book of Common Prayer, 44, 64, 70, 127, 129, 141, 150–1, 185n, 186, 205

Book of Orders (1631), 25, 35

Booth, Sir George, later 1st Lord Delamere, 68

Boroughs, 41–2, 43, 50, 57–9, 78, 99–101, 128–32

Boscombe, 127

Boston, 88

Bramhall, John, Bishop of Derry, as political theorist, 22

Brereton, Sir William, 11, 30, 47, 71, 73, 87, 88, 91, 94, 99, 118, 141, 154, 163–4, 167–8

Bretland, John, of Thornecliffe (Cheshire), 11

Bridge maintenance, 35, 117

Bridgenorth, 193

Bristol, 44, 67, 100, 115, 138, 193

Bristol, Earls of, *see* Digby

Brooke, Robert, 2nd Lord, 49

Browne, Richard, 90

Brownists, 72

Brownlow, John, ship money and, 43

213

Underdown, David, his work discussed, 5, 18, 132-3, 161, 186-7, 202
Upton, A.F., his work discussed, 4
Uttoxeter, 153
Uxbridge, peace negotiations at, 139-40, 141, 148, 159

Vane, Sir Henry (the younger), 27
Venables, Peter, 30
Verney, Ralph, 53, 76
Villiers, George, 1st Duke of Buckingham, 17, 33
Vote of No Addresses, 205
Vow and Covenant (June 1643), 76

Wales, North, 167
Wales, South, 124, 133, 140, 174-6, 204-5, 207-8
Waller, Sir William, 89, 101, 139, 141, 168
Walsingham, Sir Francis, 28
Warcopp, Thomas, ship money and, 43
Warwick, Earls of, *see* Rich
Warwickshire, 98, 102, 160n, 193
Weekly Pay or Assessment, *see* Assessment
Weldon, Sir Anthony, 162, 167
Wells, 58, 116
Wentworth, Lord, 117
Wentworth, Sir Thomas, later 1st Earl of Strafford, 27-9, 47-50, 58, 75
West Midlands Association, 87, 164
Westbury, 120
Western Association, 102, 103

Western Circuit, 60
Westmorland, 96
Weymouth, 138
Wharton, Philip 4th Baron, 19, 75, 116
White, Thomas, 127
Whitehall Palace, 36
Whitlocke, Bulstrode, 84
Wilbraham, Sir Richard, 68
Willis, Humfrey, 104
Willoughby, Thomas, Lord W. of Parham, 88
Wiltshire, 40, 56, 64-5, 88, 90, 106n, 116-17, 125, 128, 133, 137, 138-9, 141, 142-4, 144-7, 149, 150, 161, 170, 201-2
Winchester, 58
Windsor, 193
Worcester, 57, 117
Worcestershire, 40, 44, 72, 113-15, 116, 133, 135, 142, 152, 161, 203
Worden, Blair, his work discussed, 6-7, 8
Wrightson, Keith, his work discussed, 7
Wye, River, 46

Yarmouth, 131-2
Yorkshire, 39-40, 55-6, 87, 96, 107, 170
Young, Peter, and *in vino veritas*, 189-90
Young, Thomas (Clubman lawyer), 127, 144

Zagorin, Perez, his work discussed, 8-10, 26-7, 30